Book One

Against Atheism: The Case for God

Written For the Rational Believer

By Toby Baxendale

Table of Contents

FORWORD 4

Introduction 5

Section One Rationality and Faith: No Conflict 21

Part 1 The Secular Predisposition 22

Chapter 1 The (not so) Brave New World 23
    Can There Be A Rapprochement Between The Faith And Reason? 25
    Do you Have to Have Faith in Something so Obvious as the Natural Belief in the External World? 26
    Specifically Faith and the Scientists 38

Part 2 The Denial of Faith by the (Naturalist, Reductionist) Scientist 42

Chapter 2 An Apostate Scientist Dares to Suggest His Community is Faith Based 43
    The Apostate's Qualification 45

Chapter 3 Poor Methodology Exposes The Weakness of Science 50
    The Great Methodological Misunderstandings of Science 50

Chapter 4 Our Medieval, Dark Age, Primitive, Superstitious, Religious (Christian), off with the Fairies Ancestors! 54
    The Incomplete and Inaccurate View of the History of Science and its Promoters 54
    Our Much Maligned Pre-Enlightenment Ancestors 57

Chapter 5 The Surprising Friend of Theism: Evolutionary Method 79
    Synthetic *A priori*: Evolutionary Biology 79

Chapter 6 The Current Cannon of Science 88
    The Ever Moving Gospel of Science 88
    The Timelessness of Reality 97
    Time and Physics 99
    Quantum Wonderland 102
    The Arrow of Time, the Newtonian Big and the Quantum Small Potentially Reconciled 104
    Mainstream Competing Theories of The Big and the Small Worlds 107
        The 1957 "Everett Many Worlds Interpretation." 107
        A Note on Infinity 108
        The Ghirardi-Rimini-Weber Theory or GRW Theory for Short 109
        De-coherence as a Potential Solution 109
        Pythagoras' Strings to the Strings of Everything in Physics 110
        In the Beginning at Time Zero.....Gravity the Repulsive Force 112
    The Curious Case of Lee Smolin 114
    The One Man Heavy Metal Rock Band of Science: Lawrence Krauss 123
        A Digression on Hume and Kant 124
        The Fallacy of Circular Reasoning 140
        Back to Hume, Dawkins and Krauss 140
        Krauss and his Heavy Metal 144
        The Science of Krauss 147

Part 3 On Religion and Philosophy 149

- Chapter 7 On Being 150
  - The Oneness of Reality 150
  - The Scale of Forms: Success and Failure, Prosperity and Poverty, Profit and Loss, Good and Evil, Some Philosophical Concepts Explored 152
  - Enter Satan into our Thoughts on the Matter of Pure Evil 157
  - On the Matter of Pure Goodness 159
  - Postscript to Pure Being 163

- Chapter 8 Anselm's Reflective Prayer 168
  - That Old Chestnut Again: Unpacking the Ontological Argument and the Great Debate in Mind, Collingwood v Ryle 168
    - Preliminaries 169
    - Part 1. The Delusion of Dawkins 169
    - Part 2. The Collingwood v Ryle Debate 181
  - The Ontological Deduction 182
    - The Synthetic *A priori*: Economics, Geometry, Logic, Rational Thought and the Whole Collection of Facts that Make a Whole Underlying Reality 183
  - The Great Debate has not Moved on 192

- Part 4 Those Deeply Religious Men: The Atheists 200

- Chapter 9 Richard Dawkins (Plus Others) and His Creedal Statements 201
  - Daniel Dennett and His Bizarre Statements 203
  - A C Grayling the Philosophical Atheist 208
    - The Good Book: Aping Religion in Literature 210
  - The Extreme Intolerance of Atheism: On the Teaching or Not of Religion to Under 18 Year Olds 216
  - Alain de Botton and His Atheist Church 218

- Chapter 10 Secular v Religious Murder, a Silly Debate 233
  - Those Religious & Atheist Mass Murders 233
  - The Crusades 233
  - The Spanish Inquisition 237
  - The Atheist Wars 238
  - Hitler 240
  - Stalin 243
  - Mao 247
  - Child Sacrifice and the Bible 249

- Conclusion 250

- Acknowledgments 251

- Appendix: The Body Count 252

- Bibliography 254

- Index 259

FORWORD

Briefly, two things:

Firstly, you will see that I have sometimes referred to 'he' when in fact I am addressing both male and female readers. I hope you will accept this in good faith, because it seems expedient, in the circumstances, rather than using the clumsier he/she or the ungrammatical 'they' when I am talking to 'you', whether singly or collectively. I have also tended to refer to God as 'He', which is normal practice in the Christian church.

Secondly, please bear in mind that what follows isn't written as an academic text and so I haven't necessarily felt bound to follow citation practices to the letter, although all quoted sources are listed fully I the bibliography.

Introduction

> "I would be willing to bet that the present right-thinking consensus will come to seem laughable in a generation or two - though of course it may be replaced by a new consensus that is just as invalid. The human will to believe is inexhaustible." (Nagel)

I sold my principal business at the very end of 2010. I have then had enough time for the great indulgence of being able to read and research into the problem of trying to understand why, in this world or universe, there is anything at all.[1] This I call the big 'why' question.

While most of the scientific community errs on the side of caution when trying to answer the 'why anything' question, on the basis that their discipline better suits them for answering the 'how anything' question, the secular world is increasingly being taken over by champions of atheism, often noted biologists and cosmologists who seek to answer this 'why' question by proposing that a series of potentially improbable random events have all come together at the right time to make what we see around us during the passage of a very long time. The Christian religion tells us this: *God did it*. I use the Christian religion as my fundamental religious outlook here. In varying degrees of sophistication theologians over several millennia have explored what this might mean. Philosophers have often been drawn to the same God-based conclusions, although there are many who don't make a comment on the 'why anything' question, and there are many others who positively reject outright the notion of God as the cause of the 'why' of the universe. The philosophical discipline seems much more relaxed in discussing the matter than scientists who avoid the issue or condemn it as an illegitimate point of view to even discuss. However, both the scientist and the philosopher will always attest that they are using their powers of *reasoning* to deliver their pronouncements and are therefore correct. Both can't be fully right.

---

[1] Most of my life I have had this nagging need to address this questions. What also propelled into researching this book, was the reading, in the mid 00s, of Professor David Conway's book (Conway) which converted Prof Anthony Flew (Flew, 2007), prior to 'The New Atheists', the most sophisticated of the advocates of that tradition.

The moralising high priests of religion have been almost completely replaced by the moralising High Priests of Science. As you will see, when we look at the methods of the latter and the speculation they employ to arrive at their conclusions, I will be suggesting that they tend to be a poor replacement for the hectoring preacher concerning the 'why' question. I approached the reading of their works in good faith and in as scholarly manner as I could. They all bear academic titles from world renowned institutions, yet I find a staggering level of pretension on display. Their views, on the whole, are held without humility. In fact, I found I was not exploring a view point with them, but being told what to think, being deeply patronised. Their atheist 'religion' is an unthinking religion: it is the worst of any kind of religion. Yes, reader, it *is* a religion, as I hope you will discover in later chapters of this book. The scientist I challenge is the naturalist, reductionist, materialist scientist. I appreciate there are many other scientists who don't hold this view and do not conduct their science in this tradition. But for the sake of brevity, when I use the word 'scientist' it is invariably to discuss the views of such a naturalist, reductionist, materialist scientist and his atheist world view. I apologise in advance for any offence given to other scientists who do not share this view but are scientists nevertheless.

There is a certain type of theologian who will, of course, be happy stating his faith through his powers of reason which offer him the possibility of achieving some coherence in his understanding of the world around him, although many seem entirely comfortable with their beliefs alone and require no further questioning of the foundation of such beliefs. Others may rest their belief on an unquestioning faith. Some theologians and scientists will acknowledge faith first and reason second. During my reading, I have come to see that I can only understand anything via the faith I have in God - what I call the fundamental ground for being - which is absolutely presupposed, before I even start to exercise my powers of reason on anything, and that at the heart of the matter faith and reason overlap at this point as it is reasonable to hold this position of faith first to allow me to believe anything. Therefore I conclude

6

against the atheist position of no faith, hence the title of the book: "Against Atheism". You, the reader, can judge whether or not I am 'off with the fairies', a phrase atheists are prone to using about people of religious faith, or actually onto something. Like St Augustine, "I believe in order to understand," or "I understand the better to believe". Or, like another great philosopher-theologian, St Anselm, "I do not seek to understand in order that I may believe, but I believe in order to understand." I also believe I can demonstrate that by using powers of reasoning - not speculation but plain, old-fashioned reasoning - you are actually more coherent in holding a religious (Christian) world view than that of atheism. So this book is a book for the rational believer. It is about rational belief. Or maybe it is better put by saying: this book is for the person who loves to use reason in life as a key guide, and does not think that thinking about theistic matters is a more sophisticated version of thinking about witch craft.

It also became apparent to me when doing my study that Christianity needs to understand itself better as the originator of much scientific discovery and inquiry. It needs to be confident in asserting this. It needs to roll back the foundations of science, which are ultimately faith based, and own this space. It needs to reprimand Christian brothers and sisters who hold a literal, seven-day-creation belief and remind them that from the early Church Fathers onwards this view was never held *literally*. Indeed, the celebrated 4th/5th century Saint of the Church, Augustine, no less, urged a non-literal reading of Genesis. He had a very modern 'Big Bang' view of the creation event, ie that it happened all in one go. Light being created on Day One and the Sun on Day Four, on the literalist account, were contradictory to this view and thus clearly for all to be read interpretively only.[2] Let science own its own space. This is the

---

[2] Augustine writes concerning Genesis in On Genesis: A Refutation of the Manichees, The Unfinished Literal Commentary on Genesis, and The Literal Meaning of Genesis. The final three books of Confessions focus on Genesis and not to forget Book XI, The City of God. He predates Einstein by 1600 years when he allows his mind to play with the idea of time and physicality as aspects of the same thing forever linked. No 'off with the fairies' theologian was he.

space that proceeds from the creation event, with little cross-over into theological territory. This will make theology better, and science better.

One of the finest New Testament Scholars of the last century, W D Davies (Davies W., 1948), makes a point that has resonated with me on and off ever since I read it:

> "We cannot doubt that modern Christendom, if it is to survive the crisis of science, must, like post-exilic Judaism, having rightly re-emphasized the transcendence of God and human sinfulness, and without sacrificing either truth, go on also to trace in the created universe the marks of the Wisdom of God, and thus claim the perilous new world of modern science as its now."

Post-exilic Judaism needed to push out evocations of a personalised man-in-the-sky God (as do we today!), to embrace its own Wisdom tradition whereby God is transcendent, in order to combat the Hellenistic Platonic philosophical avalanche of its day, for it to survive. Correct theology must claim the world back from these pretensions, as well as from self-righteous, preaching atheists.

The book is dedicated to my three children: George, Charlotte and Henry, and my godson, Luke Jopling. All have enquiring minds. My hope is that it may help them understand the world around them a little better than they do now. Ever a contrarian, I also write, in this secular world, for those of my wider family and friends who are faithless: that hardened bunch of atheist/agnostic/sceptics who don't understand faith, in the hope that one day they might.

In the meantime, I would like to note that all the books cited in the bibliography have been inspirational to me, especially those I find myself in disagreement with. I make no apologies for quoting from them extensively; they say what they say better than I can. I am eternally grateful for their inspiration. I stand on their shoulders. All quotes from the Bible are from the New King James Version (NKJV), unless otherwise stated. I also thank my family for their support in letting me get this out of my system and onto paper.

One caveat: this book is not written for those who 'just know' there is or 'just know' there is not a God. This is written for someone who needs to question his/her beliefs, via reason, so as to be able to make any coherent assertion on these standpoints either way. This book is pretty devoid of what might be called spirituality, on the face of it. There are many well-informed people who write from a spiritual perspective and are far better than I am at exploring the spiritual disposition. I welcome spirituality, I have spirituality, but don't have anything to add in a book for the rational believer on this matter. Indeed, if anything, I hope that this book may give confidence to a certain type of person, the rational believer, to explore their spirituality.

If this book helps you as a rational believer to think more deeply about God, who is the most perfect being, then I have achieved something. Book Two of the "Against Atheism" series will look at the case for Christianity itself by examining some of the key evidential challenges it faces. The Christian belief is that God decided to place His essence in Jesus Christ, some 2000 years ago - to pay us a personal visit, if you like. The evidence or not of this will determine whether you might or might not be able to subscribe to the Christian faith as traditionally presented to us. Once again, this will not address any *spiritual* becoming which might ensue, or provide any of the spiritual food you may be looking for, but it may, hopefully, give you some very solid and *rational* grounds for pursuing those endeavours with a greater confidence than you may have had before.

The broad outline of this book is as follows:

Section One Rationality and Faith : No Conflict

Part 1
Chapter 1 The Secular Predisposition

This section is a blend of the philosophical and theological. It looks at the current state of affairs where a certain understanding of rationality is in the ascendant and faith is often scorned as akin to that oft used atheist phrase 'belief in fairies in your back garden'. To start with, when we look closer, we see that we need to have faith - even in something seemingly so basic as a belief in the outside, mind-independent world, let alone the belief we must have via pure faith in the existence of the uniformity of the laws of nature and of the universe, in order to even start to reason or do any science at all. G E Moore and his famous lecture in which he 'proves' the existence of the external world is examined to see if this claim of a mind-independent world holds true - which I conclude it does not! This was an extraordinary finding which shocked me to the core. It is a question philosophers have not answered in many thousands of years: at its foundation philosophy, like science, is faith based. Whilst I, along with perhaps the vast majority of mankind, will take the 'common-sense' position of there being an external world, I most certainly cannot formally prove it. I need to hold it as a matter of faith, in truth, much as I wrestle with using that word for something so fundamental as what I experience every day. I then look at those who more openly reject faith, such as a certain type of scientist - the materialist, naturalist reductionist variety – and how we come to see that they actually have a faith based approach to their science. In the roots of both philosophy and science there is faith, with reason as its handmaiden. A heavy debt is acknowledged in my findings in this chapter from the philosopher R G Collingwood (Collingwood R. , Reason is Faith Cultivating Itself, 1927) (Collingwood R. , Faith and Reason, 1928).

R G Collingwood

He is one of the best unknown polymath thinkers of our times. His book "The Idea of History" traces history through stages of thought when it was part of the theology, politics and myth making of the day, to now, when most of it is a branch of scientistic naturalism, a series of tedious date bashings. History, for Collingwood, is always in the present, as the 'past' which so many have sought to discover, has simply gone away. History is the historian's imaginative reconstruction. Therefore all history is the history of thought. History without philosophy is like a man devoid of his mind - a part man. You do history to understand the present better. In his masterpiece "The Principles of Art" he clearly helps distinguish craft, propaganda, utilitarian design, commercialism, art as magic, as amusement, as expressing emotion, as imagination, as language, and much more from art itself. Art is that collaborative exploration between the artist and the viewer of what is going on in the artist's mind, the idea that the artist is expressing. It's very much a live thing in the present as each individual engagement with the artist's mind is entirely unique. Look at Rembrandt's "The Return of the Prodigal Son" and you will know more about the mind of that artist and his total and utter surrender to belief in the divine, in this artwork. Collingwood's "Idea of Nature" predates Khun's 'paradigm shift' idea. He looks at presuppositions that underlie the Greek (organic and living), Renaissance and Modern periods (inert, mechanical, moving to evolving). It is hard not to conclude that the science of the day is always 'right,' but the idea of nature itself in these three distinct periods was radically different, so it can't be. It would appear that nature, and the study of it, is once again the study of the history of thought. His philosophy is commonly labelled as 'idealist.' But it is not as simple as that. Whist he did hold that the world that we are in is thought, as you can see from the above, he did have a total faith in the outside, mind-independent world. I would encourage you to look him up as there is so much more to him, if anything in this book interests you. Collingwood has had a profound influence on what I write here.

Part 2 The Denial of Faith by the Scientist
Chapter 2 An Apostate Scientist Dares to Suggest His Community is Faith Based

My proposal that reason is the handmaiden of faith is flatly rejected by naturalist, reductionist scientists. We can see this born out when a distinguished member of their community dares to suggest that all their work starts from a position of secular faith and uses reason to explore their scientific projects. Under scrutiny is the implication that all scientists are objective, rational, and can judge matters with no reference to *religious* faith whatsoever. This is challenged by one eminent scientist with much invective from his colleagues who reject the fact that they are faith-based. Against this attack, this lone scientist seems to suggest a way forward, by proposing a more rigorous application of the scientific method for faith *not* to be at the foundation of all science. He is supported by one other who actually understands what he says.

Chapter 3 Poor Methodology Exposes the Weakness of Science

This chapter looks at the method of such scientists to see if they are warranted in holding the views they do. I look at the scientific method and conclude that it is good for looking at finite things and answering the big 'how' questions, but it is hopelessly equipped to answer the 'why' questions: these are beyond its remit. Also explored are two great methodological blunders commonly called: a) the false God of induction and b) pseudo metaphysics masquerading as good science. Reader, please bear with it: this section on method may well be intensely dry, but it does underscore that you need the right method in order to look at different things in life profitably. This section is the plumbing of this book - hard work - but if you don't get this clear and right then your project falls apart. When analysing thinking humans and their actions, you need to look at a different methodology from that which you may legitimately apply to a non-thinking lump of rock or atom in order to get the right results. Both methods here have in common *reason* as their tool, both use a different methodology appropriate to what they are studying. Blur this distinction of method and you will get odd results.

Chapter 4 Our Medieval, Dark Age, Primitive, Superstitious, Religious (Christian), off-with-the-Fairies Ancestors!

This chapter takes a brief look at some relevant history. It is an exploration, based on the work of James Hannam (Hannam, 2010) and his bringing to life some of the key inventions of engineering, mathematics and science which were tremendously beneficial to mankind during this supposed dank and misty, best forgotten part of our history, according to the atheist – and often prescient of many of the discoveries of the period we now call the Enlightenment. This, of course, according to the atheist, is when the nasty Christians were burning, whipping and torturing thinking, reasonable people. The Bible says very little indeed about science, but where it does - say, for example, on the spherical earth - for some reason, we are led to believe by our atheist colleagues that the Bible propounds flat earth views, which is certainly not reflected in scripture.

Chapter 5 The Surprising Friend of Theism: Evolutionary Method

Here, the synthetic analytical thought of change through time, implied in evolution - its algorithm - is actually stated to be a real manifestation of evolution in the empirical sense and is explored a little further. An abstract proof, its algorithm, is applied to reality once more. Why this is placed in a separate chapter is because I want it to stand out. Not many people will be aware that the same epistemological grounding as the Ontological Argument and its God proof, explored in the following chapters, in particular chapter 8, lies at the heart of the theory of evolution. This may come as a surprise to the naturalist, reductionist, atheistic community. Indeed, it came as a surprise to me when I first started to think about it.

Chapter 6 The Current Canon of Science

Not being a physical or natural scientist, but a layman learner, I have tried to absorb what current cosmology says about the origins - the 'why' and the 'how' - of the universe from some of the finest exponents of science, notably the Professors Brian Greene, Lee Smolin and Lawrence Krauss, who are gifted and write books for a lay audience. As we know with science, some of the key 'facts' are always changing. Indeed, for anything to be scientific it must have the ability to be changed, to be refuted. Some believe with certainty what they write about and describe, like Krauss, and some are more careful, like Smolin when he puts forth his schema. Greene gives us a truly first class survey covering several millennia of the various mainstream views and puts the case for major current competing views, including his personal favourite, String Theory. As we shall see from the unfolding story of the various cosmological viewpoints, we can only conclude that they are making historical pronouncements, since after several generations their positions change and there is a move onto new things that make the former pronouncements relevant to that period of history only. That is why this section is called the 'Current Canon of Science,' with the subtitle: The 'Ever Moving Gospel of Science'. It *is* canonical, as it is accepted history. It is 'gospel' as it is always at the time held as truth, but it is historical, too, as all these views ebb and flow and are subject to change. It seems to me that as far as the scientific project is concerned, the only things that don't change are those things scientists take on faith: the fundamental cosmological constants: logic, reason, the coherence of the universe and, in recent centuries, scientific method. Otherwise all is up for grabs – all of the time! Sometimes they are prone to making wild speculations, or indulging in pseudo metaphysics in order to get their systems up and running in their continuing effort to avoid a God, a First Cause, The Unmoved Mover or the Fundamental Ground for Being. These scientists have some of the most imaginative and creative minds. But I find the systems they propose are often based on a fundamental contradiction, or a series of them, and in turn they are explored in this chapter. Running alongside this, I also explore why they simply can't get away from the traditional 'God' arguments, the

Cosmological Argument and the Design Argument, which have not been refuted by God's so called chief executioners Hume and Kant, although it should be noted that the latter was theistic and faith based and the former more of an agnostic. The reader can judge the effectiveness of their fertile imaginations or the cold hard logical of reason of those traditional arguments, restated a little bit by me and applied to their starting points. The Cosmological Argument is explained to show that physicality is always associated with a prior physical cause. Quite simply, I suggest, to state a causeless universe, endless or eternal - or many universes - means there is no physical cause for the physicality that we observe up and running, therefore no material factors come from nowhere. Scientists who propose an 'always something' universe, or one that is endless, or one in a series, or just that existence exists, are basing their work on an incoherence of epic proportions. The Cosmological Argument is certainly not refuted. To me, after reading their speculative (though not their scientific) musings, I can only conclude that they are actually mystics.

Part 3 On Religion and Philosophy
Chapter 7 On Being

We now arrive at a more philosophical chapter. It is at the heart of my project and forms its tentative conclusion - *that we are all part of one reality and one thing: the fundamental ground for being, or God*. When you ponder any non-hypothetical concept (as opposed to a clearly defined hypothetical one such as, for example, the concept of the number 2) - like justice, fairness, freedom, oppression, good, evil, prosperity and poverty - you will perceive the connectivity between each of these pairings, which allows you, via the understanding of the opposition contained in each, to know more about both of them. What is more, they must also contain shades of each of themselves *in each other*. These ideal forms over-lap. And <u>all</u> *of the ideal forms over-lap and are implied in the form of goodness, even evil.* It is my contention that goodness is synonymous with God. A large, sweeping claim this may seem, but I endeavour to put significant flesh on the bone to make it robust in this chapter.

15

Chapter 8 Anselm's Reflective Prayer

St Anselm of Canterbury (1033-1109) is considered the founder of Scholasticism. In his book, The Proslogion, he laid out the case for the existence of God from the argument of being. This is rather inelegantly called the Ontological Argument. Its interest to us is in its *logical construction*: that is to say, it is *rationally* thought out, completely coherent – and remains un-refuted, to this day. But he sensibly recognises that *faith* is required in order to understand it. Anselm was challenged by the Benedictine monk Gaunilo of Marmoutiers, whose attack we will review shortly. What is interesting to note is that Anselm insisted that any subsequent publication of The Proslogion must include Gaunilo's attempted refutation.

An aspect of theology and philosophy which has great relevance towards our understanding of reality is explored in this chapter. Probably the most unpopular of all the 'God proofs' - indeed it is deeply unfashionable to even give it any credence at all - is the prayer of St Anselm (Anselm, 2001) in The Proslogion. This is where the very thought of God as a pure exercise in reasoning is said to offer a proof for God. I investigate why reason dictates that this thought must actually be a real and a necessary thought. Arguments against it are also considered here. The high priest of atheism, Richard Dawkins, offers his penny-worth in trying to expose the inadequacy of this, but fails to do so, I suggest. Above all, I look at a stimulating debate between two giants of 20th century philosophy who held the same Chair at Oxford in succession: R G Collingwood and G Ryle, with Collingwood represented by another great philosopher, E E Harris. We see that the attacks on what has become known as the Ontological Argument are, in fact, baseless. The contemporary attack made a thousand years ago by the monk Gaunilo, and subsequent modern Kantian attacks, are dealt with, and the thoughts of Process Theology[3] are brought to life in the discussion of the much neglected Chapter three of the Proslogion. The parting shot from Ryle on the matter is

---

[3] (Dombrowski, 2006) This book is the inspiration here.

that unless you can prove that you can find a purely reflective *a priori* thought and apply it to the reality of fact, the argument does not hold. Here, I do just that and apply it to the foundation of economics following Ludwig von Mises (Mises L. V., 1949), geometry (Euclid) and the method of change in time of biology (Darwin C. , 1859). This I call the Ontological Deduction, which I hope really gives great credence to this much maligned proof of God. I have hope that some of my theistic colleagues will now add this to their traditional advocacy for the Cosmological and Design Arguments as an equally robust proof, instead of relegating it to the side-lines of discussion.

Like R G Collingwood, Mises is one of the best unknown polymath thinkers of our times. His book "Human Action" (Mises L. V., 1949) is the last great treatise written on the subject of economics. In time, I believe that he will be venerated as much, if not more, than Adam Smith. In fact I contend that he is more important than Smith, as he grounds the entire body of economic knowledge in the unravelling of the 'action axiom'. This states that from the *a priori* that people act, and that they act purposefully, you can start to deduce that at each moment the human actor is faced with uncertainty as to which of a multiplicity of actions that can be taken. Therefore, a ranking of preferences is made, with the most urgent done first, the least urgent last and so on and so forth. This implies you always face a downward sloping demand curve of choice. From this we get the law of demand. From this we then deduce the laws of economics, of which there are only a few, but they are certain. Like Pythagoras with his theorem of the right-angled triangle, the whole of economics unpacks itself from this one axiom, the axiom of action. The study of these purposeful acts of man Mises called 'praxeolgy'. For sure, he 'invented' a whole new science - or rather discovered it. In "Socialism" he proved that socialism (the ownership of the means of production, distribution and exchange, by the state), was impossible to sustain as it could not calculate and allocate scarce resources to their most urgent needs. In "Theory of Money and Credit" he lays out the

Business Cycle Theory for which F A Hayek, his pupil and friend, won a Nobel Prize. He is one of the few economists who actually understood that it took the entrepreneur to make something happen to land, labour, and capital, the factors of production of economic textbooks, and placed entrepreneurship at the heart of his project. The entrepreneur, observing his fellow man's urgent needs and requirements, thinks about solutions to these needs. With his refraining from consumption, commonly called savings, he mixes the land, labour and capital that he can command to make better goods and services for customers' needs, over time. His regression theorem of money, crudely put by me, is that money has objective value because of its unique attribute as a good solely used for in exchange and never to be consumed as itself. Normal goods derive their objective value from the subjective value of all consumers. As money is not consumed in and of itself (try doing that to an electronic digit on a screen), you need to go back to the last time of barter and get your subjective value then: that forms its first objective value that all subsequent values are built upon. Mises' "Theory and History" shows, much like Collingwood, that all history is ideas, and ideas in the present at that, looking at what we think is the past. Purposeful human action is what is studied, and ideas, those important immaterial elements, bring changes to the material world. Understanding those changes brings wisdom and allows us to understand our present as well as what awaits us, well, *better*. There is so much more to this man. His influence on me is tremendous. It was really thinking about his metaphysics, which he never really discusses, as opposed to his epistemology, which he does, that brought me into really dealing with idealist-influenced philosophy: that is, the hallmark of the historical, economic, philosophical and theological aspects of this book.

Part 4 Those Deeply Religious Men: The Atheists

Chapter 9 Richard Dawkins (plus Others) and his Creedal Statements

> "A religion is an organized collection of beliefs, cultural systems, and world views that relate humanity to an order of existence. Many religions have narratives, symbols, and sacred histories that are intended to explain the meaning of life and/or to explain the origin of life or the Universe. From their beliefs about the cosmos and human nature, people derive morality, ethics, religious laws or a preferred lifestyle. According to some estimates, there are roughly 4,200 religions in the world.
>
> "Many religions may have organized behaviors, clergy, a definition of what constitutes adherence or membership, holy places, and scriptures. The practice of a religion may also include rituals, sermons, commemoration or veneration of a deity, gods or goddesses, sacrifices, festivals, feasts, trance, initiations, funerary services, matrimonial services, meditation, prayer, music, art, dance, public service or other aspects of human culture. Religions may also contain mythology." [4]

The Atheists we examine at are Richard Dawkins, Daniel Dennett, A C Grayling, and A de Botton: one scientist, one philosopher-scientist, two philosophers - but the latter two are actually the systematic, theological builders of their religion, and men of great industry and vision. They each have an organised collection of beliefs. The first three are certainly materialist, reductionist, naturalist. De Botton does not say much in the one book of his that (de Botton, 2012) I have read: so I make no comment about his belief

---

[4] This is a simple definition of religion taken from Wiki http://en.wikipedia.org/wiki/Religion

system except to say that he fully practises what he preaches and as such has started his own atheist church. Grayling writes the sacred history in his own good book: (Grayling, The Good Book, 2011) They all venerate nature: they are the new pagans. Whilst I have much respect for their ability to practise what they preach, they are to me no different from the old pagans. Humanity would be better off if their *irrational* views and systems were viewed as such and were not posited as an alternative to the religion of, say, Christianity, but a cult that is in tune with a historical pulse, that of paganism, that still beats in the breast of mankind. I don't doubt they have their niche and I wish them well, but I suspect, just like the Nagel quote at the top of this Introduction, that after several generations things will have moved on. To me, after reading their musings, I can only conclude they are sophisticated (pagan) witch doctors.

Chapter 10 Secular v Religious Murder: a Silly Debate

One modern mantra is that religion is the cause of all wars. I look at two overtly religious wars and compare them to three overtly atheist wars and conclude that secular murder vastly outdoes any killing attributed to religion. At the heart of the matter, I find most wars are motivated by hatred for people who conduct their lives differently to others, territorial gain, plunder, or in pursuit of economic/political control, regardless of whatever other label is attached to them. The accusation that all wars are religious does not hold for me and I label secular ones 'atheistic wars' only in a tongue and cheek way, as atheists freely suggest this in reverse and should, I suggest, be checked on this point. The reality is that wars are caused by man and his inability to live peacefully with others.

Section One
Rationality and Faith: No Conflict

Part 1 The Secular Predisposition

Chapter 1 The (not so) Brave New World

A C Grayling, a contemporary philosopher and undoubtedly a man always worth reading, propounds in his articles for lay people the anti-God view with great vigour:

> "The absolute certainty, the unreflective credence given to ancient texts that relate to historically remote conditions, the zealotry and bigotry that flow from their certainty, are profoundly dangerous: at their extreme they result in mass murder, but long before then they issue in censorship, coercion to conform, the control of women, the closing of hearts and minds.....

> "Religious belief of all kinds shares the same intellectual respectability, evidential base, and rationality as belief in the existence of fairies."[5]

> "I think they are failing in their responsibility to themselves as intelligent beings. By not being sufficiently reasonable. If you really press them, just ask them, aren't you glad that the people who built the aeroplane you fly in used reason? Aren't you glad that the pilots were trained according to reason? Aren't you glad that your doctor or train driver thinks about what they do and uses reason? And they will say yes. Then you say, 'Well, OK, if that's the case then how about applying it to your own life as well?"[6]

How reasonable, then, we must be. Reason is the way forward, faith in matters not provable should hold no truck with us and indeed should be banished from our minds. In his first statement concerning absolute certainty and unreflective credence most religious people would agree with him: that you should not hold views on such criteria. Most people of a religious persuasion would not readily accept or take kindly that their belief in a deity is akin to belief in the existence of fairies. Rather, they would agree with the third statement of Grayling's (above) concerning the reliance we all (theist, agnostic, atheist, or none of these) prefer to place on those trained, with reason, to the highest standards in order to do things or provide things for us, that manifestly

---

[5] http://www.telegraph.co.uk/news/features/3631819/Believers-are-away-with-the-fairies.html

[6] http://www.theguardian.com/books/2011/apr/03/grayling-good-book-atheism-philosophy

improve our lives such as the technological knowledge that allows us to fly in aeroplanes and the medical discoveries that treat us and give us a better quality of life.

Grayling stereotypes a religious person as always an extremist rather than as a fellow human being who uses the faculties of reason - just as he does. This is all good for the rhetorical moment, and the fundamentalist type certainly does deserve a verbal lashing, but this does not lead us really to understand why the overwhelming majority of religious people will agree with those points I have highlighted above while still holding some belief in a deity as a matter of faith.

So why does such a chasm exist between those who have a religious faith and at the same time hold the tenets of reason dearly and sincerely, and those who hold that it is impossible to maintain a religious view point in accordance with those same tenets of reason?

Strange though it may seem I submit that faith and reason are both aspects of the same project and that at its most fundamental level is us exercising our reason. Faith is held on reasonable grounds. This is contrasted with blind faith, or faith not held on reasonable grounds - the blind 'faith in the fairies' proposed by Grayling. The attack on blind faith is often an attack on the straw-man view (such as belief in the tooth fairy, Santa Claus, fairies in the back garden etc) of what it means to hold a belief on faith alone. That propagators of this line of attack fail to realise is that they miss the target and demonstrate what blind faith they themselves have in their own belief systems. This is explored in Chapter 9 when we look at those deeply religious men: the atheists. I duly contend that faith and reason are not in conflict with each other at all. Reason has, and always will be the handmaiden of faith and you cannot have reason without faith. This may seem odd and in tension with our common sense use of the two terms, so before I attempt to convince you, the reader that I am indeed not off with the Grayling fairies, I will unpack a little further why I assert what I do.

Can There Be A Rapprochement Between The Faith And Reason?

The conventional story told in our schools today is that in the western world it would seem that man was asleep until the arrival of the Greeks two and a half thousand years ago when what we call 'western Thought' suddenly became up and running. Plato uses the word 'faith' to describe our belief in the realities of the world around us, the objects we see. If anyone denies that these exist we can't prove him wrong, but we 'know' him to be wrong with great conviction. He uses the word faith as St Paul does: as the absence of any proof, or otherwise. So the absence of proof by reason alone is what is attributed to faith.

It is startling that when you ask philosophers to *prove* that there is something as mundane as a cup of tea just made in front of them, they can't, as they can only describe things via the lens of their mind. They say, "well, I can touch it, so I know it is there". That perception of touch is a mental construct embedded deeply somewhere in the mind is lost on most people, but nevertheless the thought of touch comes before the thing you touch. People say, "well, I can see it, I know it is there." Once again, the seeing is done via the lens of the mind. We are all trapped in the prism of our mind through which we filter all manner of information. We can suppose an external world, we can have faith in an external world, we can *believe*, but we can't prove it in a formal sense. Like Plato and St Paul, we take it on faith, or the absence of proof, that there is a mind independent world.

By this formal sense I mean understanding something deductively or inductively. We can acquire knowledge *deductively* when we put forth a hypothesis such as: 'Socrates is a man, all men are mortal, therefore Socrates is mortal,' and know that if the premise is true the conclusion that follows from it will also be true. With *induction*, we can put forth a hypothesis such as: 'water has a boiling point, when it turns to steam', and we can test it again and again and conclude something contingent about the boiling point of water. Concerning that cup of tea, every descriptive word you use to say you can touch it to prove it, requires a prior idea or thought of your mind to describe the feeling of touching the cup. Likewise, to even describe it as a cup must presuppose the thought of a cup that is internal to the mind. I resolutely hold the belief that there is a world around me and it exists objectively, but I sure as hell can't prove it, independently of my mind, so I take it as a matter of faith; I presuppose it, if you like. If you can prove otherwise, you solve a most perplexing 2,500 year puzzle, and for sure no one has done this yet.

Do you Have to Have Faith in Something so Obvious as the Natural Belief in the External World?

> Luther in his "Sermons" defined faith: "It is the nature of faith that it presumes on the grace of God .... Faith does not require information, knowledge, or certainty, but a free surrender and a joyful bet on his unfelt, untried, and unknown goodness." (Pelikan, Reformation of Church Dogma (1300-1700))

There have been many attempts in philosophical literature to ground the external world in reason alone. The last major attempt was done by the analytic philosophers G E Moore, Bertrand Russell, Gilbert Ryle and A J Ayer, who burst upon the philosophical horizon in the late nineteenth/early twentieth century to overturn the prevailing philosophy of idealism. They are said to have dealt deadly blows to Luther's thought (above). They absolutely dominated this field of enquiry during the twentieth century. Much of their analytic method has great merit in sharpening the mind in order to help us extract more information from our surroundings and progress our understanding of the world. But they utterly failed to prove the outside world exists and left it the biggest elephant in the room of philosophy. We still have to hold a belief in the external world on faith and faith alone and not via reason, which they sought to undisputedly install as the champion of all knowledge.

Among the most famous of all the attempts to refute the belief that you can't prove the existence of a world external to oneself, was that of G E Moore, in his Lecture, Proof of An External World Read 22nd November 1939 (Moore)

He opens by noting that the preface to the 2nd Edition of Kant's Critique of Pure Reason says:

> "It still remains a scandal to philosophy ..... that the existence of things outside of us .... must be accepted merely on faith, and that, if anyone thinks good to doubt their existence, we are unable to counter his doubts by any satisfactory proof." (Moore, 1939)

Moore decides that Kant is in error and that he can give proof of the external world. The proof of objective reality must mean proof of 'the existence of things outside of us' or to offer more clarity, 'the existence of the things outside of us.' (Moore) He then does his best to prove the external world. In binary and precise prose, he lays out his case. Then, in a magnificent piece of theatre - and, oh, how brave and daring this must have seemed to the audience at the time, I wish I could have seen it - he said the following:

> "I can prove now, for instance, that two human hands exist. How? By holding up my two hands, and saying, as I make a certain gesture with the right hand, 'Here is one hand', and adding, as I make a certain gesture with the left 'here is another'. And if, by doing this, I have proved ipso facto the existence of external things, you will see that I can also do it now in numbers of other ways: there is no need to multiply examples." (Moore, 1939)

Moore asks himself: is this a rigorous proof? In accordance to what most logicians would agree, it needs to satisfy three conditions:

(1) Was the conclusion that followed what was expected from the premises stared with?
(2) Did I know the premise was true?
(3) The conclusion must follow the premises.

Essentially he posits he knew what he was asserting when he said his hand is here and here is another one: it would be absurd to say that he only believed it!

> "How then can I prove that there have been external objects in the past? Here is one proof. I can say: 'I held up two hands above this desk not very long ago; therefore two hands existed at some time in the past Q.E.D'." (Moore, 1939)

27

However, he concludes that his case fails in the strictest interpretation, but notwithstanding this - it does not matter!

> "Of course, what they really want is not merely a proof of these two propositions, but something like a general statement as to how any propositions of this sort may be proved. This, of course, I haven't given; and I do not believe it can be given; if this is what is meant by proof of the existence of external things, I do not believe that any proof of the existence of external things is possible." (Moore, 1939)

For such a rigorous thinker, Moore seems to be saying he is allowed to make these pronouncements as he is a philosopher, and he just believes it is so. His reason sits in the diplomatic bag of immunity accorded to the philosophical and scientific few who alone have these privileges - but not to those who explicitly and, in many ways humbly, accept their lot and acknowledge the substrata of faith that REASON tells us we rest within.

Ayer picks up this oversight by Moore, showing that he can prove that he held up his hands by acknowledging that he perceived it and he *remembered* it. Whilst this is brilliant wit on Ayer's part and as daring as the Moore lecture itself, sadly we still can't prove the existence of the external world just by the fact that we remember, via the lens of our mind, some event that happened in the past. We prove, if anything, that we hold that the external world exists by faith alone. In many thousands of years of thinking about it, we are no further down the line at solving this issue.

Moore, however, still pushes the debate about the external world further, trying to prove the existence of it and says:

> "In order to do it, I should need to prove for one thing, as Descartes pointed out, that I am not now dreaming." (Moore, 1939)

Ayer says also that in a lecture called "Certainty" published in *Philosophical Papers,* Moore discusses how, if anyone argues that they did not know if they were dreaming or not - they certainly can describe situations when they are for sure dreaming - they can thus do so when they are not, ie, proving the ability of man to distinguish between the real world and the dream world. Ayer thinks this is an "ingenious argument." (Ayer A. , 1971) He thinks this gets over the Cartesian problem in that it allows us to distinguish between what is real and what it not, what is mind-dependent and what is not. He concedes that it is possible to hold a view that is not self-contradictory which says that all your current sense experiences are in fact one big dream, but the fact that you can distinguish past ones means you must assume there is a distinct difference between the two. Ayer points out that this could also apply to your memory senses as well. This would seem to give hope of the external world existing as mind-independent, but it is still only the mind sifting through what is real and what is dreaming. I believe this line of argument is doomed, just like all the above arguments put forward to try to establish the external mind-independent world.

Moore would appear to be saying it is a 'definite mistake' to say that just because you can't prove the premise you must bin the proofs given, as you could not reason anything if you did not make this over-riding assumption. You may not be able to think anything at all about the external world if you only believe it is a figment of your imagination, that is certain, but why not just humbly accept that we mere mortals have to take this on faith, and faith or absence of proof alone? It is perplexing why so many are reluctant to do this. I think his reason now gives away to a blind prejudice that refuses him the humility to accept the limitations of his reason, and that his reason rests on a rock solid bedrock of faith, and faith alone. To a rationalist like Moore and, indeed, Ayer, this would put them in the same camp as those who believe in pixies at the end of the garden, if there are such people, and I suspect this is something they seek at all costs not to be associated with. The straw man of irrationalism forces them to not accept that reason demands that they accept, by the absence of proof, the existence of the external world, just as a religious person accept his faith, by the absence of proof.

> "This view that, if I cannot prove such things as these, I do not know them, is, I think, the view that Kant was experiencing in the sentence which I quoted at the beginning of this lecture, when he implies that so long as we have no proof of the existence of external

things, their existence must be accepted merely on faith. He means to say, I think, that if I cannot prove that there is a hand here, I must accept it merely as a matter of faith - I cannot know it. Such a view, though it has been very common among philosophers,, can , I think, be shown to be wrong – though shown only by the use of premises which are not known to be true, unless we do know of the existence of external things. I can know things, which I cannot prove; and among things which I certainly did know, even if (as I think) I could not prove them, were the premises of my two proofs. I should say, therefore, that those , if any, who are dissatisfied with these proofs merely on the ground that I did not know their premises, have no good reason for their dissatisfaction." (Moore, 1939)

I am dissatisfied with this! Whilst I am delighted he knows that he can't formally prove the outside world - that he does not want to accept this is held by faith and faith alone - I have laboured the point regarding the existence of the outside world simply to expose the fact that although I believe very much in the external world - indeed I think it no other way - I believe it by faith and thus faith is actually a tool so close to me, so important to me, that I often take it for granted. If I take this most fundamental and seemingly obvious thing , the external world, as a matter of faith, then faith must actually be a very important thing and not the parody painted by A C Grayling at the start of this work.

I have much sympathy with wanting to root our understanding of the world in something much more solid than faith would appear at first blush. The Greeks were very much for putting reason at the forefront of our knowledge-gathering enterprise. Aristotle put forward his idea of syllogistic proofs where everything could be proved by argument except first principles (such as the Socrates example above). The Greek mind wanted a demonstration for everything, and as such it was a highly intellectual mind-set. From first principles, all deductions were made, all demonstrations were arrived at. These first principles were not matters of faith, they were demonstrable in the negative, by noting any attempt to disprove them produced a contradiction.

In contrast to the Greeks, Christianity arrives in the Western world and puts faith at the top of the agenda. The conventional view is that religion dealt with the immaterial, the spiritual, the murky world of mysticism, whilst the former dealt with the syllogism of Aristotle. The method of the syllogism was to be applied to any finite object, to root out its causes. Suffice to say, reason is the proper tool for all scientific discovery, it deals far better with matters of the finite than faith. The proper application of faith is to explore the given, or those brute facts, such as the existence of the outside world, and the infinite. The 20th century's foremost advocate of this line of thought was the philosopher R G Collingwood. He best expressed it in his article "Reason is Faith Cultivating Itself" (Collingwood R. , Reason is Faith Cultivating Itself, 1927) where he observed:

> *"It was because the object of faith is God; and God being infinite , has no relation to anything outside himself by which he can be indirectly known. A finite object – a chair or a geometrical figure- has causes outside itself. Hence, in order to know it completely, you must start outside it, you must know it by its causes, for the cause, in Aristotle's own words, is the middle term of the syllogism. Thus Aristotle's own doctrine proves that, if there is an infinite uncaused being, this being cannot be known syllogistically, its existence cannot be proved by argument; it must be grasped by some kind of intuitive act." (Collingwood, 1927)*

And:

> *"The Greek view of life involved cutting human thought into two parts, the one scientific , syllogistic , argumentative , and intellectually respectable ; the other intuitive, immediate, irrational, and in the last resort merely superstitious. Under the first head fell philosophy and the sciences; under the second,, religion and everyday perception." (Collingwood, 1927)*

For Aristotle he proposes a uncaused cause, the unmoved mover, to get all of physicality up and running. From this start point, we then have very little of what attributes Aristotle can place to his God. Instead he concentrates on the world of our material things. All objects are finite whose causes are outside themselves. Each and everything is moving teleologically to its predetermined end point. To know a thing is to know its causes. For the Christian, God is uncaused and infinite, much as He is for both Plato and Aristotle. God cannot be demonstrated syllogistically as you can't think of God in relation to cause and effect. Christianity came into world and said faith was actually superior to reason as it showed that on matters of the infinite you had to intuitively grasp only as we intuitively grasp all the ultimate truths of science. The fact that the ultimate big truths of science rest on faith may sound bizarre to the modern mind we will be exploring this more in the next chapter - just as there being no formal proof of a mind independent world. The fact that we take all of this on faith is so counter-intuitive to the contemporary mind; nevertheless, it is the world we occupy and if we reflect on this a bit, we might recognise that for all our reasoning we need faith in order to understand anything at all. The fact that the foundation of science rests on faith and has the same status as faith in a deity, openly expressed by theologians, seems lost on most. For Collingwood, faith was the wellspring of all beliefs in the Deity, and the bedrock of all understanding.

We can see that Christianity, being rather more Aristotelian than Aristotle, was in fact the at the birth of the scientific revolution to come, as it asserted that faith, by which we grasp the infinite, was totally different from how we use sense to grasp the perceptions we do of the finite world. For the Greeks, the infinite world was a world of superstition. For the three Great Christian Saints , Augustine , Aquinas and Anselm of the Middle Ages, they put faith at the top of knowledge and reason underneath it. You were to have faith in order to understand the fundamental ground for being , or God, from which all of reality cascaded forth. Your faith allowed you to explore the outside world and all your surroundings in pursuit of understanding this creation. However, it would appear on a cursory look that they were mutually exclusive - that is, the Greek intellectual bifurcation between scientific thought and the irrational, the former being concerned with philosophy and the sciences, the latter with intuition and superstition corresponding with everyday perception and religion. With Christianity, we now had a third element: faith. Faith was not to be concerned with the finite world of sense perception, but of the infinite only. Faith of supreme reality is the first organ of knowledge, reason flows from it and was subordinated to it. This was the dominant, but not exclusive Christian position, and still is today. So changed the world view, away from bifurcation and into a synthesis. It was truly revolutionary. Collingwood explains it well:

> *"The main principle is this: the finite falls within the infinite , not outside it; therefore the sphere of faith and the sphere of reason are not two mutually exclusive sphere, but the sphere of reason falls within the sphere of faith. Faith is our attitude towards reality as a whole, reason our attitude toward its details as distinct and separate from each other."*
> *(Collingwood, Faith and Reason)*

He claims that failure to observe this will lead to no settlement in the dispute between faith and reason but a continuing polarity, when, in fact, as we have seen, we need faith to even begin to understand the outside world. This was evident in the Middle Ages, when many believers argued for demonstrable proofs of God and the three Saints realised that they were in the final analysis un-provable, as even the most rational proof, still sits full square on the bedrock of faith we have in the first place, to even begin to reason about the external "real world" we have total faith we live in. Anselm devised the famous ontological proof, but in reality proof, in the formal sense, it may well be, but in reality it is just a strong indication of God as he knew it. In the final analysis, he realised his great, rationally thought out 'proof' rested in the substrate of faith. Indeed, Anselm says: "I believe, in order that I may understand; for this I know, that unless I first believe I shall never understand." (Anselm, 2001) Faith is given absolute authority and priority over reason. He realised that the very demand for a proof of God contradicts this by applying reason over faith. If you do that, reason can only deal with finite cause and effect objects of reality. Keeping the finite separate from the infinite makes the infinite actually a finite thing, and if this was so, then reason takes precedent over faith, God becomes a finite thing with cause and effect and ceases to be the un-caused cause of all things.

In Chapter 7, On Being, we will explore more fully various philosophical concepts that seem opposed and hard to conceive as being ever reconciled. There is great opposition in them. In the common sense usage of the words 'faith' and 'reason', we are content to see each as opposite. However, if you accept the thought process above, you can see that reason is a component of faith, it sits embedded in the very fabric of faith. No, faith in the conformity of the universe to its laws, the commitment to logic, the outside mind independent world itself, all rely on a faith in them, as you certainly can't prove them. At the heart of the matter, reason is a child of faith; they overlap right at the very genesis of their existence.

It is also worth a pause here to reflect that if you think you are a materialist, and that dispensing with God or Gods is the role of reason, and that reason has latterly done a good job with only one God left to get rid of, you hold your materialistic world view as a matter of faith only in the first instance, as we have established and not as a matter of faith and reason. But far more worrying for you should be the fact that you hold this matter of faith not on grounds of reason, but blindly, unquestioningly, and undoubtedly on a fatal contradiction. To hold a conception of a material and finite world or universe, you must accept causality of anything material. If you then jump to an assumption of an infinite series of finite physical things just existing to explain why we observe what we do around us, your project commits intellectual suicide, as to be physical and finite you must have a cause to get up and running. You can't just postulate a prior physical cause and so on an infinitum. Why? Because you must have a cause to get the whole of physicality up and running in the first place in order for it to be physical. So what you are saying is that the universe does in fact have no cause. If it does not have a cause, it is not physical. If you are presupposing an infinite series of prior physical causes, in reality you are saying that the material universe we observe is causeless and indeed does not exist as the material universe we observe. You are conclusively impaled on your contradiction. This is why theologians, in conjunction with certain philosophers since the dawn of time are lead, seemingly paradoxically, by reason, to assume, as there is nothing left to put in its place to start a physical cause, as it needs a prior one, an uncaused cause. Indeed, an immaterial cause is required to get the whole of materiality up and running: there is no other conclusion that stacks up, according to logic or reason. This is precisely what theologians assert as God. Philosophers may take out the religious connotations associated with the word God and substitute what I call the understanding of the fundamental ground for being as the first cause. I will use the two to mean the same thing. This thing must be infinite and uncaused. From this, robustly, reason established a firm rock, indeed a mountain of God, from which we can build our understanding of the world and the form it presents itself to us. We can then start to explore the world. This is the power of faith and its handmaiden, reason. Truly, it is what Christianity gave us: a rational synthesis of faith and reason! Without this understanding it is doubtful any of the wonders of the Western World would have progressed. This understanding allowed the dawn of science to start to flourish and is implied in the thought process of all scientists, even the most militant atheist ones, though they seem unaware of it as I will demonstrate in coming chapters. At this point, it is worth pausing for thought re who is off with the fairies?, the theologian who accepts the logic of an immaterial first cause, or the Atheist, who is truly religious and irrationally faith based who accepts a causeless universe that implodes in on its own contradiction: a material property (the universe) that has no cause and thus no materiality (a non-universe)!

If you hold that the infinite is worth thinking about, the finite must be absorbed into it. Thus, reason must be absorbed into faith, but, as stated at the outset, the two may still appear to be in conflict with each other, as the modern secular view would attest. So how is this puzzle resolved to the modern mind, if you are not satisfied with the older solution? Rene Descartes in the Cogito [7] provided the start of the solution. He held that the conviction of one's own existence as real - that you can't help but have it - is a coincidence of both faith and reason. Collingwood, again, states:

> "In the certainty of my own existence I have a conviction which is rational in the sense that it is universal and necessary , but a matter of faith in that it rests not on argument , but on a direct conviction .' (Collingwood, 1927)

It does not depend on proof to be believed, that is for sure. It is a fact that it cannot be denied. It is a performative contradiction to do so. To try and deny you exist, your thought or utterance regarding this confirms your very existence. This is precisely why we know we exist.

---

[7] Cogito ergo sum, "I think therefore I am" From the Principles of Philosophy 1644.

And:

> "Descartes has shown that our knowledge of our own existence is of exactly the same kind as this direct knowledge of God by faith, with this difference, that it can never desert us when we acquire its presence ." (Collingwood, Faith and Reason)

To be more precise: in either acknowledging that I exist or trying to deny it, reason and faith coincide. My belief that I exist rests on faith arrived at by intuition but also via reason, in the sense that it is a universal necessity and cannot be denied by any thinking being, as when you think, you presuppose you. It is unlike first principles in that are all invariably all deniable and there are as many of these are there are points of view. All natural rights - for example, the right to life, liberty and the pursuit of happiness, as enshrined in the constitution of the United States, as first principles - these can be denied. Always. a different collection of start points can equally be inserted, depending upon the authors' subjective preferences, for example the right to freedom of speech, religion and private property rights - or take your pick. However, the cogito of Descartes, "I think therefore I am" certainly can't be denied. It is undeniable and is held via reason. But also by total unquestioning faith do we hold on to it. It would appear to be a 'given' at first glance - or it is just immediate to us, although examine this and you realise it is held on faith and reason in an inseparable way, as, at the heart of it, faith and reason are the same. Kant elevated such understanding away from a faith/reason conflict, but placed it in the grounds of metaphysics proper in that he correctly laid down the trinity of the un-provable: that God, freedom and morality were the subjects of metaphysics and not proofs. Proofs are for the finite things:

> "We do not demonstrate them, not because they are too uncertain, but because they are too certain: they lie too close to our minds to be proved, they are too inextricably interwoven with our experience to be argued about . To prove them is like buttoning up your own skin." (Collingwood, 1927)

The whole world and the whole universe are taken on faith. The details of the specifics of that world and universe are the preserve of science. Science tells us the details. Just as science can't assume that there are not laws of nature, and that untrue premises cannot logically follow from true premises, so science can't deny that its research project is embedded in this unity, resting on faith. Once again, to deny this, science denies itself. The scientist, if he is honest to himself, should not hold the very substrate of the universe and its laws as a "mere" matter of faith. Collingwood tells us, and I agree:

> "Not at all: faith they are, but not mere faith, because the faith which they express is a rational faith in the sense that it is universal in everyone – even in you, who pretend to doubt it - and necessary to all thought, even the thought by which you pretend to criticize it." (Collingwood, 1927)

The intuitive certainty outlined by Descartes is actually the foundation of all knowledge. When I am reasoning, I know I am not talking nonsense, and my premises will bind my conclusions. Reason depends for its very coherence on the article of faith which is indemonstrable. Reason springs forth from faith. The certainties of reason, according to Collingwood "are certainties of precisely the same kind as Descartes' cogito ergo sum. They cannot be proved, because they lie too close to us". These are absolute presuppositions of all proofs whatsoever. They are the conditions from which all syllogistic arguments begin. Faith can never be the product of reason. You can't lump together finite quantities to reach the infinite. What is more, "faith is presupposed in argument itself." (Collingwood, 1927). By this I hold that Collingwood is stating that to argue, or to even think this presupposes mind as a fundamental irrefutable axiom that as mind you can't deny, but one that cannot positively prove itself except by contradiction, so you hold your very mind as a matter of faith:

> "Reason cannot generate faith, but reason alone can reveal faith to itself, can display it to its own nature." (Collingwood, 1927)

To add understanding to faith means faith revealing itself. I quote Collingwood at his little known best:

> "And anybody who thinks he is perfect in his faith may logically and morally refuse to torment himself by following the stony path of reason . But anyone who finds his faith less clear and strong would wish it must take steps to amend it; and these can only be finite

> kind. Faith, in and by itself, cannot be cultivated; and if I have made myself clear, I shall be understood when I conclude by saying that reason is nothing but faith cultivating itself." (Collingwood, 1927)

In summary: reason is the *thinking* aspect of faith.

Specifically Faith and the Scientists

> "If it is true of the scientist's belief that his researches are not pointless, may it not also be true of the Christian moralists' belief that his morality is not pointless? The scientist does not know that even the most long-established hypothesis may not be refuted by new evidence tomorrow. All that has been written about induction has not altered the fact that belief in the nature of regularity of the universe is an act of faith; and yet we base all our actions on this faith ." (Hare)

As said, faith is a religious attitude of mind and that is also the same attitude we hold towards the universe. Most of the publically vocal scientists wince at the thought that they are 'faith heads.[8]' On the contrary, they are the masters of rationality, to which no challenge is too great. Whatever their great achievements in helping entrepreneurs provide better, faster, stronger goods and services, doctors better, more effective treatment for aliments and all the life enriching this implies:

> "The scientist may be unconscious that the experiment which he is making rests upon his certainty that the universe as a whole is rational; but his unconsciousness of the fact does not alter the fact. Without absolute confidence in the "uniformity of nature," or whatever name he gives to the rationality of the universe, he would never try experiments at all." (Collingwood, 1927)

Grand unifying theories of everything seem doomed to be elusive to man. In each age of humankind, the scientists have presupposed they were nearly there to finding an equation representing everything, only to be amended or refuted by some other great discovery. I can't help feeling there is a pattern repeating itself here, whereby the holy grail of a unifying physical

---

[8] The insult used by Dawkins et al against those recognize their limitations and embrace faith. As we will explore later , the handle may be more appropriate for himself.

theory gets tantalisingly close, only for a subsequent discovery to come along - or maybe three at once, like London buses - when this endeavour shifts further out of reach. That said, in the pursuit of such a definitive discovery, findings filter down from the ivory towers of research that have very useful application to the modern world, which we all enjoy and often take for granted. Long may those discoveries continue, but if scientists deny the role of faith they deny their own discipline: they deny science. To set themselves up against faith, they attack themselves. Perhaps scientists and openly faith-orientated people should focus their dispute on eliminating superstition. This is where there is a true synthesis between the two camps of faith and reason. In fact, reason should rightly champion the elimination of superstition and allow faith to better understand itself. Superstition occurs when one sections off part of finite reality and refuses to let reason enter in to perform an analysis. True religion ought not offer any hiding places for superstition and those religions that do should be labelled superstitious, like the Atheist Religion (material universes that don't have a cause, that just exist, and thus can't be material, for example). Reason is always at loggerheads with superstition, but so is faith: faith and reason which are actually necessary for each other. Faith can't exist without reason, reason without faith. More focus is needed to understand this deep and inseparable unity.

> "To look for the infinite by throwing away the finite would be very much like making the players stop playing in order to hear the symphony. What they are collectively playing is the symphony; and if you cannot hear it for the noise they are making, you cannot hear it at all." (Collingwood, Faith and Reason)

Theologians need to recognise their scientist brothers, and scientists their theologian siblings:

> "A person who says he believes in God, but shrinks from developing his belief into a science of theology, or a person who professes faith in the rationality of the world but will not say how exactly this rationality manifests itself in detail, is like the man who says, "I believe this bridge will bear me, but I would rather not walk across it." (Collingwood, 1927)

More than ever before, as reason seems to be separating itself from faith in our secular world, do we need this reuniting of faith and reason if we are truly to get a better picture of the whole of reality. Reason cannot exist without faith. Science rests on universal laws embraced by acts of faith. Reason has done a great service to its master, faith, by relentlessly ridding mankind of much of its superstitious mumbo jumbo. The mumbo jumbo of the mystic, the witch doctor, and all the peddlers of quick fixes and conjuring tricks are impaled by the deadly arrow of reason. When scientists recognise that this sharp arrow of reason is sheltered in a rich bath of warm comforting and reassuring faith, and they embrace their faith, they will surely produce better science. The theologian must never be afraid to let reason into his innermost sanctum. It must be allowed to root out, refute and destroy superstition. If he does this, he procures for his faith a great service. Scientists must acknowledge its substratum of faith and recognise this is the enabling factor that allows it to investigate anything finite at all.

> "Three things, therefore, must happen simultaneously. Religion must set its house in order by scrupulously searching for superstitious elements within itself and seeking to eradicate them. Science must set its house in order by abandoning mythologies and occult forces and being truly scientific. And these processes go forward – they are not things that can be done once for all – the quarrel between religion and science will die away, and each will gradually learn to find in the other not a rival enemy, but a friend and ally." (Collingwood, Faith and Reason)

It may be that Collingwood was too premature in stating the following:

> "Reason has won every battle; but faith has won the war, because by its defeat it has learnt to be itself and to claim for its own not this detail or that within human life, but human life as a whole." (Collingwood, 1927)

I think this was well, but hastily, written. As faith has been hounded out by our increasingly secular society, it is sometimes hard to believe that faith has won the war. We will see in the following five chapters that some scientists in recent years are desperately trying to deny their faith and float effortlessly, objectively, like all-knowing angels, detached from our reality but able to observe in a way uninfluenced by anything other than their reason, and to opine on matters relating to man and his environment.

Now, theologians of Christianity have always known that they need the faith discussed above, in the uniformity of nature, the uniformity of the universe and all its laws, to help make meaning, or to come to an understanding of man and his surroundings. The religious disposition develops from this - as does the scientific one. Both of these we will be exploring later. However, Richard Swinburne (Swinburne, Faith and Reason, 2005) argues that the modern mind demands inductive evidence as opposed to the theories of natural religion if it is to bolster the argument of religious faith. This inductive method, familiar to every scientist to the extent that it is his bread and butter, is where the scientist-cum-historian can probe into and test out all the reported instances of God manifesting Himself in our material and finite world. This is where the scientist and the historian can meet the philosopher and theologian at the Inn at the World's End to find that unifying peace - that is, of course, if you accept the evidence presented in such things as scripture. But scripture, insist the champions of the secular world, is nothing more than fiction. It is a contention in this book that all the observation, historical, oral and written records of the history of Christ, for example, suggest strongly that God is more likely than not to satisfy the modern mind of its existence. The empirical evidence of God in the world is explored in Book Two of the Against Atheism series in the 'Controversies in Scripture' sections. For now, we will turn our minds towards grounds scientists have for saying anything. And also: is what they say is reason-based more relevant to our attempt to discover the truth about the universe and all that exists - or not?

Part 2 The Denial of Faith by the (Naturalist, Reductionist) Scientist

Chapter 2 An Apostate Scientist Dares to Suggest His Community is Faith Based

> "We must expect and demand a scientific spirit in our professional men of religion and a religious spirit in our professional men of science " (Collingwood, 1927).

It is a valid point that reason will never get rid of faith, as if it did it would get rid of itself. But the consensus in the scientific and philosophical community, for now, does not acknowledge this. Anyone from such a community who even alludes to it, as we will explore now, comes under a barrage of invective. Not much seems to have moved on since Collingwood was writing in the 1920s. Large sections of the scientific community presuppose, unquestioningly, the rationality of the universe as a given; they take it as a matter of blind and unthinking faith. A recent debate highlights this. When Professor Paul Davies wrote a New York Times Op Ed called: "Taking Science on Faith" he attacked the absolute presupposition of science: ie, that the uniformity of the universe and its laws was just assumed as a given. You can see the full article here [9] Dangerously, but modestly, he suggested that his scientific community might like to look at other possibilities to help explain the universe. You may think that for other scientific minds he would be welcomed as a revolutionary and a free thinker, but he was attacked by no less than ten other eminent scientists for suggesting that they should question their static faith - which they, of course, refuse to recognise as faith. Their responses are contained here [10] Probably the most binary and unthinking attack from a fellow scientist was made by Sean Michael Carroll, Ph.D. a senior research associate in the Department of Physics at the California Institute of Technology:

> "Human beings have a natural tendency to look for meaning and purpose out there in the universe, but we shouldn't elevate that tendency to a cosmic principle. Meaning and purpose are created by us, not lurking somewhere within the ultimate architecture of reality. And that's okay. I'm happy to take the universe just as we find it; it's the only one we have."[11]

---

[9] http://www.nytimes.com/2007/11/24/opinion/24davies.html?_r=0
[10] http://www.edge.org/discourse/science_faith.html
[11] http://www.edge.org/discourse/science_faith.html

One of the undisputed benefits of the scientific frame of mind has been its relentless quest for knowledge. It does seem strange that at this particular juncture we just unquestionably accept the given of the universe as we find it, never seeking to find out *why* it is. His faith is of the unquestioning kind, indeed of the superstitious kind. It seems like a gross intellectual oversight that Carroll and his fellow disputants seem to not understand this fact. The shades of the mystic, the witch doctor, permeate through Carroll's view of the origins of the universe and the enduring uniformity of it.[12]

The Philosopher R M Hare in his essay "The Simple Believer" (Hare, 2004)[13] recognises the quality of the scientist when doing science properly, but goes one step further to confirm the religious nature of the scientist:

> "Suppose that a scientist has a hypothesis which he is testing by experiment, and the experiment shows him that his hypothesis was false. He then, after trying the experiment again once or twice to make sure there has been no silly mistake, says 'My hypothesis was wrong; I must try a new one.' That is to say, he does not stop believing in, or looking for regularities in the world which can be stated in the form of scientific 'laws'; he abandons this particular candidate. Thus, whatever happens, he still goes on looking for laws; nothing can make him abandon the search, for to abandon the search would be to stop being a scientist. He is just like the religious believer in this; in fact, we may say that belief of the scientist is one kind of religious belief - in kind, moreover, which is not incompatible with what is called Christian belief, for it is part of it.
>
> "I want to emphasize this point, because it is the most important I have to make. When the scientist refuses to give up his search for causal explanations of things, even when any number of proposed explanations fail, he is acting in an essentially religious manner." (Hare)

---

[12] One of the most informative and easy to read books addressed to the layman audience concerning the Higgs Field was written by this scientist, I do thoroughly recommend it despite his wanderings into areas he knows little about regarding the why of the universe. Nevertheless, he is a gifted scientific pedagogue.

[13] I am grateful for an email exchange with Dr David Gordon of the Mises Institute for drawing my attention to this book.

Hare explicitly notes the empirical fact that:

> *"It is rather a part of Christian belief. It is part of Christian belief to believe in the possibility of explaining things by means of scientific laws." (Hare)*

This will be explored later when we challenge the view which has gained credence that places religion in a hostile relationship with science. For now, we will maintain that the best scientists approach their science in a religious manner. At heart, the white coat of the laboratory is coming from the same place as the white smock of the clergy. Despite the fact that the he high priests of science now appear to carry more authority than the High Priests themselves, their methods are the same. Their faith, in this matter, is the same, wherever you find it.

The Apostate's Qualification

In a rejoinder at the end, Paul Davies re-clarifies his position to his colleagues who have missed his point that their enterprise rests in faith. I suspect that in order to be more scientifically respectful to his colleagues, after pointing out the obvious (which they take faith for granted), he provides the suggestion of a little 'get out of jail free card' for his community of non-believing believers:

> *"My article pointed out that the widespread belief in immutable perfect transcendent prior laws underpinning the physical universe, while not necessarily wrong, is nevertheless held as an act of faith, similar in character to belief in an all-perfect divine lawgiver. Let me be clear about the sense in which I am using the word faith here. Obviously faith in the laws of physics isn't on a par with "faith" in the popular religious sense (such as belief in miracles, prophecy, the bible as historical fact[14], etc., all of which I personally regard as completely ridiculous). Rather, in using the word faith I refer to the metaphysical framework, shared by monotheism and science (but not by many other cultures), of a rational ground that underpins physical existence. It is the shared faith that we live in a universe that is coherent, a universe that manifests a specific mathematical scheme of things, a universe that is, at least in part, intelligible to sentient*

---

[14] I would refer the learned Professor to my "Section Two The Real Evidence for Faith Provided by the Bible" and would challenge this aspect of this statement of his.

> mortals. These tacit assumptions running through science, that stem from monotheism, can all be challenged. The universe doesn't have to be that way! But most scientists believe it is that way." [15]

> "My interest in pursuing this project is to critically examine ultimate explanations of existence, for which there is a long tradition within religion, and a rather short one within science. I plead guilty to Lawrence Krauss' complaint that I am sidestepping some hugely important issues, such as the moral dimension of religious faith, the tragedy of human existence and suffering, and the question of purpose in the universe. My concern is admittedly with a restricted physics/cosmology agenda, as that is the only area in which I can claim some modest authority. However, the conceptual framework I am developing can accommodate a universe with something like "purpose," albeit one that is inherent in, and emergent with, the universe, rather than imposed upon it from without." [16]

Lee Smolin is the only one of Davies' respondents who recognises that Davies is suggesting to his colleagues that by looking at emergent theories you can perhaps move science away from this belief that all scientists reside, unbeknown to most of them, on a bedrock of faith, in their physical laws. This is because if they have emerged they are not given and taken on faith, but can be subjected to testing. It is odd to me that neither of these two more enlightened scientists on the matter - who have grasped the fact that the laws of nature seem to spring forth from (secular) faith - do not also grasp the fact that the reasoning they use to justify their investigations spring forth from a substratum of faith as well. So even if the emergent schema they propose does seem to stack up in the future, do the laws of reason get subjected to the same emergent thinking? Can it be possible that actually one plus one might have equalled one? But then it has slowly drifted to equalling two, or emerged as two over many cosmic unthinkably large time spans? I think not. The latter would be called polylogism: asserting that logic and your powers of reason can be different, that A can be non A. The former emergent natural law is called polynaturalism. Whilst scientifically intriguing, I feel it would falter in a similar way. Why? As one move of one of the fundamental cosmic constants one way or other wipes us all out of existence in the blink of an eye, there is nothing *emergent* about it. That the evolutionary algorithm works within these

---

[15] http://www.edge.org/discourse/science_faith.html
[16] http://www.edge.org/discourse/science_faith.html

constants should not be confused with their black-and-white nature and how they appear to operate, to us. Unless, of course, we suppose this has happened multiple time sand our random moment in all of it is just the 'now' we occupy. This is pure speculation only and will be discussed further in chapter 6 called 'The Current Cannon of Science.'

To reason, we assert the law of reason and the uniformity of nature. Smolin's attempt to ground science in laws that have emerged are not timeless, but change and evolve, just like biological systems which can be falsified and made subject to proper scientific inquiry along the lines of: make hypothesis, induce test, get result or not. This will be looked at in Chapter 6 as well. Suffice to say that I find it a truly heroic effort to move science away from its faith-based grounding. In my opinion, it does completely fail as he needs to assume a 'meta-law' that provides the *conformity* to allow you to *reason*, to expect to observe a *uniformity* of the universe and its laws and induction (which he calls 'precedent') that is assumed to make his emergent, evolving system work. Anyway, more of that later when we discuss 'The Curious Case of Lee Smolin', below. Let me say once more: science is never free of faith. Like Lee Smolin, Paul Davies seems to miss the point that even if the universe can be looked at via the lens of many emergent aspects, and speculated upon via reasoning, it all still rests on the same bedrock of faith. If there are emergent evolutionary laws and pathways of the great cosmic fundamental constants, then they will be laws explained by an unchanging reason and logic that in turn need explaining. Smolin, revolutionary pioneer that he is, I have no doubt, by suggesting that the immutable and transcendent laws imposed from without may have a rationality imposed from within, misses the point that that same rationality allowing him to postulate other emergent systems is still held as a matter of faith.

So faith is so much a part of their fabric that they don't see it, even with a sophisticated thinker like Davies who grasps this in part, and Smolin, who wishes to find a way to reject it. Yet they reject *themselves* if they were to succeed - which is, of course, impossible. The atheist philosopher Terry Nagel noted that for science to happen at all rests on an assumption that there is a basic intelligibility underlying the process:

> *"The view that rational intelligibility is at the root of the natural order makes me, in a broad sense, an idealist - not a subjective idealist, since it doesn't amount to the claim that all reality is ultimately appearance – but an objective idealist in the tradition of Plato and perhaps also of certain post-Kantians, such as Schelling and Hegel, who are usually called absolute idealists. I suspect that there must be a strain of this kind of idealism in every theoretical scientist: pure empiricism is not enough."* (Nagel)

Nagel may well be right. Empiricisim is but a method of looking at specific things, but never a method suitable for understanding the whole of reality. The cosmologist, whose endeavour is to explore the foundations of the cosmos, will never be able to answer the questions demanded by man as to 'why anything' at all. Science can only ask and answer the questions of science via its method and show us the 'how'. Its remit, properly understood, is not the ultimate questions of the 'why'. This seems to elude many scientists, with the result that when they pursue this line of questioning they all too often conclude it is either pointless, or unanswerable. This is not a surprise, as science is only looking at one aspect of our experience via its own methods of hypothesis, measurement and quantifying. It can't answer the 'why' question, nor should it try to as it is ill- equipped to do so: it is a round hole to a square peg. A classic illustration is to read Dawkins on science: he is magnificent when he delves into questions of why, but he is like a rabbit in the headlight going hither and tither, despite the fact that he thinks he is going somewhere! They are even more ill-equipped than most when they don't realise that every time they make an utterance it is on the assertion that there is a bedrock of faith in the conformity of the universe and its laws, of the laws of logic, the existence of the external world with all of us in it, and they don't realise that what they believe is their exercise of considered reason is in fact sprung from the substratum of faith.

Anyway, if I am right that science can't yield up fundamental answers concerning why we exist, whether God exists, why the universe exists - what branch of knowledge can answer these ultimate questions? For this, I fear we must delve into the very murky and at times unsatisfactory world of metaphysics and theology. That won't be until the next Chapter, and Chapters 7 and 8. The scientific method of induction and trying to postulate for itself a metaphysics renders scientists who try to answer the why anything in the universe question rudderless, and this in turn puts into question the integrity of their own scientific projects. We will consider these methodological errors next.

Chapter 3 Poor Methodology Exposes The Weakness of Science

The Great Methodological Misunderstandings of Science

"Metaphysics is the finding of bad reasons for what we believe upon instinct, but to find these reasons is no less an instinct." (Bradley)

The proper start point of science is to have a credible absolute presupposition which is untestable - neither right nor wrong – but that can't be *not* assumed. This is a true metaphysical proposition. As we have seen, at the conjunction of faith and reason exemplified in Descartes' Cogito, we have a universal truth: I exist. This is arrived at via reason which can't be denied, because as you start to reason and perform that act - that you might not exist - you contradict yourself. That you can't positively prove it surely means, therefore, that you hold firm by faith alone. This is a good absolute presupposition with which to start your system of reasoning. Likewise, the conformity and uniformity of the laws of nature and of logic are universally assumed, but can't be proved. We do, however, have good reason to take them on faith. To be clear: it is reasonable to absolutely presuppose them. Once more at this conjunction, we see faith and reason overlapping. These are true metaphysical absolute presuppositions. When a scientific scheme purports to start from something, we then need to examine whether it is a metaphysical proposition proper, or a pseudo metaphysical one. If it is the former, it is good science, if the latter, it is fiction – and, indeed, good science-fiction should not be equated with real science, being composed of stories created to deliberately evoke magic and mystery in the mind. Those that relate to cosmology, we will deal with in the Chapter 6 called 'The Current Canon of Science.' For now, we will look at a case in biology. Some scientists in this area are prone to lapse into starting their systems with some pseudo metaphysical utterances, which will mean their conclusions are bound to be inaccurate and rather more akin to some of the best science-fiction. These, really, are unsupported propositions that should be put to the test of science and not actually metaphysical propositions that form the foundation of science. This often happens when the scientist is better off remaining silent rather than trying to root his system in a bigger narrative. We see this in Richard Dawkins' book, the "Selfish Gene" (Dawkins, The Selfish Gene, 1976)[17]. He engages in a kind of metaphysics. Here is his 'In the Beginning' Genesis type moment:

> *"At some point a particularly remarkable molecule was formed by accident. We will call it the Replicator. It may not necessarily have been the biggest or the most complex molecule around, but it had the extraordinary property of being able to create copies of itself. This may seem a very unlikely sort of accident to happen. So it was. It was exceedingly improbable. In the lifetime of a man, things that are that improbable can be treated for practical purposes as impossible. That is why you will never win a big prize on the football pools. But in our human estimates of what is probable and what is not, we are not used to dealing in hundreds of millions of years. If you filled in pools coupons every week for a hundred million years you would very likely win several jackpots."*

The probability of accidental causes, molecules that just have a self-replicating ability emerging out of nowhere, will be looked at in Chapter 6, 'The Current Cannon of Science', when we examine what empirical grounds we have to believe what these high priests of science tell us. For now, I want to look at Dawkins' metaphysics, followed by his pseudo-metaphysics. Concerning the former, as is usual with all scientists, he takes on faith the orderliness of the universe and this allows him to conduct science in a predictable way, as a given, unquestioningly, and as a matter of blind, unthinking faith. Underlying logic and reason are assumed, with good reason - taken on faith alone. He asks no questions about why: they just are. His pseudo-metaphysics proper would seem to be his assumption that trillions of trillions of actions of non-conscious random matter can lead to the creation of conscious life, and that this

---

This book, from a collector's perspective, is a true gem. It will be read in many hundreds of years' time as it is a book that has helped shape the ideas of this period. Although he builds on Darwin, he advances new understandings about the evolutionary method and phenotypic effects that are now in common usage. I had my first edition signed by the great man himself and inquired if he still had his first edition with the iconic dust jacket. He said no. So I got him one. Opposite page 247 in his autobiography, I presume this must be my gift to him! (Dawkins, The Making of a Scientist, 2013)

randomness seems to work in a completely ordered way. All this, theoretically, can be tested empirically. Eat your heart out CERN, this would be the mother of all experiments - forget the 'God Particle,' actually the Higgs Field, and think the Genesis experiment, the ultimate Tower of Babel experiment. Needless to say, as we are dealing with material non-introspecting matter, and it could all be subject to the sort of test-and-refutation that the scientific community excel in. It may *become* science, but science it is not now. None of the points he makes are either proven or anywhere near to being proved, but as they relate to finite matter they are subject to the lens of science which, to date, provides no reason for believing such speculations. His start point is based on a pseudo metaphysical presupposition: that's the technical and polite wording for it. In the vernacular, we would call this wide speculation.

He further states from his pseudo-metaphysics:

"What does matter is that suddenly a new kind of 'stability' came into the world. Previously it is probable that no particular kind of complex molecule was very abundant in the soup, because each was dependent on building blocks happening to fall by luck into a particular stable configuration. As soon as the replicator was born it must have spread its copies rapidly throughout the seas, until the smaller building block molecules became a scarce resource, and other larger molecules were formed more and more rarely" (Dawkins, 1976).

"The next important link in the argument, one that Darwin himself laid stress on (although he was talking about animals and plants, not molecules) is competition. The primeval soup was not capable of supporting an infinite number of replicator molecules. For one thing, the earth's size is finite, but other limiting factors must also have been important. In our picture of the replicator acting as a template or mould, we supposed it to be bathed in a soup rich in the small building block molecules necessary to make copies. But when the replicators became numerous, building blocks must have been used up at such a rate that they became a scarce and precious resource. Different varieties or strains of replicator must have competed for them." (Dawkins, The Selfish Gene, 1976)

So - order from randomness occurs at some point, on a sufficiently large scale for life to occupy a whole planet, and competition for scarce resources thereafter abounds. This is a scientific proposition that is just *supposed*. The Genesis of the Hebrew Bible is just supposed, too, and I think this passage from

Dawkins will sound just as mysterious 4000 years after it was written as Genesis does today. The difference between the two is that Genesis never purports to be science, but rests as a story, a backdrop surrounding the even more mysterious event: that of the creation of the entire cosmos, explained to our ancestors in language they could understand thousands of years ago. Never has this been taken literally by any mainstream theologian, but rather read and understood metaphorically. Dawkins' creation of the life moment is pseudo metaphysics masquerading as science and he wants you to take it as serious fact. I submit he is better off saying something like: "I don't know how life was created, but I do know by what method it moved in time, from one incremental change, slowly, to the next, by the process of natural selection, and this natural selection is driven by the selfish replicating gene inside of us". Stepping outside his science, and trying to plug the gap in our knowledge of the 'why' of creation, attempting to slip in science - which in reality is pseudo-metaphysics - undermines the credibility of his whole project in which he does not need to be exposed to such a weakening of his work. Science and scientists do their best when they stick to their own particular knitting.

Methodology can be tedious, I agree, although, as we know, if you build your house on sand, it will be blown away in the first flood/storm/big event, leaving you houseless. Economists, if they have learned anything at all, will surely attest to this. We now move on to the next chapter to consider historical motivations which led scientists to explore, and what they subsequently found, from the advent of Christianity to the Enlightenment, through the Dark Ages and the Middle Ages, when we are taught at school that nothing much happened as those pesky Christians obliterated our ability to reason. Only to be heroically rescued by those great scientists whose guide was solely reason.

Chapter 4 Our Medieval , Dark Age, Primitive , Superstitious , Religious (Christian) , off with the Fairies Ancestors!

The Incomplete and Inaccurate View of the History of Science and its Promoters

There is a general view that seems prevalent in the modern scientific canon - again, you can see this best expressed in the Edge.org blog article referred to above - when discussing faith and the scientists. It is that there were Greeks, 2,500 years ago, who were largely focused on maths and who laid the foundations of science. Christianity came along and halted this progress. There was a little flourish from the Islamists 1500 years later, building upon work done by the Greeks, so it goes. Meanwhile, in the Western World, after the fall of Rome, the Dark Ages and the Middle Ages descended upon us, during which religion and superstition reigned supreme and when, it is often supposed, little or no progress was made. Then the Humanists and the Enlightenment spectacularly arrive on the scene to shake us up, to wake us up from our peasant-like and rather primitive and pitiful existence by giving us science! Glory to those rationalists who have saved man from his witless existence!

During this period, it continues, religion actively persecuted the probing, questioning, inquisitive, scientific mind, restricting areas of free thought. Religion of all forms was thought detrimental to progress and fought tooth and nail against any scientific progress, executing heretics as you would swat flies along the way. Reason triumphed and we are in a better place today. So says the gospel of modern scientists and historians. One of its own High Priests comments:

> "Gibbon ....In the revolution of ten centuries,, not a single discovery was made to exalt the dignity or promote the happiness of mankind." (Pelikan, The Spirit of Eastern Christendom)

Gibbon was one of the first to proselytise this view. According to Gibbon, in 529 Justinian closed the Classical School of philosophy in Athens. In commenting on this it is clear that the theologians are the bad guys. According to the historian Gibbon they:

> " ... superseded the exercise of reason, resolved every question by article of faith, and condemned the infidel or sceptic to internal flames. In many a volume of laborious controversy they exposed the weakness of the understanding and the corruption of the heart , insulted human nature in the sages of antiquity, and proscribed the spirit of philosophical inquiry, so repugnant to their doctrine, or at least to their temper , of an humble unbeliever." (Pelikan, The Emergence of the Catholic Tradition (100-600

This statement, unfortunately for Gibbon, is not supported by the facts. According to Pelikan:

> "The closing of the Athenian academy was more the act of a coroner than an executioner. The establishment of the imperial University of Constantinople by Theodosius II, or perhaps by Constantine himself, had already transferred the centre of Greek learning from Athens to the new capital of the Hellenic world." [18]

So the pagan school in Athens had moved to Constantinople, and indeed the pagan scholars did get safe passage by Justinian to effect this.

If we take a look at some of the statements of the scientists made in their attack against their fellow scientist above, we can see that the picture I paint of their views, albeit simplified and incomplete, nevertheless stands up quite well. For example, the scientist Scott Atran writes:

---

[18] http://www.bede.org.uk/justinian.htm Here the historian James Hannam hunts down an actually translates this decree and it seems that public funding was removed from heretical teaching but no ban on it.

> "The scientific revolution began in earnest when a Polish cleric, Nicolaus Copernicus, bucked his faith and theorized that the earth turned around the sun. The Church did not pay much mind as long as the theory remained in the realm of speculation. But when Italian philosopher Galileo Galilei empirically confirmed the theory with a telescope, the Church banned Copernicus's teachings as "false and altogether opposed to the Holy Scripture. " In 1633, Galileo himself was brought to trial by the Holy Inquisition and compelled to recant.
>
> "Given the supposed risk of society's moral degradation in the face of the free choice to make up one's own mind ("I think, therefore I am"), the Church violently insisted that ideological faith in absolute authority ("In the beginning, God created the heavens and the earth") must always trump the more tentative teaching that goes with clear reasoning and experimental observation. When the Enlightenment unshackled scientific thinking from lingering religious control, religion opted for a separate realm where science would not operate. Science, for the sake of its peace and independence, generally accepted this division into separate "Magesteria." In 1992 the Catholic Church cleared Galileo's name and in 2000 Pope Jean Paul II apologized to God (not to Galileo) for the trial." [19]

And:

> "Einstein, like Newton before him, believed that the universe was structured with deterministic mathematical regularity; Bohr and most of Einstein's later colleagues did not. Einstein did not ignore Bohr, or want to try him or burn him at the stake, but continued to argue with him and to provisionally accept his findings," [20]

Are there any facts to support this? James Hannam takes such a view to task in his book "God's Philosophers How the Medieval World Laid the Foundations of Modern Science," (Hannam, 2010), and lays down a very serious challenge to this common world view:

> "The achievements of medieval science are so little known today that it might seem natural to assume that there was no scientific progress at all during the Middle Ages. ..Writers use the adjective 'medieval' as a synonym for brutality and uncivilized behavior ..... Even historians, who should know better, still seem addicted to the idea that nothing of any consequence occurred between the fall of the Roman Empire and the Renaissance." (Hannam)

---

[19] http://www.edge.org/discourse/science_faith.html

[20] http://www.edge.org/discourse/science_faith.html

> "Closely coupled to the myth that there was no science worth mentioning in the Middle Ages is the belief that the church held back what meagre advances were made."
> (Hannam)

Following in the tradition of the writings of The American Lynn Thorndike (1882-1965) and the German Anneliese Maier (1905-71), who did much to revive this lost part of our history, so Hannam launches his counter-blast. With reference to between 500 AD and 1500 AD he discusses modern inventions and notable knowledge-enhancing events. He starts with a simple story of the modest, but revolutionary invention of stirrups and ends in a little straightening out of the facts surrounding the trial of Galileo.

Our Much Maligned Pre-Enlightenment Ancestors

We learn that the laws of Rome had restricted how much load you could get a horse to pull. The peasants, by this time, had developed a horizontal wooden log chained to the front of the plough cart with the horse attached to it, thus equalising the load and allowing more to be pulled by the animal for less energy. The invention of the horseshoe added durability. Mill technology grew. All of this allowed a massive productivity increase in the land under cultivation.

The population of the UK rose from 500,000 at the fall of Rome to 5m by the time of the Normans. Just this alone shows that Gibbon's remark at the start of this section was well off the mark. The Domesday Book draws our attention to the fact that peasants on the land were tilling the soil, which implies a plough, digging, turning and relaying the soil, burying weeds and the remainder of last year's crop, increasing fertility and productivity with far less labour required.

The Normans had stirrups, so they could balance their weight and propel their full force behind their weapon, making them more effective in battle than the stirrup-less rider who had to concentrate more on being mounted than effectively fighting. No uncivilised, theologically oppressed, Dark Age/Medieval peasants were these ancestors of ours. Now that they used these stirrups when they went into battle, their experience of horse riding was significantly improved. Not a massive earth shattering invention, but religiously oppressed people they were not.

Meanwhile, while our agricultural ancestors were making great innovations in their sector, medicine, maths (algebra, algorithms), philosophy, art and literature were advancing. At the same time, much more was being progressed under the Muslims, inspired by Christian teachings and Greek learning. These conquerors of the Greek lands were the inheritors of that ancient tradition of rationality. In the 5th Century, Probus of Antioch translated much of Aristotle for the Arabs. In the 9Th Century, the Assyrian Christian, Hunayan iBn Isaq, translated Plato's Republic, Aristotle's Categories, Physics and seven books of Galen's anatomy. The latter must have been a very brave undertaking as no pictures of the body are allowed by Islam. At the same time, the Syriac Christian, Yahya ibn Adi, translated into Arabic, Plato's Laws, Aristotle's Topics, Theophrastus' Metaphysics and more. That is not, of course, to say that the Byzantines did not preserve their own heritage and literature and keep learning from it, just that the Muslim world were better exploiters of that work at that time. Whilst the Muslims helped preserve the Greek texts that they translated into Arabic and later into Latin, we must remember they were always extant in the Eastern Orthodox world. There is a myth that it was the Islamic world which preserved these texts, but one small reflection on the 1000 year history of Constantinople, with its Greek culture, should expel that myth easily. I picked up the works of the Greek St John of Damascus, who is generally classified as the last of the Church Fathers. His Orthodox faith, which is loaded with references to Aristotle, was first translated into Old Slavonic in the 10th Century, then, in the same century into Arabic by Anthony, the superior of the Monastery of St Simeon Stylites by Antioch. Pope Eugene III in the 12th Century was ordering translations from Greek to Latin. The Muslims has the Greek philosophy because of Christian translations into Arabic. The myth of them preserving Western thought should be resisted as it is simplistic and not true. Meanwhile, earlier and over in the Latin world, the 'Carolingian Renaissance' of Charlemagne employed the services of Alcuin of York (735-804) to preserve all the classical works of literature in the Latin. No rationalitysupressing religious hot-head was he, either. So much of the original works of the Eastern Empire of Rome were translated into Latin long before the rest were translated from the Arabic. That is not to downplay the Arab injection of knowledge into the Western World - just that it was not the 'everything' that modern writers would have you believe. For example, few might know that the on-going development of the understanding of the cosmos and maths was led by the Pope: The 'Mathematical Pope' Gerbert of Aurillac. He helped introduce Arabic numerals to the West (including zero). These were incorporated into the abacus to help people calculate, thus improving their lives.

The Astrolabe was probably introduced to Europe from Persia by Gerbert: it could predict lunar eclipses and movements of the stars. The medieval world view was actually very knowledgeable, as we can see from Boethius (6th Century), who wrote in his "Consolation of Philosophy":

> "It is well known and you have seen it demonstrated by astronomers, that besides the extent of the heavens, the circumference of the earth has the size of a point; that is to say, compared to the magnitude of the celestial sphere, it may be thought of as having no extent at all." (Hannam) [date?]

Much confusion exists when moderns point to the Mappa Mundi, like that in Hereford Cathedral showing the circular earth with the sea around it, Jerusalem at its centre, along with the Mediterranean. This, of course, only illustrated what they knew at the time was the whole of the inhabited world. Gerbert calculated the circumference of the earth to be 29,000 miles, so he was not that far off. The area they knew was inhabited was mapped on a flat surface - but this did not mean they believed in a flat earth!

> "The falsity of the presupposition does not, therefore ... affect the truth-value of the sentence which uses them. Psalm 104 praises God for many marvels of nature including that 'he laid the foundations of the Earth, that it should not be moved forever.' (104:5). Now the earth has no 'foundations' in some other body, as the Psalmist supposed. But what he was getting at was the earth was not wobbly, you can build on it, it is firm; and he expressed the claim that God is responsible for this stability, the sentence is true."

(Swinburne, Revelation, 1992)

It was also considered that were the bible to be conflicted with current science, a non-literal view should be taken in favour of the science of the day. St Augustine had long ago in the 5th Century pointed to the conflict in Genesis, when, on the fourth day, the sun is created, but on the first day light was created, illustrating that the Bible should not necessarily be read literally, but metaphorically.

Another saint of the Church, St Thomas Aquinas, was also an advocate of this approach:

> *"Thus Aquinas doubted in whether there were in the literal sense 'waters above the firmament' (Genesis 1:7) on the scientific grounds that any water in such parts would be compelled by its weight to fall down to the Earth. He therefore interprets the text in accord with the principle that 'God was speaking to ignorant people and out of condescension to their simpleness presented to them only those things immediately obvious to the sense.'"* (Swinburne, Revelation, 1992)

Summa Theologiae 1 a 68 3 translation William Wallace OP (Blackfriars 1967)

Aquinas in "De Genesi ad litteram" specifically says it is a metaphorical interpretation that the sun was only made on the fourth day when light was made on the first day and you needed the sun to make what we know as a day, as opposed to a literal interpretation underscoring the flexible way you need to read the Bible, as was common with all works of man at the time.

Psalm 96:10 is often used to show that the biblical view is of a flat earth fixed in space:

> *"The World also is firmly established. It shall not be moved."* It then continues in verses 11-13 " *Let the heavens rejoice, and let the earth be glad; let the sea roar, and*

all its fullness; let the field be joyful, and all that is in it. Then all of the trees of the woods will rejoice before the Lord."

Now, do we really think the Psalmist was asking us to believe the sea had a voice and that it roars? Or that the earth could be glad like a human could be glad? Or that the trees themselves could whoop with joy as people might when watching an uplifting film? Or is the Psalmist trying to evoke emotion - dare I say it, a feeling of enchantment - in the reader? For surely it is absurd to read this literally. We will see later how in the Book of Job, when some very precise scientific things are said in a factual way concerning a spherical world we can read them literally. This contrasts with writings like the Psalm mentioned, demanding our discernment between the two modes. Interestingly, some 500 years before Christ, the Bible was very explicit in warning readers against the study of astrology. Jeremiah 10:2-3 states:

"Do not learn the way of the Gentiles; Do not be dismayed at the signs of heaven, For the Gentiles are dismayed at them. For the customs of the peoples are futile;"

The instruction was clear: it's a no to astrology![21]

In the 12th century, universities were established free from royal interruption so they could concentrate on the scientific study of God's creation, nature itself. This study of nature or 'natural philosophy' blossomed during this period.

"Most significant of all for the future development of science was the movement to translate into Latin an enormous body of newly discovered scientific and medical writing from the ancient Greek and Islamic worlds. This flood of new knowledge meant that Western Europe could assimilate it and then progress from all that had gone before." (Hannam)

"If any period deserves the label of 'renaissance' then it is the twelfth century." (Hannam)

---

[21] Amos 5:8 also condemns the worship of the stars as does 5:26 and Zephaniah 1:5. The rationalist / Humanists of the Enlightenment would appear to be one on this matter of star gazing.

Adelard of Bath during this time translated Euclid's' "Elements", the foremost book on geometry. Clear axioms elaborated the whole of geometry with inescapable conclusions. Logic could do the same in other areas, it was held. At this time from Greek and Arabic into Latin went most of the key texts of Western antiquity to be translated and not lost to the Western, Latin part of the World. In the West, the universities, based on monastic convention, formed themselves into corporations, independent of either Royal or State control. These corporations eventually became the forerunners of the modern corporation which allowed, as it did with the universities, groups of individuals to form one united body with its own legal status separate from its constituent members. Here we see the founding principles of the establishment of that very essential element of modern life, the corporation! The Law School of Bologna in 1158 was the first of these corporations. In 1222 the University of Padua was set up to accommodate disgruntled students from here. The early 13th century saw the establishment of Oxford and feeder 'public' schools, all religiously inspired, to introduce a new and wider intake of people to the education system.

As with all human institutions, both now and in antiquity, the Church itself has periods it might rather forget. Ironically, the Inquisition used the new techniques of law, promulgated by the Law School of Bologna to investigate heresy. If The Inquisition found a heretic guilty, he was invited to do penance and repent, which was usually a very lenient option, contrary to the blood and guts, torture images of the Protestant Reformation. Later, in chapter 10, we will assess the scale of the Inquisition v the scale of secular deaths at the time, and up to the present day, to see who was the most blood-thirsty - the Church or the secular authorities. The reason for this is if you take seriously the much-touted atheist assertion that all wars are created by religion, and that religion is the disease permeating humanity and the last vestige of a pre-rational mind we should be rid of, we should expect to see the Inquisition as the champion in the death and destruction stakes. More of that later. However, the church, at this time, had no power to execute, but had to hand over to the secular powers the charged heretic, who would invariably receive another, lesser punishment.

Over a number of centuries, about 5% did end in executions, to the shame of the Church. Deaths were in their low tens of thousands over several centuries with the largest estimates being circa 300,000 deaths over nearly 400 years[22]. Still disgraceful, but compared to the fanaticism of the National Socialist killers in Europe during the Second World War, the killings by the Socialists in Russia/the Soviet Union, the mass murders in China under the Socialist Mao, and the socialist killing fields of Cambodia, to name but a few, this is a mere drop in the man-on-man-made blood-letting of humanity. The numbers here are in excess of 125m human deaths in less than a century, against which deaths caused by the Inquisition pale into insignificance by comparison. Totally devoid of any belief in God were the Socialist, rationalist, planned systems which set them in train.

However much of a digression this is, the authority on the matter seems to be James Buchannan: "Inquisitions in Medieval Society: Power Discipline and Resistance in Languedoc", 1997. Most members of the Church realised that it became apparent that large parts of the population were not taught properly, therefore it was better to focus on teaching in these matters than prosecuting poorly held and thought out beliefs. This lead to the establishment of a whole new education movement. It is a paradox that this cruel part of church history led to a massive educational mission on behalf of the wider population, but it did.

As with modern warfare, we often hear from the state sponsors of war that the expenditure of £X taxpayers' money is justified in the military arena as the technological spin offs that result get picked up by the private sector and given to the wider use of humanity. In the Crusades, we also had the physics of war at play, showing us that the direction of man's endeavours have not necessarily changed during the interim. The Crusades against the Northern heathens, and the appalling pillaging of the Byzantines allowed the development of technology. The levers of the Trebuchet were great example of

---

[22] See the detailed body count in the notes in the Chapter 10 called "Those Religious & Atheist (Genocidic) Mass Murders"

this. Later on we see that at The Fall of Constantinople in 1453, Mehmet had engaged Urban, the Hungarian engineer, to deploy his gigantic canon to knock down the walls: warfare and technology going hand in hand, just as it always was and still is today.

During this medieval period, we are led to believe little good could emerge as the toxicity of religion ensured all rationality was supressed by the church. We have a Dominican monk, (St) Guzmen, founding the Order of the Preachers in 1216. He taught that representatives of the church must live their lives like Jesus, or how could anyone expect to learn from them anything about the Christian message? The black habit they wore led them to be called Blackfriars. They became involved with the emerging universities, reversing the short ban on the teaching of Aristotle in 1231, and established firmly that natural philosophy was the hand maiden of theology. Friar St Thomas Aquinas made the teaching of Aristotle essential. Thomas Aquinas's Scholastic Method and his 'Five Ways' to know God were not proofs to God, but showed how reason could be used to fully bolster your faith. The Greeks were now becoming more than ever fully integrated into the Western Church, sowing the seeds for the Enlightenment. At this time, to protect the quality of their standard of teaching, theologians took a leaf out of the medical profession's book and established minimum standards. It took seven years to qualify as a theologian. Medical doctors and other professions had a similar period of training before being qualified. The latter even prosecuted people who were not trained properly and now theologians did the same. They got very serious about their educational mission at this time. They also forced a long over-due separation between philosophy and theology teaching. New graduates of philosophy had to swear they would not enter into the realms of theology. If they wanted to get involved with theology, then they must train in theology: this was the answer. The same would apply for the discipline of philosophy discipline.

Although much progress was made with the enlightenment of church teachings and their educational mission, it was not a clear run home for reason from here on into the Enlightenment itself. In 1277 The Bishop of Paris had prepared 219 condemnations of the teachings of Averroes the Aristotelean. This was summed up by the Bishop prohibiting anyone from saying: "God cannot do anything that is naturally impossible." Much of the credit for making sure the condemnations did not get much traction was that, although recently dead, St Thomas Aquinas had constantly referred to Averroes in his works. The Dominicans had lobbied hard for raising Aquinas to sainthood. This eventually happened, and from thenceforth no one could argue that Christianity and Aristotle could not be taught together. As he was a saint of the Church, you could therefore not teach his works without reference to Averroes. Short lived regressions such as these pop in and out of our history, but by and large the Church was very much at the forefront of pushing through the education of as many as possible, with faith allowing reason to be its chief lead. This 'Averroes episode' demonstrated that it was not a banning of philosophy, but a curtailment of its role so that the disciplines of philosophy and theology, along with all the other disciplines, could be taught separately as masters of their own areas with the view that all could go about their business in peace and within properly accepted intellectual demarcations.

At this time also, what become known as 'the Merton Calculators' - based around Merton College Oxford - of Bradwardine, Heytesbury, Swineshead and Dumbleton, all accelerated the learning of mechanics in the early 14th Century, helping pave the way for Newton. The mathematician Archbishop of Canterbury from Merton Collage Oxford, Thomas Bradwardine, invented logarithms 300 years before Napier was accredited with inventing them. He also speculated about how, in a vacuum, a light and a heavy object would drop at the same speed. Over the English Channel, the Rector of the University of Paris, Buridan, was another nominalist who was also busy laying the foundations of Newtonian mechanics, as was his Archbishop cousin Bradwardine. Contra Aristotle, he said that the hand moves the ball by giving it impetus. The concept of momentum was developing its own momentum! He thought, with Aristotle, that up in the heavens there was no friction. He also thought that if something did not interrupt this impetus the moving would last forever. This was the start of questioning what causes the planets to move and stay in motion. Inertia would stop everything, if subject to force. We see here the outlying thoughts underpinning the Newtonian system. In fact, with two notable theologians practising science, we observe the groundwork for the birth of logarithms and the Newtonian system.

Buridan knew the night sky made it appear that the earth had all the stars rotating around it. He did not like the thought of the immensely large universe turning around the tiny earth. God's plan was inelegant. He used the analogy of a boat going down the river with an observer on the boat and on the bank and to each, the other would appear moving. Buridan said the whole atmosphere moved with us. We see much in modern science about relativity emerging here as well. He pre-dated Copernicus by two centuries. He mathematically proved the mean speed theorem via his graphs. The church sponsored universities were the *only places responsible for progressing science.* Contrary to the modern notion that all the Church did was step on free thinking and at worst burn people at the stake, it actively encouraged the scientific discovery process. At this time, Cardinal Nicholas Cusa was arguing in his "On Learned Ignorance" for a non-earth-centric universe with planets rotating relative to each other.

At the turn of the 14th Century came the philosopher St Dun Scotus to carry on the work of Aquinas in advocating reason as a tool for understanding God. He did not argue that God was constrained by the natural laws of the universe He created, but that He could do anything. Thus science should be encouraged to look for any explanation in nature. In fact, Science was positively encouraged to look. We must not forget that at that time the monk William of Ockham also arrived on the scene with his famous "Razor," he was a Franciscan. William of Ockham was a supporter of the nominalist position, as opposed to the universalist position of St Duns Scotus. Against Scotus, he actually stated that we can explain all things - individual things - without need of inventing imaginary universals. This was the famous "Ockham's Razor" that *"multiple entities should never be evoked unnecessarily."*

As said, this is often used by modern science to reject more complex theories. However, species, electrons, are all universals that have real properties to the scientist, though they would not be universals to Ockham. He would have razored out all of their key tools of universal and metaphysical explanation/ speculation if he were alive today making it a paradox, as he is held in such high esteem by modern science which so frequently uses universals plucked from their Platonic, universal heaven! Collingwood (in his "Philosophical Method") makes a similar point about using the analogy of a medical student being taught about a text-book case of tuberculosis. In this, we learn about a universal case. However, the practitioner of medicine should always be mindful that it is just that - a text-book, hypothetical case. If you speak to any doctor, he will tell you that any diagnosis is patient-specific and as such is always marginally different for each patient, therefore unique. Some of the blandishments of scientists would do well to take this into account and carefully distinguish between when they are talking in abstractions to assist them with understanding, and when they are referencing reality. More attention to Ockham could well have prevented the current global recession, as we have seen, and could have led Dawkins to conclude what I would consider a much more observable and indeed reasonable suggestion: that we are not driven by our selfish genes, but by our self-interested genes, and above all by our rationally-orientated consciousness.

On a more practical note at the time medieval medicine was making emergent progress, one myth that is common and worth shooting down is that the church banned human body dissection. "De Sepulturis," the Papal Bull of 1300, banned the boiling of bodies, not their dissection. Human dissection was on the syllabus of every major university, most theologically founded and run at the time, needless to say. No, human dissection was not banned by the church. Bleeding was not considered irrational. It does to us today and I don't doubt that in 500 years' time, cutting off body parts, subjecting patients to heavy doses of radiation, and much more of modern medicine will be thought of as totally barbaric. However, we must remember that it was these 'medieval barbarians' whose shoulders we have stood on during each generation, progressed to the point of being able to prevent and cure what we can today. It should also be remembered that by 1306, when sight-enhancing spectacles were in existence - refracting the light in order to produce 20/20 vision and showing us how truly path-breaking our ancient ancestors were - this is the so-called period of history when nothing much happened! During this period, not only reading glasses were made, but a monk from St Albans, the clock-maker Richard of Wallingford, developed a mechanical clock which could chime in any of the 12 hours. This was a new invention. Wallingford's clock is what you can see in all its glory on public display at the Abbey Cathedral of St Albans today.

Let us also not forget that the invention of the printed book occurs toward the end of the medieval period. Although most bits of printing technology existed already, Gutenberg, a great entrepreneur, invented moving typeface and a non-smudging ink, and putting the two technologies together achieved the ability to print books on a large scale, to the great benefit of mankind. Thousands of books were printed in this period and distributed to a much wider audience than ever before. Today, this leap forward is akin to the impact of the technological/Internet revolution.

Why was most of this understanding lost to us? The emergence of the Humanists turned the word 'medieval' into an insult and attempted to consign to oblivion all their predecessors' works. These were not atheists as the word has been associated with in modern times, but religious people who had a belief in faith and especially liked the teachings of the Greeks and the Latins. They idolized Latin in the 'pure' form spoken by Cicero, despite the fact that no one ever spoke as he wrote. Plato's work started to be translated and was promoted above that of Aristotle. Then there was the systematic destruction of medieval scholarship. Logic was taken off the syllabus. The protesters condemned Scotus ("dunce" became a play on his name – Cromwell banished his works) as the worst of the Scholastics and marginalized Aquinas, Ockham and their like. The Humanists held back the development of their predecessors' thoughts and undoubtedly held back the progress of science. But printers kept the old alive. And progress did still continue, though now at a slower pace.

We are often told that medieval folk believed the earth was flat and that the Bible had told us this was so. Astronomers from the time of the Greeks always knew Mercury and Venus were only visible at sunrise and sunset and some speculated that these planets must rotate around the sun. From the Greeks, all planets were meant to move in perfect unison. This did not reflect the changing brightness of some or the apparently erratic and at times backwards movement of others. Puzzles very much remained out there to be discovered and resolved during and after the Copernican revolution. However, many theologians openly professed the spherical nature of the earth and took a non-heliocentric view of the universe, contra the Greeks' and the Romans' so-called proto-Enlightenment teachings.

Let us start with the Bible. The Old Testament Book of Job asserted that if you looked from the northern hemisphere you could see a very different set of stars to those visible in the southern hemisphere. The implication is that during this time they must have travelled into the southern hemisphere and been aware of the spherical nature of the world and quite possibly what it rotates around.

Job 9:9 "He made the Bear, Orion, and the Pleiades, and the chambers of the south"

This is reinforced in a later chapter:

Job 26:10 "He drew a circular horizon on the face of the waters, At the boundary of light and darkness."

Form this same chapter we also have this suggestion (that God):

Job 26:7 "He stretches out the north over empty space; He hangs the earth on nothing."

And:

Isaiah 40:22 "It is He who sits above the circle of the earth"

The phrase "foundations of the earth" is to signify nothing more than the solidity we stand on and is used metaphorically in the Bible, as we have seen. The Bible is clear on its teachings about a spherical earth and Copernicus leaned on the ancient teaching of the Bible. As part of the Old Testament, the Talmud tradition suggests Moses as the author of Job but we will probably never know. The traditional view is that since the Book of Job was set in an adjacent territory, and as the Chaldeans mentioned in the story are marauding raiders, this suggests a time of writing before they were city dwellers, placing it around 1500 BC. It is good to know that knowledge of the southern hemisphere and a completely 'new' set of stars in the heavens of the southern hemisphere, with all the implications this has, predates the Enlightenment 'discovery' of this by probably 3000 years! At the latest, Job was post the Flood (approximately 4500 BC), so this knowledge could have been with us for us much as 6000 years before the Enlightenment. Isaiah was an 8-7th Century BC prophet, so even if Job is set aside, then for nearly 2100 years the spherical earth has been biblical teaching. Either way, the writer of this ancient book had a clear understanding of a circular world, set in space. In the Book of Job, you will see much usage of language suggesting the world and all creation was built on solid foundations, on "pillars" and so on. Also, as if there has been a great big construction project based on *terra firma*. I tend to view these passages as talking in the language of the time to communicate to the target audience who, more than likely, were unaware of the implications of the passages quoted above. After all, we sophisticated moderns still say the sun is 'rising' in the east and that it is 'setting' in the west, rather than suggesting that when we use such common expressions we should qualify them with: "actually, look at the sun disappearing over the horizon, we must have rotated around our axis again". I tend to also view passages which say the earth is stationary and we are on solid footings are still are used in common language to provide ease of communication. This, of course, would be easier than having to say: "well, actually what I mean is we are still relative to something else moving, and from its perspective we are moving and it is still" all the time .

The modern scientist uses language in a particularly qualified manner which, if you are not aware of it, or do not pick it up in their writings, you can end up imputing things they don't necessarily mean which often turn out to be the opposite of what they actually mean. The philosopher Mary Midgley's "Gene-Juggling"[23] review (Midgley, 1979) of the scientist Richard Dawkins' "The Selfish Gene" is a classic case in point. Dawkins in his opening remarks says:

> "The argument of this book is that we, and all other animals, are machines created by our genes. Like successful Chicago gangsters, our genes have survived, in some cases for millions of years, in a highly competitive world. This entitles us to expect certain qualities in our genes. I shall argue that a predominant quality to be expected in a successful gene is ruthless selfishness. This gene selfishness will usually give rise to selfishness in individual behaviour. However, as we shall see, there are special circumstances in which a gene can achieve its own selfish goals best by fostering a limited form of altruism at the level of individual animals. 'Special' and 'limited' are important words in the last sentence. Much as we might wish to believe otherwise, universal love and the welfare of the species as a whole are concepts that simply do not make evolutionary sense."
> (Dawkins, The Selfish Gene, 1976)

The word 'selfish,' in common usage, implies a self, a consciousness if you like, which would seem to imply that genes have consciousness. Their selfish behaviour within us guides us, or at least influences us to proceed in a selfish fashion. As there is no consciousness specific to our genes as far as we are aware, it would appear to Midgley, that Dawkins has invented an imaginary construct to describe his views: that of self-aware genes replicating, whereas Dawkins is actually saying it is the actions of the mindless genes that are giving us the impression at the individual human level of selfish behaviour, which of course is something quite different.

If you read Aristotle literally, you may well make the same mistake due to the limitations of language. He theorised that nature had its nisus, its pulling

---

[23] Although I do not quote from this article, or the response from Dawkins and the reply by Midgely, I list them in the Bibliography as they are very instructional in understanding Dawkins.

towards, its impulse, its teleological end point implied in all things. All live things were responding to some final cause, ie a Platonic Form or some other immaterial thing which it was trying to emulate. The *final cause* is also the *efficient cause* with Aristotle. If the plant is growing to the full potential of the adult plant, the form is actually pulling it this way and must be responsible for all action in every respect of the plant: it is the efficient and the final cause of the plant's growth. For Aristotle, although the plant cannot think (as in Dawkins' use of the phrase 'selfish gene'), it does not imply there is consciousness in that plant making it grow as it has a desire to reach this perfect goal of the immaterial form of the plant. For Aristotle, this was the immaterial being which is the unmoved first mover of the natural world. Darwin used the word 'selection,' which evokes a teleology in nature. Modern Darwinists - those who promote the selfish gene and survival of the fittest theories - imply a teleology that I suspect their authors would deny!

Very early in "The Selfish Gene," Dawkins qualifies his point, as follows:

> *"It is important to realize that the above definitions of altruism and selfishness are behavioural, not subjective. I am not concerned here with the psychology of motives. I am not going to argue about whether people who behave altruistically are 'really' doing it for secret or subconscious selfish motives. Maybe they are and maybe they aren't, and maybe we can never know, but in any case that is not what this book is about. My definition is concerned only with whether the effect of an act is to lower or raise the survival prospects of the presumed altruist and the survival prospects of the presumed beneficiary." (Dawkins, In Defence of Selfish Genes, 1981)*

If this qualification were not clarified at this point, it would appear that a common sense interpretation would render Dawkins a complete mystic in supposing, with no evidence, that chunks of chromosome have personality and think in the full sense that the complete 'you' does. Understand his qualification on the use of language and the book is coherent on this point.

> *""For brevity, we shall again use the convention of thinking of the individual as though it had a conscious purpose. As before, we shall hold in the back of our mind that this is just a figure of speech. A body is really a machine blindly programmed by its selfish genes." (Dawkins, The Selfish Gene, 1976)*

> "Anybody can see that, as a matter of fact, genes do not control their creations in the strong sense criticized as 'determinism'. We effortlessly (well, fairly effortlessly) defy them every time we use contraception" (Dawkins, The Selfish Gene 30th Anniversary Edition)

> "We, that is our brains, are separate and independent enough from our genes to rebel against them. As already noted, we do so in a small way every time we use contraception. There is no reason why we should not rebel in a large way, too." (Dawkins, The Selfish Gene 30th Anniversary Edition)

As with any books, biblical or scientific, you really need to get close to the authors' intentions and make every effort to understand how they are using language in the way they do before you leap in to condemn them. If you read the Bible, just as you need to read Dawkins, you will see that the flat earth view advocated by many atheists, especially those who blog on the Internet and as suggested by unthinking dullards, is not in the Bible at all. For Dawkins, as I read him, the suggestion is that acts of stimulation by the genes to generate X,Y or Z effect on the outside world lead to some strategies being effective and some not. Those that are not, cease to be effective for the genes in question and they die out while those that are effective and prolong survival will survive. Such give the outward appearance of being consciously moved, but in reality they are mechanically driven, blindly and by chance. The conscious mind may well have developed this way, over many billions of years, giving us the appearance of an ability to think for ourselves, but really we are just the beneficiaries of zillions of trial and error interactions with antecedent gene battles which give us the optionality to think through scenarios of various choices in order to enhance that survival. We can even appear to ourselves to overcome these blindly programed replicators and defy them. This view has almost completely taken over the scientific academy to become the mainstream view. Offer opposition and you are rabidly shouted down.

Dawkins also argues we are just like the Deep Thought computer chess programme that has learnt to think and can play and beat human interlocutors. His analogy is that although man built the Deep Thought programme, it needs no creator nudging it along. Given a view billions of years, the random interaction of molecules could well have created such a thing as a thinking machine and his attestation is that it did, and that thinking machine is us. On this point, I think he is wrong as well. I am reminded of a passage in F A Hayek's work on psychology: (Hayek, 1952)[24]

> "8.67. Apart from these practical limits of explanation, which we may hope continuously to push further back, there also exists, however, an absolute limit to what the human brain can ever accomplish by way of explanation-a limit which is determined by the nature of the instrument of explanation itself, and which is particularly relevant to any attempt to explain mental processes."

And:

> "8.69. The Proposition which we shall attempt to establish is that any apparatus of classification must possess a structure of higher degree of complexity than is possessed by the objects which it classifies; and that, therefore, the capacity of any explaining agent must be limited to objects with a structure of possessing a degree of complexity lower than its own. If this is correct, it means that no explaining agent can ever explain objects of its own kind, or of its own degree of complexity, and , therefore, that the human brain can never fully explain its own operations. This statement possesses, probably, a higher degree of prima facie plausibility".

Essentially, as I understand it, the classifying unit, or the human being, needs always to have a bigger capacity than the classifying object, that is, the Deep Thought chess programme in Dawkins' analogy. So as to what robots we set in motion, it must be presupposed as a matter of logic that it is a lesser intelligence than we, the creator. This is why we can never explain God in full, and artificial intelligence generating an intelligence greater that the human mind is not possible.

We can see that our ancient Biblical writers were very aware of the spherical structure of the world, the enormity of the size of the universe. The multiple-millennial non-literal reading of Genesis with a literal reading where something specific is said in the Bible should therefore be the way it should be

---

[24] Although Hayek is best known for his Nobel Prize winning works on Economics (Business Cycle Theory), his exploits in phycology were generally met favorably, according to his Biographer , Professor Bruce Caldwell who confirmed this in conversations with me.

read. We have also seen how the use of language by a noted modern practitioner of science can be very confusing to the intelligent layman as well as to other scientists. However, the deductions of the ancients, whilst accurate, were not accepted as scientifically proven by the scientific method until millennia had passed, partly as scientific method was only just starting to get into its modern full swing. Copernicus, in 1507, circulated his first ideas about the heliocentric universe, then came "Revolutions of the Heavenly Spheres". He looked in detail at the problem of the parallax of the universe which meant that wherever you were on earth the whole of the universe always appeared the same. Copernicus magnified it by one billion to show that it was so large that whatever we did from our observational status on earth would never change its appearance. He had no proof for this and indeed he could not convince many of its necessity. At no point in time did he give any acknowledgment to Aristarchus of Samos who, in the third century BC, wrote about this and seems to get no credit for it. Neither did the priest Buridan get any mention for his observations about the rotation of the earth, and he may have even directly plagiarised from the Bishop:

> "if anyone is in a moving ship who imagines he is at rest, then should he see another ship, which is truly at rest, it will appear to him that the other ship is moved....And so, we also posit that the sphere of the sun is everywhere at rest and the earth in carrying us would be rotated. Since, however, we imagine we are at rest ..... the sun would appear to us to rise then to set, just as it does when it is moved and we are at rest." (Hannam)

Copernicus, 200 years later:

> "When a ship sail on a tranquil sea, all the things outside seem to the voyagers to be moving in a pattern that is an image of their own. They think, on the contrary, that they are themselves and all the things with them are at rest. So, it can easily happen in the case of the earth that the whole universe should be believed to be moving in a circle [while the earth is at rest]. (Hannam)

Nor does Cardinal Cusa's full scale book we mentioned earlier (Hopkins, 2001), some 60 years prior to a placing of the spherical world within a gigantic universe, with no specified place at its centre, get a mention by Copernicus.

Galileo is now lauded for the discovery of many great things while the Church was against him all the way, as we saw in the Scott Atran quote earlier. But re-reading Hannam (Hannam, 2010) , you get an alternative view which can be summed up in the following. The common perception is that Galileo was responsible for being the first to say that objects of different weights fall at the same speed. We should note that John Philoponus in the 6th Century had argued this already. Thomas Bradwardine had suggested it in a vacuum. Giovanni Battusta Benedetti in 1553 published his own results showing incorrectly that density was the determining point in objects falling re: their speed. This is incorrect, and Galileo agreed with him. The Dominican Domingo de Soto in 1551 had published his text book giving an accurate description of objects falling under gravity. This book was widely used by the Dominicians in their teachings. The meant speed theorem had been developed by the Merton calculators and Nicholas Orseme. Likewise, it is held by the cannon of science that Galileo established that vacuums really exist. The Papal appointed teacher Francisco Patrizi, not Galileo, wrote how vacuums could be real. Curiously, it is held that Galileo proved Copernicus right. Kelper did this .

Our modern scientists holler that the cruel Inquisition put him into prison for his scientific allegations. Correct, in part, but with some critical qualifications to the usual story. Firstly, in 1610, Galileo publishes "The Sidereal Messenger," showing what he had discovered with the telescope. Since Aristotle, all celestial orbs were considered perfectly formed. He showed the Moon had craters on it and Saturn had 'ears' and other imperfections. Cardinal Bellarmine asked the Jesuit Christopher Clavius to confirm this for the church, which he did. Kepler confirmed how the telescope worked. The counter-Reformation had showed that modern Catholic Doctrine maintained that in matters of faith and morals, the Holy Scriptures were sacrosanct. Cardinal Bellarmine was taking a literalist approach to the Bible, despite over a thousand years of understanding since Church Fathers like Augustine indicated that this was not the correct way to understand what had been written for the common man. Copernicus's book was subject to a ban and Galileo was warned not to advocate the heliocentric view. Galileo then went on a mission to have this decision reversed. This was actually a very un-Catholic way of doing things, brought about by the infusion of aspects of the Protestant Reformation into the Catholic Church, notably its focus on solely that which in scriptures may be taken as the truth, versus the wider interpretations the Catholic Church was allowed to deploy in its understanding of theological matters. This stupid move by a stupid Pope is still having its ramifications played out today as we can see by the half-formed comments from our scientists in earlier chapters on the matter.

Events moved on and a year later The Congregation of the Index made ten adjustments to Copernicus, making his work hypothetical, not factual (as with all science, that is subject to refutation and was not a bad move by the Church). Corrections were to be inserted into the books already issued. The new Pope Urban VIII was sympathetic to Galileo, especially if this system could be described as a 'model' way of describing the workings of the universe, comparing it to other models and how they worked. In 1624 Galileo had six meetings with the Pope to discuss this work. Urban explained how he thought it was beyond any man's ability to truly explain the workings of the universe, and this model was the best they had at that point. In 1632 Galileo published for the lay person - in Italian and not Latin - his Dialogue proving the Copernican system. One character, Simplicio, is a naïve simpleton who is modelled on Pope Urban, no less. With a humiliated Pope, trouble was sure to happen. The Congregation of the Index had approved the writing of this book so it seemed at odds for the Inquisition to then investigate it for heresy. Prior to the trial, it became apparent that Galileo had been told not to teach any of the views of Copernicus, even as models. He claimed he had no recollection of this. There was an unsigned memo concerning it. During his trial, in order to save his life, he lied outright to the Inquisition, saying he did not believe in the Copernican system. An Inquisitor went to visit him to point out the incoherence of Galileo's position as it was very clear he *did* believe in the Copernican system. He refused to admit this, but said he would subject himself to any punishment the church should administer to him. They found him seriously suspected of heresy. Life imprisonment was the sentence. This was immediately commuted to house arrest. The insulting of the Pope seems to be more to the point concerning his arrest and imprisonment.

Hannam believes that, at best, 'creative tension' is the way to describe the Church's interaction with science, but certainly not one of conflict:

> *"This book should lend some support to the sceptic claiming that the term 'scientific revolution' is another one of those prejudicial historical labels that explain nothing. You could call every century from the twelfth to the twentieth a revolution in science , with our own century unlikely to end the sequence". (Hannam)*

And concerning our medieval ancestors:

> *"We should not write them off as superstitious primitives. They deserve our gratitude."*

I am minded to agree with him on both points.

Chapter 5 The Surprising Friend of Theism: Evolutionary Method

Synthetic *A priori*: Evolutionary Biology

The current crop of evolutionary, naturalist, reductionist scientists propagate a myth - much like dismissing the medieval period as being a backwater of history stoked full of religious intolerance to scientific rational-only progress - when they assume that the Theory of Evolution is incompatible with theism. It is assumed that the evidence for evolution is so overwhelming that you must finally ditch your theism [belief in God]. In fact, at its heart, it is based on an *a priori* thought, that of an algorithm working away. This is much like Anslem's idea of a being (God), than that which nothing greater can be thought of. It is an *a priori*, consistent and logical in thought, and so is evolution: they spring from the same thought process. So a theist may welcome this as it does not conflict with anything he holds dear and, what is more, he may welcome its empirical findings - whilst clearly disputing that it answers the 'why' of life-or-anything question.

The leading atheist Daniel Dennett, whose religiosity is explored in Part 4, 'Those Deeply Religious Men: The Atheists', describes the method of evolution as an orderly algorithm which you can draw directly from the work of Darwin himself:

> *"If during the long course of ages and under varying conditions of life, organic beings vary at all in the several parts of their organisation, and I think this cannot be disputed; if there be, owing to the high geometrical powers of increase of each species, at some age, season, or year, a severe struggle for life, and this certainly cannot be disputed; then, considering the infinite complexity of the relations of all organic beings to each other and to their conditions of existence, causing an infinite diversity in structure, constitution, and habits, to be advantageous to them, I think it would be a most extraordinary fact if no variation ever had occurred useful to each being's own welfare, in the same way as so many variations have occurred useful to man. But if variations useful to any organic being*

do occur, assuredly individuals thus characterised will have the best chance of being preserved in the struggle for life; and from the strong principle of inheritance they will tend to produce offspring similarly characterised. This principle of preservation, I have called, for the sake of brevity, Natural Selection. Natural selection, on the principle of qualities being inherited at corresponding ages, can modify the egg, seed, or young, as easily as the adult. Amongst many animals, sexual selection will give its aid to ordinary selection, by assuring to the most vigorous and best adapted males the greatest number of offspring. Sexual selection will also give characters useful to the males alone, in their struggles with other males." (Darwin, 1859)

"Darwin had discovered the power of an algorithm. An algorithm is a certain sort of formal process that can be counted on-logically-to yield a certain sort of result whenever it is "run" or initiated." (Dennett, 1996)

"Life on earth has been generated over billions of years in a single branching tree-the Tree of Life-by one algorithmic process or another." (Dennett, 1996)

This can be interpreted as follows:

1. There is lots of life in lots of time.
2. Events happen in time and those life-forms that survive such situations have characteristics suited to survival more so than those species that do not survive.
3. This variation is useful to the well-being of this particular member of the species.
4. Inheritance insures these traits are carried through to the next generation.

And so it goes ever on.

There is deep irony in Gilbert Ryle's student Dennett, whose teacher was so dismissive of an *a priori* argument being capable of establishing a fact, and here we have one at the heart of the evolutionary process. I say this because in Chapter 8 we explore an argument that is purely *a priori* and establishes that God, if he rejects its premise and conclusion, then out must he bin the Theory of

Evolution. Darwin gives us a method of how, with mechanical logic, life moves from one part of the evolutionary arrow onwards to next part. However, he does not attempt to give us an answer to the origin of life or why there is life at all. The Bible tells us life was created from dust. Over 3,000 years ago, King Solomon is recorded in Ecclesiastes 3:1-8 reflecting upon a beautiful poem about the order of creation. In 3:20 he notes

> *"All go to one place: all are from the dust, and all return to the dust."*

I don't think we can expect a king from 3,000 years ago to know about amino acids and other building blocks of life, but he had a fairly good grasp of the beginning. In 12:7, he also adds:

> *"Then the dust will return to the earth as it was, And the spirit will return to God who gave it."*

Perhaps Dennett will not agree with this last. However, I would have thought he could support Solomon as being very modern in his thinking. Moreover, I would have thought that is the *only* way to interpret Genesis 1:31 and 8:22 concerning regularity, and Genesis 2:7 and 3:19 concerning being created from such a substance, probably the smallest known item that 3,000 years ago was known to man: a speck of dust. Here is my prophecy, then: in 3,000 years' time we will view amino acids as the equivalent of dust and there will be a multiplicity of other discoveries our best scientific brains will have made and will keep on making, taking us to even more interesting places. A literal reading of Darwin, then, may well be unfulfilling and very primitive. Nevertheless, I hope he is still given great respect within the cannon of science.

We know that the Greeks came tantelisingly close to being able to explain the evolutionary process; but what is little known is that the Bible actually touches upon evolution itself as well. The author of the Book of the Wisdom of Solomon, writing some 2000 years before Darwin, chooses words in a similar way to Pythagoras when he says how the elements of the world change - similar to the way notes change to produce different sounds, the elements reconmbine in a harmony, and in 19:19 (KJV)[25]

> "For eatherly things were turned into waterey things, that before swan in the water, now went upon the ground"

Dennett does not give us an answer as to the 'why' of creation, neither does Darwin, but they do point the creative process to *a priori*, undeniable logic. Concerning Dennett's philosophical ancestors, Plato was a creationist, as was Aristotle, and there was a logical process at play in their reasoning. Aristotle, the master founder of the rules of logic, reasoned that there must have been an unmoved mover, but that this eternally unmoved mover had no actuality in the physical world because to think of Him being involved in praxis or action in the finite world compromised Him. This is all laid out in his books "Nicomachean Ethics" and "Metaphysics." A very useful book by David Sedley outlines this:

> "The reason why in Aristotle's view no directive mind can be at work in natural processes is not any preference on his part for "scientific" over theological modes of explanation. It lies rather in the conviction that the Platonic account gets the theology wrong. God's causality in the natural world is omnipresent, as Plato held, but must be such that all the operative drives and impulses belong to the natural entities, leaving god himself eternally detached and self-focused." (Sedley, 2007)

If there was no divine craft in nature, as Plato supposed, why then was nature grafting to get to its teleological end point? Nature was just set to do this of its own volition.

In nature we find the four causes:
1. Material.
2. Moving.

---

[25] http://www.kingjamesbibleonline.org/book.php?book=Wisdom+of+Solomon&chapter=19&verse=19

3. Formal.
4. Final.

In order to explain these four elements, Aristotle discusses the case of the pig, thus:
1. Its material matter or cause is its mother's and father's prior material matter.
2. Its moving cause is the day to day changes the pig undergoes.
3. Its essential form of a pig is its formal cause.
4. Being a fully developed pig is its final cause.

Although not articulated by Aristotle, I will speculate how the current pig in question must have been implied in the first pig: just as Pythagoras's number is implied in the concept of a right-angled triangle, so is the pig, and all the existing pigs we have today are actually implied all the way back to the original singularity of creation. This thought is implied in every species. The formal cause is always implied in its parents and all the way back to the beginning – what a singularly magnificent thought! To be clear, this means that a few billion years ago, at the very moment of the creation of the first life form, you and I were implied in it, as was every living thing that he come both before and after us. Sedley says, in discussing Aristotle's form, that it is eternal. In this way, in nature, an organism's form pre-existed you in your ancestors. To throw light on this, Aristotle compares the pre-existence of form in nature to the way that in a craft the artefact's form pre-exists the artefact itself, by being already present in the mind of the Craftsman. I would really push this point a stage further and say your genetic code is presupposed in the moment of creation as is everything else. If chance was the cause of this, it would have had to have miraculously organized all of creation and its potential outpourings - in that moment. Yes, the nanosecond of creation, ready and pre-programed with you and every living life form that has been, is, and will be already implied, in that moment. Wow! What a mind- bogglingly wonderful thought. To be clear, this makes any calculation of any existing molecules being able to arrange themselves into the first simple cell structure with a self-replicating mechanism already implied in it as well, to kick off all of life, to then start the process to self-select against each other, for all possible combinations of life forms in the past, present and the future, at that moment of creation, to be so large ... no, I don't think it is possible to sustain the line that chance caused this alone. I simply don't believe this is at all possible by chance alone.

This contrasts with the atomists' views, who stress that all atoms have causal motions which are necessary, in that they follow a mechanical sequence fortuitous for us, in that they allow us to exist and don't suppose any purposive re-programming. Aristotle would argue that that pre-programmed nature of cause and effect does in fact show the original purpose. This contrasts with Lucretius, a Roman atomist who, in "On the Nature of Things," writes about which faster, cleverer, more agile, dexterous creatures survived and prospered and out-competed, if you like, the others, to survive and prosper. Although he demonstrates a sense of the Darwinian process, there is no notion of one gradually changing to another thing over vast passages of time implied in his only known work. The Epicureans, like Lucretius, had no conception of the gradualist approach to evolution over many centuries, evoking the power of infinity to explain how changes take place. Modern Darwinists, like Dawkins and Dennett, also assume an infinity of time is needed, or certainly billions of years, to randomly make these changes happen. If you do hold that the finite can be infinite, then of course any and every set of combinations of things happen and this could be the case as in an infinity of events. This improbable event would have been one of these. So complex systems of the body likes eyes can be accounted for, according to the atomists, by accident. As we have discussed before, to be material and finite implies a prior cause and, unless you want to jettison the law of causality from the picture, an original, finite thing must have a prior cause that is immaterial *at some point*, otherwise there is something finite that is un-caused, which is absurdly contradictory. That materialism implies a prior physical cause is glossed over to sustain this incoherent picture of the origin of life. This did not occur either to the atomist epicureans of the time or to our modern naturalist scientists of today, some twenty one centuries after Lucretius. They are all the heirs of Lucretius and as

continuing error of method. In fairness to Darwin, I don't see that he was arguing that if you assume infinity you can get the whole of life up and running. He was not arguing like the atomists that infinity had ensured the current arrangements of life, just that the method of life, once it was moving, was more than likely the evolutionary axiom. Modern Darwinists jump from the axiom of evolution to the conclusion that it explains the origin of life. The philosopher high priest of atheism, A C Grayling, on Darwinism, writes in a similar vein:

> *"Religions apologists who say their views are compatible with Dawinism accept that biological evolution occurs over great periods of time, yet say that a deity is involved in designing and sponsoring this process. Consider a parallel. Suppose it was once believed that flowers are coloured because fairies paint them while we sleep. Once we understand the natural process by which flowers come to be coloured, it would not merely be redundant but contradictory to claim that in addition to the biological process that causes floral colouration, it is also part of the explanation that they are painted (in the very same colours) by fairies. For if the biological account is correct, the fairy-tale account is false (and vice versa): one cannot hold both to be true together."* (Grayling, The God Argument, 2013)

He likens his fairies to God in analogy, as we have seen from the start of this book! However, he does not answer the 'how' of how creation started, and the 'how' of it is the proper domain of the scientists, certainly.

The Christian view of St John written at the same time as Lucretius states:

> *"In the beginning was the Word, and the Word was with God, and the Word was God. He was in the beginning with God. All things were made through Him, and without Him nothing was made that was made. In Him was life, and the life was the light of men. And the light shines in the darkness, and the darkness did not comprehend it." [John 1:1-5]*

There is nothing contradictory to evolution theory in this. The first cell like structured contains the blueprint of all life in it thereafter. The theist claims the trigger point is God (as his reason tells him, as discussed in the proceeding chapters especially concerning faith, on being and below regarding the Ontological Argument/deduction). The atheist makes hypothetical speculations about a primordial soup with packs of cell structures getting together to kick of life as we know it, things popping in and out of existence yet not caused by anything, and a whole host of other matters. As the Bible makes no direct claims, other than that God created everything - unless you take a very literal reading, which none of the apostles or church fathers ever did - the theist can hold a very consistent account of creation via God as the creator and evolution as its prime method. Ockham's Razor is much used to razor *out* the need for a deity, but I find it a more compelling case to use the razor to rule the Deity *in*.

To me, there is a compelling logic to evolution: it is similar to the compelling logic we see in the geometry and economics models which will be discussed in Chapter 8; it is also the same logic that can establish the existence of God. Here again, we see, and will see in Chapter 8, that the logical thought of something can in fact be very useful to understand evolution and God. Science and theology will be shown to be at one on this point.

However, there is an illogical start point in the Greek and Roman atomists' start point, as there is with modern day Darwinists', that is: if you accept physicality in anything, it must have a prior cause, and that to be causeless is not to be material at all. The infinity assumed is not logically possible. Without a start point, that must be an immaterial first cause, reason dictates you can't even get onto the runway, let alone lift off with explanations that purport to explain the origins of the Universe and life as we know it. To use Grayling's analogy, the fairies are not dispensed with by the logic of evolution. As his analogy relates to God, I can only conclude that God (un-caused non-material cause) is implied in the evolutionary process as the start of it, the immaterial first cause that must be at the foundation of all physicality to make physicality coherent for the reasons we have discussed, and the programmer of the whole of that moment of the creation of life past, present and future. No words can really describe the magnitude of this.

Whilst evolution plays its role in the unfolding of the plans of creation, it is not the complete answer to the *method* of the creator. For if we assume the method of the creator is evolution, these incremental variations over time can't possibly account for why we, as a species, stand not just incrementally above the most intelligent animals, but way, way ahead of them in terms of cognitive abilities. Do we need to know the speed of light to be one step ahead of the ape? Do we need to know complex calculus to keep one step ahead of the dolphin? Do we need to appreciate Shakespeare to keep the animals in a subservient position to us? I know that this is a deeply unfashionable view to hold. If you suggested it in an academic forum you would be considered a cretin; if you said it on a public platform like a web blogging site, you would get a torrent of bad-mouthed insults. But these are not reasons for not saying it. Conversely, it could be argued that we need these finer attributes of man to compete against our fellow man in the survival of the fittest game. There is never a case of one man against all men and vice versa, as the rationality of man produces the climate for overwhelming co-operation. It is this co-operation that allows to accelerate leaps and bounds above all creatures. This is not driven by evolution as currently described by any of its advocates that I am aware of. There is an *a priori* logic to evolution, but undoubtedly it is not the be all and end all of the explanation for the why and how of life. We explore in the next chapter the even bigger scientific searches for the why and the how of the cosmos itself. Theism and science can help each other here as well - but not according to the naturalist, reductionist scientist towards whom now we move.

Chapter 6 The Current Cannon of Science

The Ever Moving Gospel of Science

> *"Some treat science as if it were a sort of infallible oracle, like a divine revelation – or not infallible (since it seems so regularly to change its mind), at any rate such that when it comes to fixing belief, science is the court of last appeal." (Plantinga)*

> *"Two of the most important and overarching contemporary scientific theories are general relativity and quantum mechanics. Both are highly confirmed and enormously impressive; unfortunately, they both can't be correct ". (Plantinga)*

In Chapter 4, we saw how our scientific ancestors did not really speculate that much about the creation of the universe, but that they used their science to create things that improved the wellbeing of people's lives, on the whole. Theologians dealt with the nature of 'why anything at all?' questions; science dealt with the 'how' of the matter. Chapter 5's focus on evolution is a great example of science addressing the how but falling foul when they think it addresses the why. Scientists became progressively better at answering the how question - and wonderfully speculative in their pseudo-metaphysics in attempting to think out the 'why' question. Their inability to distinguish what is metaphysics proper and what is pseudo-metaphysics leads to very sophisticated attempts to collapse metaphysics into science and provide us with an answer for the ultimate 'why' question, a question I don't think the tools of science are equipped to answer. In my life time[26] I was born into the understanding of the Judeo-Christian creation story in its non-literal sense. The Big Bang was the how it was done (by whom or what science could shed no light), and evolution was the process by which life moved along. As science has changed its spots we now have suggestions of a multiverse, a universe from nothing, and emergent universes. Concerning evolution, we have a much stronger advocacy for something-from-nothing in the primordial soup, a moment of magic where spontaneously life just emerges under the right

---

[26] As for my grandparents, they were brought up with the Universe being steady state, eternal.

conditions and it does so to stimulate matter to turn into matter with consciousness. Biologists have shifted from evolution as the process through which life moves from one place to the next, to match their contemporary physicists in order to postulate how the 'all' of life just pops into being, all by itself, out of nothing much. I aim now to take a look at some of these things.

It should be noted that I am no natural or physical scientist, so all I can do at this stage is to read books by the best in the class of the physical and natural scientists and try to understand them. More importantly, I always carry with me an inquiring mind which wants to really try to understand why and how they view the world, the universe and everything in it, and whether can they answer any of the big questions such as the 'why' of the universe and the 'how' of it.

Brian R Greene's opening remarks in his Magnum Opus "The Fabric of the Cosmos" suggest the following:

> "The overarching lesson that has emerged from scientific inquiry over the last century is that human experience is often a misleading guide to the true nature of reality. Lying just beneath the surface of the everyday is a world we'd hardly recognize. Followers of the occult, devotees of astrology, and those who hold to religious principles that speak to a reality beyond experience have, from widely varying perspectives, long since arrived at a similar conclusion." (Greene, 2005)

The occult, religious aspects are, of course, not what he has in mind when thinking of progress, but his scientist colleagues are the heroes of the play, as their hard work in peeling back layer after layer of what we see as reality to uncover something paradoxical and at time quite bizarre shows.

Newton proposed that his laws of motion, governing what we observe, and capable of predicting the movements of the starry heavens above us with great accuracy, operated in relation to a static and fixed absolute space. Leibniz put up his hand in firm protest and said all talks of space are meaningless unless they are about relations between things. Space, being empty, is meaningless as it has nothing in it. Space did not exist as Newton proposed, but only as a collection of relations. The Newtonian juggernaut ploughed on and sunk Leibniz's views.

It is worthwhile taking a short pause from the science part now to reflect upon this point Leibniz makes as it has much relevance to later discussions about scientists, as we will see in particular with Lee Smolin. I decided to look at F H Bradley and his views as they were more recent and predate the Einstein revolution by some 20 years, but they have relevance to this episode as well.

In the opening section of "Appearance and Reality", Bradley says:

"I shall point out that the world, as so understood, contradicts itself; and is therefore appearance, and not reality." (Bradley, 1893)

Bradley starts out by trying to work out how we can understand anything distinct, and by following this line of reasoning he, like Leibniz, concludes that everything - space included - is relational, and nothing is truly distinct. He starts by thinking about primary qualities being those we perceive or feel; the secondary ones, their residue of feelings in us. This is exemplified thus: if we think of a thing: say, a table, having a unique property in and of itself, this implies that the secondary quality that lingers in our mind - the description of its firmness, its shape, its texture, its supporting nature, its shapeliness - does not exist as these adjectives are applied by our minds to describe it. Yet without these descriptions, the table ceases to exist - or the secondary qualities, and we, the perceivers, cease to exist. We have an apparent contradiction that makes him conclude that we only have appearances that relate to reality and not reality relating to appearance. He goes on: an ear will hear, but it is not audible itself. A thing will have a property of heat, but it is meaningless unless brought towards our skin to feel it. Our organs have these 'wandering adjectives' appended to them, these secondary qualities that help us describe the extended world. It is important to note that as we can dream and be delusional, it shows we can have the secondary sensation without the experience of the primary, which in turn means, we can only really think about 'stand-alone things', as an abstraction of the mind, and: "the secondary qualities must be judged to be merely appearance."

We may put many adjectives around a thing - for example, we say the table is hard, supportive, has room for a chair to go underneath, made of wood, is upright, odourless etc. Yes, it is all of this, but if you take things in isolation it falls apart. Thus a table is a mixture of these adjectives and not any of them in isolation. So the relations are not identical with the thing which still makes the thing very illusory:

> *"If you predicate what is different, you ascribe to the subject what it is not; and if you predicate what is not different, you say nothing at all."* (Bradley, 1893)

We would seem to have a collection of adjectives that gives us the illusion of describing a property of something we consider real, but that has no single adjective on its own and can't exist on its own. So its independent unity, the material reality of it, arrives as appearance to us, as a collection of adjectives, which in turn, upon analysis, makes the independent thing in question, of materialism, commit suicide:

> *"Our conclusion briefly will be this. Relation presupposes quality, and quality relation. Each can be something neither together with, nor apart from, the other; and the vicious circle in which they turn is not the truth about reality."* (Bradley, 1893)

You can't think of qualities without evoking distinctions; you can't think of distinctions unless they are in relations; and you can't think of relations unless you are thinking of qualities. So we have a circle of reasoning to describe what we perceive as reality.   Qualities without no relation to thought are meaningless. Qualities then on their own become meaningless without thought so it seems we are doomed to say they can only be appearance and not reality. The way we look at things:

> *"It is a makeshift, a device, a mere practical compromise, most necessary, but in the end most indefensible. We have to take reality as many, and to take it as one, and to avoid contradiction. We want to divide it, or to take it, when we please, as indivisible; to go as*

> *far as we desire in either of these directions, and to stop when that suits us."* (Bradley, 1893)

Materialism, upon which modern science is based, implies that the qualities of an extended body are really what it is and our secondary senses are subjective to us and add-ons that help us understand the primary world. Bradley, as we have seen, asks: do these external relations between them hold? We seem to be in a vicious circle as we can't do away with the adjectival without doing away with the extended quality. And we can't do away with the subjective thought without doing away with the thinker. Materialism is appearance only. What is more, our body only exists in this relational set-up and not as a distinct thing in and of itself. Our body:

> *"... itself is no exception, for we perceive that, as extended, solely by the action of one part upon another percipient part. That we have no miraculous intuition of our body as spatial reality is perfectly certain. But, if so, the ex-tended thing will have its quality only when perceived by something else; and the percipient something else is again in the same case. Nothing, in short, proves extended except in relation to another thing, which itself does not possess the quality, if you try to take it by itself"* (Bradley, 1893)

Materialism needs to separate the bodily organs from the observation of extended qualities and grant them an independent existence - and it can't.

> *"In short, it is the violent abstraction of one aspect from the rest, and the mere confinement of our attention to a single side of things, a fiction which, forgetting itself, takes a ghost for solid reality."* (Bradley, 1893)

> *"Yet the materialist, from defect of nature or of education, or probably both, worships with-out justification this thin product of his untutored fancy."* (Bradley, 1893)

There is a quasi-religious quality to the materialist's understanding of the world of qualities. He holds it as a matter of faith (not reason). In truth it is just an abstraction, with the materialist holding onto his atomised view of nature not just by warranted faith - the faith that believes in the constants of nature, its fundamental laws - but by blind, unquestioning faith.

It is tempting to view all relations between things as internal relations. However, these fall into contradiction as they imply a unity of internal relations, or a wholeness of reality, which I have much sympathy with. But their internality is blown away in the unity of the oneness of reality, which makes the internal relations fall apart. External relation is just an abstraction without an external hook to anything real; until it hooks onto anything real, then it becomes internal, thus it stands on a contradiction. Therefore, contra Leibniz - or building upon him - I believe Bradley concludes that there is just appearance, not Newtonian space or Leibniz with his relations. This third way is not discussed as an option by scientists; it does not appear to be anywhere acknowledged although the Cox/Forshaw quote at the start of Chapter 7 may indicate, knowingly or not, that some scientists may be considering this.

G E Moore, in his essay "Nature of Judgment" (Moore G. E., 1899), attacked such a line of thinking and said there is a mixing of symbol and symbolised within Bradley's belief that the idea is implied in the thing itself and can't be separated. Moore said the idea was a concept, and that different ideas have common content that represent the same concept. This connection of concept is independent of the idea. I personally think that even if we try to create this distance in order that we can analyse things in isolation, we are kidding ourselves if we think this complex series of connections concerning the concept itself can ever exist outside of any notion of connectivity to the mind as we need to think of this new, independent relationship in the first place. This does not mean that if a tree falls down in a wood and nobody observes it, it does not exist - just that man can't conceive of it existing until, well, he conceives it.

Bertrand Russell, inspired by Moore's "Nature and Judgment", proposes (Russell, 1903) external relations in maths as they need to be asymmetrical for them to proceed. So: 4 must be independently bigger than 2 to have any meaning whatsoever, and must stand in relation to it externally. However, a mathematical construct is only an abstraction and taken on its own it remains that way and can't be used to suggest independent external things just by being abstract and external in that abstract state. He further argues that if we consider something as simple as A being taller than B, it would imply a relationship. If everything is relational, you end up in a situation where to be coherent you can only have a whole in which A & B are in it and not distinct. As they are distinct, they must be related externally and therefore this relational edifice of Bradley and co must be rejected, and a plurality of atomistically-minded, independent things must exist. In abstract, I can concur with this, but when I actually think of a real A man being taller than a real B man, I can't separate out what I mean by 'man' until I populate him with real characteristics and attach a number of adjectives to that man that are related to me the describer, so they would still appear to be internally related at first blush, then appearance only when thought about a little bit harder, as not being distinct causes them to collapse away from being independent of the mind. I can only conceive in isolation a man as being embedded in the whole oneness of reality.

So I believe, despite whatever our common sense tells us, that we are stuck with our reality of appearance and not a concrete and mind-independent world that we can rationally believe in; we can only have a faith that it exists. When we look at the quantum world, we will see that physicists divide themselves along the same lines as philosophers have historically done since the dawn of time, as those who would seem to suggest that human observation is the trigger to something in the quantum world becoming a thing as opposed to a potential thing, and those who think there are definite external things; it's just that we don't know how to prove this yet.

For now, we go back to Bradley as he turns his mind to discuss space, that entity we like to think of as 'out there 'endless' or a least mind-bogglingly big. But to have an 'endlessness' to it, it must be necessary for it to have a beginning. It seems contradictory from the starting gun of our reasoning, as endless implies no beginning because this would get in the way of its infinite nature. If it is endless and beginning-less, it is not space at all. A space of nothing is nonsensical as it has some solids in it, be they even a force field, and this, then, makes it relational and a something that has some solidity - which makes it not space. It is relational. If it is relational, as Leibniz suggests, it's a collection of things or collection of spaces, which makes space itself meaningless. So materialism and space would seem to be mere abstractions at best, convenient and common ways of viewing things. The Leibniz way of viewing things may well be the more coherent way, although that, as we have seen, comes with its own problems.

We have seen how briefly, post Newton and Leibniz, philosophy took a different turn regarding how it was going to comprehend reality. Sir Isaac Newton, however, had conclusively won the day, with his publication in 1687 of his "Philosophiæ Naturalis Principia Mathematica" proposing the notion of there being an absolute space, totally independent of anything - out there, if you like - to which all things moved in relation. His famous laws of motion that govern all things we observe, certainly with the natural eye, seem perfectly predictable by an understanding of the operation of these laws. If you can factor in all the causal variables, you can understand anything it moves and anything that moves thereafter as a result of its movement. His world is mechanistic and thoroughly deterministic. His world was also mind-independent and externally related.

Some 230 years or so later, Einstein proposed that space and time were in fact not separate, but rather one and the same – space-time - and that this indeed occupied everything[27]. The gravity of Newton, the apple falling to his head, was not the correct way of thinking about things; what was, was the warping of space-time itself, whose depressions and impressions moved things towards or apart from each other. If you think of jumping on a trampoline, then at the bottom of your downward jump the fabric of the trampoline is like a "U" shape under your feet. This is what we are asked by standard physics text books to hold in our minds - with your feet being replaced by a planet like earth, and light being forced not to go in a straight even line around the planet, but going down, then around to go back up and carry on its journey. This does not happen

---

[27] I note the opening of the Bible in Genesis 1:1, *"In the beginning God created the heavens and the earth."* Time starts (the beginning), the cosmos is birthed (the heavens) and the earth and all material things are established. Not bad for a 3500 year old book.

on a flat dimension, but everywhere, all the time. Everything is moving in relation to everything, warping the fabric of space-time, of whose fabric we are an intricate part. The clear and distinct boundaries of Newton's absolute space and absolute time were merged into one. However, in this relational merger of Einstein, there was one absolute. Einstein declared that the speed of light moves at 670 million miles per hour relative to everything; this indeed is his absolute. You often hear it described as the only truly independently observable thing but, as we have seen, it is impossible for the term 'light' to mean anything unless attached to a human thinker. That aside, light is a constant to which we and all material things march, or move, if you like, to its drum beat. I pondered this during a 1.5 hour root canal surgery episode, so perhaps my thoughts are jaded in the matter, but if light is constant everywhere for everything and it is always moving at 670 million miles per hour, then each time anything moves it would appear to adjust back, or to still stay in its constant relationship, automatically, and if this did not happen, we would just see a very blurry world. Consider this: if you could hypothetically hitch a ride on a photon and were to flash a torch whilst moving at the speed of light on this photon, the later batches of photons would not travel at the speed of light of the photon you are riding, plus its speed of light. You would not get the speed of light x 2, but the torch would just automatically adjust to riding at the speed of the photon you were hitching a ride upon. It would be still *in relation to* the photon you were riding on.

Added to this, his theory of Special Relativity showed us that if you are still, watching a still bird, you are not moving through space, but moving through time, but if a bird flies off in front of your eyes, it is having some of its motion diverted from moving via time to moving via space. If it could fly at the speed of light, it would be timeless, not moving though time. The fastest speed in the universe is indeed no speed at all, as you are timeless and stationary within that time! At distances under the speed of light, we all move relative to each other and to everything. Our times are the same if we are not moving in relation to each other, but as soon as we move relative to each other, as light takes time to get from A to B, my reality of what is happing now to me would be marginally different to your perception of it.

For Einstein, space and time are one and forever always inseparable and we move in the fabric of space and time simultaneously or, as I prefer to think, we are actually part of that fabric. Interestingly, from this he develops the view that our laws of physics do not distinguish between past, present and future; there is said to be symmetry in the laws. Crack an egg open and as far as the laws of physics is concerned if you know the trajectories of each and every particle of that exploding egg, you can reverse its trajectory. Yet we observe so much asymmetry in the way we say time's arrow always moves from past, present to the future, that the egg is never reassembled, our arranging does not reverse. Do an experiment, all things being equal, in London, Paris or New York: it will deliver up the same results. Do it on a moving train, or in a stationary lab, it will still yield the same outcome. The laws of physics are said to be indifferent to time and apply themselves in the same way all the time making no past, present, future distinction. The laws of physics seem to be timeless.

For Newton, the clock ticked off time for everybody everywhere in the whole of space with the latter being absolute. For Einstein, each and everything has its own clock ticking away, and different speeds relative to everything else. The laws of physics can still be applied in this predictable but relative world with space-time and the speed of light being the new absolutes. This space-time is just a lot of 'nows', with no past, present future distinction - just a now, that now being the whole of everything. This is what we will look at next.

The Timelessness of Reality

Greene, at his explanatory best in this You Tube clip https://www.youtube.com/watch?v=vrqmMoI0wks and in his book mentioned above, explains to the layman how, if you line up all these moments and posit an alien billions of miles away and have him moving backwards/sideways and forwards at varying speeds, his 'now', that includes everything of yours and vice versa when you were stationary (albeit due to the speed of light not being simultaneously aware of it) now slices up the moments differently and looks diagonally to other moments that would be past or future, depending upon the direction of the movement. Meanwhile, our physical laws are spectacularly indifferent to this: they simply don't distinguish between past, present and future. If you are far enough away, moving fast enough in space-time, and if you could theoretically see what was going on, you would be able to observe past, present and future things. Physical laws are oblivious to our anthropomorphic conception of time, thus they are time-less and time insensitive. To them, there is only the whole of space-time, a oneness of reality. There is no flow for these laws. [28]

Proceeding more in support of the common sense view of the arrow of time flowing towards the future, we have the second law of dynamics which states that all things in the universe are tending towards a more disorderly state. This does not say that all things are moving towards this state, but that they are tending to. Greene uses the example of taking apart "War and Peace", page by page, producing 10^{1878} ways of potential page arrangements. So whilst

---

[28] If we are both motionless, my now is the same as your now. If we move, our nows will be slightly different, although of course both equally as valid. This new relativity-based understanding of the world suggests that our common sense version of time as past, then now, moving into the future, is a mental construct that does not reflect reality, as my now, at one end of the room, will be slightly different from your now. For someone in the UK and someone in Australia, actions may be happening seconds apart. Momentarily, you could be dead in one place and viewed to be alive in the other place, and both views would be right. Following relativity, we can only deduce from this that we have a series of nows from the start of the Big Bang encompassing every moment, in what seem to us the past moments, the present moments and indeed the future moments, or nows. A theist would sit very comfortably with this evocation of reality as if God is the cause of it. He sits alongside it, or encompasses it, as the causal agent, and thus can observe all moments, being therefore omniscient. Or, another type of theist would argue that these real moments emerge from its creator and thus are all capable of being known to it.

it is not impossible for you to randomly throw them up in the air for them to rearrange themselves in the original formation, it is highly unlikely this will happen. Thus time's arrow would appear to flow from order to disorder, on the whole. Meanwhile, these laws of physics apply in a timeless fashion. Since the Big Bang we have been moving at varying degrees, asymmetrically, towards greater disorder.

Once again, I will pause and consider what philosophers have long discussed regarding the nature of time, as this has relevance to what their scientist colleagues have to say.

Time and Physics

In recent years, post Einstein, scientists have been grappling with the concept of time - its reality or otherwise, the everyday concept of reality being something 'out there,' atomistic, finite, and clearly separate and independent – or, looking at reality another way as inter-relational, always related reality. Or: looking at reality as none of the above, but just as appearance. Pre Einstein, one of the last philosophers to really address these issues were F H Bradley in his "Appearance and Reality" (Bradley, 1893) and J Ellis McTaggart in his famous essay in the Journal "Mind", "The Unreality of Time" (McTaggart, 1908). Bradley asks us to think of time in the common sense way of past, present and future, like a stream flowing. This is relational. If you view time as the whole of this passage of discrete units, then it has no duration at all and ceases to be time, but if you give each unit in time duration, it ceases to be an independent unit. So they all become a matter of relation. And, once again, if you specify time as a quality of a moment, it sits in relation to something and ceases to be a moment. It seems impossible to maintain a coherent conception of plain-speak time. If you think of 'now' as during and into the past, and the future as becoming, any process within the now destroys it and makes it a 'not now':

> *"It perishes in ceaseless oscillation, between an empty solidity and a transition beyond itself to-wards illusory completeness."* (Bradley, 1893)

If you imply a relationship in order to get the concept of time up and running, past is related to now and you destroy the quality of past. The now of present and future don't stand alone for the same reason, and if you then follow this reasoning to impose a unity on the whole of time, it becomes timeless, as physicists like Einstein and beyond would suggest. We spin around, therefore, in a vicious circle of contradiction.

J Ellis McTaggart (McTaggart, 1908) also shocked the pre-Einstein world-view with his total denial of the reality of time:

> *"And it is because the distinctions of past, present and future seem to me to be essential for time, that I regard time as unreal."* (McTaggart, 1908)

This is what he boldly declared in the opening of his famous article in "Mind".

What he calls the "A series" is a series going from past, present to future. The ordinary man's view, or the common sense view, is what characterises this.

What he calls the "B series" goes from earlier to later and never changes:

> *"A position in time is called a moment."* (McTaggart, 1908)

McTaggart suggests that in reality, when we perceive an event in our mind's eye, it is always relational in terms of the A series, and fixed in terms of the B series. Indeed, it is always both:

> *"It would I suppose, be universally admitted that time involves change......A universe in which nothing whatever changed (including the thoughts of the conscious beings in it) would be a timeless universe."* (McTaggart, 1908)

No change would render the B series timeless, therefore it becomes incoherent. According to McTaggart, if we move to the A series, we can see an event of, say, the death of Queen Anne Stuart (the example he used) to see once it was a future event, then a present, then a past event, but also always a fixed event never changing once the event has happened:

> *"Thus we are forced to the conclusion that all change is only change of the characteristic imparted to events by their presence in the A series, whether those characteristics are qualities or relations."* (McTaggart, 1908)

However, the death of Queen Anne, still as an event, never changes would seem to be incompatible with the A series notion of change in time.

> *"The B series, however cannot exists except as temporal, since earlier and later, which are distinctions of which it consists, are clearly time-determinations. So it follows that there can be no B series where there is no A series, since where there is no A series there is no time."* (McTaggart, 1908)

A 'C series' of events, M, N, O, P could be introduced, but in reality it just remains as static as the B series and therefore there is no change and time is again illusory.

If you look at the C series in a non-temporal way, you can view it any which way and it remains coherent. This is what I expect Einstein and his physics followers really mean when they look at the 'Block Universe,' the universe of everything in the moment, as non-temporal, with all other moments of being having become already, or will be becoming soon. In the temporal world, the series always has a reality and the appearance of an arrow going from past to present to future. However, this is only an appearance, as the reality of the concept of time seems to be incoherent upon close examination; like so many concepts for mankind, it is a happy and convenient construct that gives sense and meaning to our world.

You can view one position in the C series as always present. You have established the arrow of time with one position always having either side going off into the past and directly opposite into the future as it moves down that series. The A series would seem to become coherent once more. Then the event can sit in the B series and an event in that moment. But, as we saw, it then became timeless.

It would seem that each event has the term applied to it of either past, present and future, as it will always have all of these characteristics. It is impossible for these mutually exclusive things to be co-instantiated in the one event. A property holding both futurity, present-ness and past-ness is incoherent. It was past, it is present and it is future. If it has these all at once, this would be contradictory, but if it has these separately from moment to moment, as in the C series, it would seem to become coherent. However, McTaggart concludes:

> "But this explanation involves a vicious circle. For it assumes the existence of time in order to account for the way in which moments are past present and future. Time must then be pre-supposed to account for the A series. But we have already seen that the A series has to be assumed in order to account for time. Accordingly the A series has to be pre-supposed in order to account for the A series. And this clearly is a vicious circle."
> (McTaggart, 1908)

You may say time is an absolute presupposition but, as you know, there is a contradiction, so it must fall away.

It is interesting to note how both philosophers and physicists come to the same conclusion, but from different starting points, which is that time is unreal. We only have a series of nows. We will also see this in the next major break though in physics, the discovery of the weird and wonderful world of things so small, the quantum world, were anything seems probable.

Quantum Wonderland

Following Einstein's early work, quantum mechanics then bursts onto the scene and shows with great precision how we can't know the exact location or speed of a single particle with certainty, and that we only have a series of probabilities that a particle will be doing this or that when observed at a fixed point in time. What is more, following Bohr, or what we call the 'Copenhagen Interpretation' of quantum mechanics, we can only establish anything about a particle when it is observed by a human or an instrument controlled by a human. Before there is any talk of a thing's position, it does not actually have one until you have made it have one. This would seem to support the famous empiricists of the Enlightenment: Bishop Berkeley's view, for example, that a tree is only there because it is thought of or perceived of as there. Berkeley did not deny an external world, he proposed that there was the grand observer of all things - God, hence when individuals are not thinking about, say, the moon it is still there in reality, as an objective thing, since the great architect of the universe is always observing it. Like Einstein, he did not seriously consider that if the moon was not looked at, it was not there. Strip this of its religious connotations on behalf of the modern, secular mind - which might make this view moderately more palatable to 21st century folk - the fundamental ground for Being was doing the observing, or a collection of finite minds observing pretty much everything relating to humans could also keep the whole show on the road of our reality. Philosophy and physics would again be seeming to look at the same thing by approaching from different ways.

Heisenberg bowled us a googly when he showed how, when you observe a particular particle, your very act of observation – even to the extent of one bit of light bouncing off it - affects its position. Your observation contaminates the very thing you wish to observe. You can fix its position at the expense of knowing its velocity, and vice versa. Also, particles seem to act with each other. When we fix, say, the location of one, we fix that of its partner particle and, what is even more bizarre, this partner particle can be anywhere in the universe, suggesting that a great connectivity that has hitherto evaded us. Greene (Greene, 2005) comments:

"We used to think that a basic property of space is that it separates and distinguishes one object from another. But we now see that quantum mechanics radically challenges this view. Two things can be separated by an enormous amount of space and yet not have a fully independent existence. A quantum connection can unite them, making the properties of each contingent on the properties of the other. Space does not distinguish such entangled objects. Space cannot overcome their interconnection. Space, even a huge amount of space, does not weaken their quantum mechanical interdependence.

"Some people have interpreted this as telling us that "everything is connected to everything else" or that "quantum mechanics entangles us all in one universal whole." After all, the reasoning goes, at the big bang everything emerged from one place since, we believe, all places we now think of as different were the same place way back in the beginning. And since, like the two photons emerging from the same calcium atom, everything emerged from the same something in the beginning, everything should be quantum mechanically entangled with everything else. While I like the sentiment, such gushy talk is loose and overstated."

Although such science does point to the oneness of reality, Greene clearly sits uncomfortably with this and displays his material and atomistic preference or metaphysical underlying (pseudo) absolute presupposition (as the uncaused material universe becomes the non-material universe), but he does not propose an alternative to conclude this.

The Arrow of Time, the Newtonian Big and the Quantum Small Potentially Reconciled

Time via the Quantum lens gives us future probabilities only, but still, this sits with our common-sense view or notion of there being an arrow of time. The incisive mind of Feynman in the late 1940s applies his 'Sum Over Histories' approach to grasping this aspect of the Quantum wonderland and it may well provide a solution to this seeming paradox of a timeless universe, pre-determined, with laws of physics being indifferent to all. He said that if we know that an electron can pass through both a left and a right hand hole in a screen through which it is being shot, to arrive both at the same point on the receiving screen, an experiment performed time and again in the laboratory, then to some extent all its probabilities are contained in this one outcome. They happen simultaneously. So the probability wave contains all possible histories, all potentiality, if you like, to arrive at the one possible outcome, determined by you.

The mechanical predictability of Newton's laws of motion, with their seeming perfection when measuring large objects, becomes more understandable now in the seeming chaos of the Quantum Wonderland. Here, a microscopic thing, embedded as a potential thing in its quantum field, can be a wave or a particle, can have many potential instantiations of itself in many paired, multiple locations around the universe, giving us the prediction of unpredictability. If we take the sum over histories approach, we accept the apparent chaos, but recognize that the grouping together of all these probabilities is lost in the rounding on the big scale and is simply unobservable.

Long ago, Cardinal Nicolas of Cusa displayed shades of this thought process of Feynman's. He was a theologian and philosopher during the 15th century. In Book I of "On Learned Ignorance" (Cusa, 2001), he asks us to consider a circle and a straight line - seemingly very different things. If you imagine the circumference getting bigger and bigger - so much bigger that at some point you can't even notice that part of the circle you now observe as a straight line – it is just like the 'big' of the Newtonian world of mechanical prediction: the big makes the small un observable, but still very real. Just as that circle of Cusa is very real, even though it is so big, it appears as a straight line. He called this a "coincidence of opposites." This is a very apt phrase for the apparent paradox of the big and the small world of Physics. Cusa was using this as a metaphor for explaining how the finite thing gets lost in the Oneness of the creator.

Concerning time, it would seem to me that we can have that loaf of time that Greene so eloquently and ably explains in the You Tube clip, but the past would be fixed and the future would be that which is quantumly possible: not a moment that is fixed already, but potentially fixed. Certainly, the architecture of the Quantum world is the limiting factor in what can, or cannot happen. However, it provides us with the comforting view that free will within this potentiality is very much there, and real. We are not a Newtonian-determined object occupying our part of absolute space, trundling through the cosmos at a predetermined mechanical pace. Nor are we a fixed moment, one of many in that Einsteinian paradox. The Quantum Wonderland does give us a hint that the future is dominated by it, and our free will works to trigger causality in the mix of the future. Being able to manipulate the potentialities of the quantum world gives great potential for making other possibilities beyond the norm. We are determined only in the very loose sense that we can only do what is quantumly possible. This gives hope for a great new future for science to manipulate the quantum world to create a whole new range of things to serve mankind. For those theists who believe that a creator created the universe, it is child's play for that creator to mess about with quantum probabilities to produce any variety of miracles which, paradoxically, would then be perceived to be natural and not unnatural events.

Lee Smolin (Smolin, 2013) about whom I write more later, proposes that you must do away with the concept of timelessness in similar vein:

> "That is, quantum mechanics describes a universe in which you can make probabilistic predictions of how systems behave, but in which those systems have as much freedom from determinism as any physical system described by probabilities can have. So in the sense that quantum systems are free, they are maximally free." (Smolin, 2013)

> "This formulation cannot be expressed outside a framework in which time is real, because it makes essential use of the distinction between past and future. So we can abandon the idea that there are time-less and deterministic laws of nature without losing any of the explanatory power of physics." (Smolin, 2013)

Cusa, in book II (Cusa, 2001) also introduces us to the metaphor of "enfolded" and "unfolded." He was using the former to argue that we differentiated beings and finite things are all part of this Oneness in the fundamental ground of Being or, as he would put it, God and we are unfolded in terms of becoming in time. You can strip this of all its religious connotations and it will bear a secular relevance to understanding the Einsteinian version of a timeless universe incorporating all past enfolded into it and all quantum actualities pruned down to being instantiated and real. Moving into the future, we have our ongoing unfolding quantum probabilities, fixing themselves in the now.

In this book, Cusa was well ahead of his time. He proposed that motion being everywhere, with its centre being the Oneness of God, implies that the earth is not its centre and also that no finite thing can ever be viewed as its centre and that everything is relative to it in space and time. Once again, if you strip this of its religious trappings, his views stand as a precursor to the dumping of both the geocentric and heliocentric picture of the starry heavens and the emergence of the Leibnizian relational view of the world, with the seeds planted for an understanding of the relative world of Einstein.

Mainstream Competing Theories of The Big and the Small Worlds

The 1957 "Everett Many Worlds Interpretation."

Here, we see an eminent scientist deny the collapse of the wave function into an instantiated thing. He proposes that each and every wave function happens. You are dead and alive, but in different universes. Yes, each and every potentiality from the zillions of variations of you being alive and doing all the potentially zillions of things, for all of the billions of us and every finite thing, each individually has a parallel universe. There is no evidence of this, but a noted high priest of science advocates it, so it is taken as a serious potential solution to the quantum possibility outcomes that would seem to conflict with our certain world. This, surely, is the wildest attempt to avoid a creation moment, be it the secular Big Bang or a theistically created Big Bang.

Its hope of carrying truck with anyone is whether the concept of infinity carries any substance in reality to accommodate any of these zillions of combinations.

A Note on Infinity

By infinity, I think we mean that we can conceive of a series of zeros unfolding off into infinity. If we add a series of the numbers of ones to the series of zeros - which is now infinite? I can only conclude that each compromises the other's infiniteness and thus they become finite. The concept of infinity has no relevance to the objects of the finite world. Indeed, even concerning constructs of our minds such as mathematical constructs, it is incoherent. All we know about the universe confirms it has a boundary and thus is finite in some way. Even if you just propose endless matter, this is in fact always a material something that is differentiated from a material something else. As we have said before, even though you can say the words 'endless matter', matter without a cause, is in fact not matter at all, but nothing. Take away its causality and it ceases to by physical. In positing endless matter, in effect you propose it as causeless, which ceases to make it matter. Immateriality might be the only potentially unlimited thing. In fact, theologians from the dawn of mankind have always argued that the only infinite thing was the immaterial creator of the universe; it is hard - indeed impossible - to think of anything material as being infinite. The infinite, when applied to our finite physical world, is forming an abstraction of reality, a mind construct, and making the mistake of applying it to the real world, and by doing this making a statement about the real world of things. This is surely a mistake. The "Many World Interpretation" must be incoherent because of it.

The Roman poet and philosopher Lucretius summarises the atomistic view of the universe and puts it to a wider audience in this way: if there are an infinite number of atoms combining in an infinite number of ways, following clear laws of nature, we don't need a creator. Later evolutionists would propose that significant time and infinite combinations provide the mindless, chance driven world and universe we occupy but, like the atomists, I believe their start point, their founding axiom of the reality of infinity, is contradictory at its core, so their conclusions carry no truck with me. I can't quite take the Everett "Many World Interpretation" any more seriously, just as I can't evolution by chance and creation by chance alone.

The Ghirardi-Rimini-Weber Theory or GRW Theory for Short

This is a very recent (1985) attempt to remove the human observer as the trigger that, at the point of observation of a wave, forces it to become a determined particle of some kind. By proposing a modification with some equations that govern this, it seems they can deduce that a wave will spontaneously collapse (with no requirement for a human to observe it). This may be a billion-year event for a wave, however, as all things seem to be entangled and a lot of this is going on all the time. As this happens in tiny fractions of seconds, large objects always exist as they appear to us. What is more, unlike Everett and, indeed, Schrödinger's famous cat, you can't be dead and alive, but always either/or. It would seem remarkable that unless these spontaneous collapses are not working to some other law to give us the conformity we observe, we would be in an entirely random world, which is not what we observe.

De-coherence as a Potential Solution

In 1970, the scientist Heinz-Dieter Zeh asked us to look at the electron that passes though the left and right slit of the detector, to be picked up by the detector at a single point. In this classic experiment, we see quantum interference on the detector as there are lighter and darker strips appearing. Some paths the electron takes reinforce the final result, some don't. So macroscopic things are even marginally affected by these things and are made a tad more incoherent - but we can't see it. The macroscopic stays in its familiar world, we all observe, but is coherent with its Quantum cousin, now Quantum brother. The act of human measuring then disappears from this mix as nothing is needed to substantiate the instantiation of a wave to a particle: it's happening all the time. Whilst this may appear to remove the assumption of a human observer causing a probable outcome to actually happen, we only know that it may be the case due to that fact that there have been observations made by humans that might support this. I suspect this theory will die in a vicious circle of contradictions.

Pythagoras' Strings to the Strings of Everything in Physics

The latest development in physics is String Theory. I feel like we are back to the acoustics and geometry of the Greeks. Scientists like Greene (Greene, 2005) favour String theory. It has similarities to the Pythagoreans, and in particularly Pythagoras himself, after whom they are named - who put forward an assertion to kick start his reasoning that the world is a sphere. With our modern knowledge, we can upscale this to the universe of everything. Borrowing from the Hebrew Biblical understanding of the world as a sphere, as we have seen in the older Book of Job, the orb is floating in the substance of space. He assumes the rotation of the orb creates the various opposites: hot cold , dry wet etc. This is rather like when we spin blood to force it to separate into other things, such as plasma. Pythagoras presumed this on a global scale to arrive at the material separations we observe. However, matter was proposed as one substance - matter was one homogeneous blob from which all things came until this process, this method of spinning, started. He also postulates that differences in nature are based upon their differences in geometrical structure, which defines how matter ends up as it does. So you need not get involved with saying what differentiated what from what in the general substance of Being, just that what we observes conforms to a reliable, and therefore predictable, geometry. So these relationships were mathematically quantifiable.

What is more, the Pythagoreans showed that in acoustics it is not the properties of the musical instrument being played by the music master, but the vibrations resulting from the strike of the strings that determine the nature of the sound. Different sounds were spaced out in a mathematical relationship. So this mathematical method can be applied to all sorts of physical things. Vibrating stings expressed as a mathematical formula can indeed account for sounds in reality and they and the instrument itself is determined by this mathematical formulation. Vibrating stings forming in strict and predictable patterns manifesting themselves in matter seems to be what modern String Theory is about. Greene suggests:

> " ... superstring theory starts off by proposing a new answer to an old question: what are the smallest, indivisible constituents of matter? For many decades, the conventional answer has been that matter is composed of particles— electrons and quarks— that can be modelled as dots that are indivisible and that have no size and no internal structure. Conventional theory claims, and experiments confirm, that these particles combine in various ways to produce protons, neutrons, and the wide variety of atoms and molecules making up everything we've ever encountered. Superstring theory tells a different story. It does not deny the key role played by electrons, quarks, and the other particle species revealed by experiment, but it does claim that these particles are not dots. Instead, according to superstring theory, every particle is composed of a tiny filament of energy, some hundred billion billion times smaller than a single atomic nucleus (much smaller than we can currently probe), which is shaped like a little string. And just as a violin string can vibrate in different patterns, each of which produces a different musical tone, the filaments of superstring theory can also vibrate in different patterns. These vibrations, though, don't produce different musical notes; remarkably, the theory claims that they produce different particle properties. A tiny string vibrating in one pattern would have the mass and the electric charge of an electron; according to the theory, such a vibrating string would be what we have traditionally called an electron. A tiny string vibrating in a different pattern would have the requisite properties to identify it as a quark, a neutrino, or any other kind of particle. All species of particles are unified in superstring theory since each arises from a different vibrational pattern executed by the same underlying entity." (Greene, 2005)

The 2500 year old problem Pythagoras was trying to resolve is still unresolved but, interestingly, the mathematical relationships expressed in music and mathematical shapes, or relations proposed by geometry and this new string theory, all seem to come together now in this new idea of a series of strings, the smallest things in reality vibrating and producing particles of L,M,N and O depending on the pitch of the vibration. Pythagoras would be happy. However, as I understand it, the majority of this theory is still in hypothetical formation and not deemed provable yet by scientific method.

In the Beginning at Time Zero......Gravity the Repulsive Force

What is a potentially even bigger hurdle to get over to scientists is to explain to us what actually happened at the time of the Big Bang. The point of singularity has more mystery than the Virgin Birth. It's a point so small as to be nothing yet this no-space or nothing contains everything and is infinitely dense. You have to have a strong, blind, and unquestioning faith in this for it to be the start point from which all your deductive and induced reasonings are to emanate concerning the creation of the Universe. A sceptical psychologist scientist J B Davies (Davies J. B., 2013) comments (and with this I have much sympathy) that the Big Bang starts off from an impossible position of zero volume and infinite mass, two contradictory things. Such a start point is nonsensical - this is not to imply that the process described nano seconds after (or what is called Plank time , 10^{43} seconds after) the Big Bang is nonsensical, but surely its conventional start point is. A particle must have space, so it can't have no volume into which infinite mass must pile itself. If this was offered by a priest, you might nod you head and say "yeah right, silly faith-head mystic, why does he not stop preaching this drivel and go out and live the life like Christ and serve the poor as he is meant to do." As it is scientists who assert this as fact we say instead: "wow, these boffins are far more intelligent than me, so they must know what they are taking about, especially with all these billions and billions of bits of kit and technology around to assist them, they are surely right." The white coats of the scientists now replace those of the priestly cast to present to us our new high priests of science.

Greene passes no comment on that contradiction at the heart of the Big Bang and just assumes it, but he does say concerning the Big Bang, that it:

" ... says nothing at all about time zero itself And since, according to the big bang theory, the bang is what is supposed to have happened at the beginning, the big bang leaves out the bang. It tells us nothing about what banged, why it banged, how it banged, or, frankly, whether it ever really banged at all. In fact, if you think about it for a moment, you'll realize that the big bang presents us with quite a puzzle. At the huge densities of matter and energy characteristic of the universe's earliest moments, gravity was by far the dominant force. But gravity is an attractive force. It impels things to come together. So what could possibly be responsible for the outward force that drove space to expand? It would seem that some kind of powerful repulsive force must have played a critical role at the time of the bang, but which of nature's forces could that possibly be?" (Greene, 2005)

The answer was developed in the 1980s and is called Inflationary Cosmology. This suggests that in certain conditions, gravity can be repulsive and not attractive. The thought process seems to suggest that compression into a small point – let's leave aside the idea of an infinitely small point of nothingness having everything in it for now, and run with this - compresses energy adding more and more weight into the mix. This pressure (a sort of negative gravity) builds up and up until BANG! she goes inflating away, rapidly, with unimaginable power, to what we continue to see today: an expanding universe with all of us within it. I am sure that Greene knows what he and his colleagues are talking about in all these matters they write about, and take this in good faith. He tells us how, as the universe expands, matter and radiation lose energy to gravity while inflation gains energy from it, and so the Big Bang show rolls on and on, faster, bigger, quicker, self-reloading. One of the most liberating passages in his book (Greene, 2005) in summing up Inflationary Cosmology is this:

"This means that at the onset of inflation, the inflation field didn't need to have much energy, since the enormous expansion it was about to spawn would enormously amplify the energy it carried. A simple calculation shows that a tiny nugget, on the order of 10^{-26} centimetres across, filled with a uniform inflation field —and weighing a mere twenty pounds—

> *would, through the ensuing inflationary expansion, acquire enough energy to account for all we see in the universe today.'* (Greene, 2005)

> *"Thus, in stark contrast to the standard big bang theory in which the total mass/energy of the early universe was huge beyond words, inflationary cosmology, by "mining" gravity, can produce all the ordinary matter and radiation in the universe from a tiny, twenty-pound speck of inflation-filled space. By no means does this answer Leibniz's question of why there is something rather than nothing, since we've yet to explain why there is an inflation or even the space it occupies. But the something in need of explanation weighs a whole lot less than my dog Rocky, and that's certainly a very different starting point than envisaged in the standard big bang."* (Greene, 2005)

Children, don't try this at home please!

Also, I am delighted he is humble enough to realize that the 'why' question remains unanswered. But what may well have been answered is why the arrow of time streaks out from the Big Bang, to us, and on into the future.

The Curious Case of Lee Smolin

In his book "Time Reborn", Smolin recounts how, in his younger years, he yearned for the timeless world of physics and set his heart on a search for an equation that would explain everything. After a lifetime of research at the cutting edge, he concludes:

> *"I used to believe that my job as a theoretical physicist was to find that formula; I now see my faith in its existence as more mysticism than science."*

In many respects, he is showing a revolt against Platonism, whereby transcendental pure forms are presupposed from which all reality is a mere imperfect image of it, mathematical forms being the finest clear expression of the forms, timeless and indifferent to everything and existing 'out there'. Smolin has, in many respects, revolted against this priesthood of conventional science in observing that if the Universe is everything, then, truly, the laws that operate within in it can't come from beyond it. In my opinion, he is being more of a scientist by working exclusively in the scientific method, when he rejects transcendental crutches to start off his quest and proposes just the rules of induction and therefore empirical testing to yield results. In fact, for nearly 20 years he has been doing this. He is quite correct to say that a scientific cosmological theory must be able to make falsifiable predictions for it to be, well, scientific. Just accepting the laws of nature as a 'given', or 'brute fact' carries no truck with Smolin - in this respect, he really is a methodologically true scientist. Any metaphysical crutch, or transcendental forms and deductions from it, is anathema to him. If his research programme is successful, he can do what no other scientist has done and move science completely out of its philosophical groundings founded over 2500 years ago. This is a big task.

"In my 1997 book, The Life of the Cosmos, I proposed a mechanism for laws to evolve, which I modelled on biological evolution. I imagined that universes could reproduce by forming baby universes in-side black holes, and I posited that whenever this happens, the laws of physics change slightly. In this theory, the laws played the role of genes in biology; a universe was seen as an expression of a choice of laws made at its formation, just as an organism is an expression of its genes. Like the genes, the laws could mutate randomly from generation to generation. Inspired by then-recent results of string theory, I imagined that the search for a fundamental unified theory would lead not to a single Theory of Everything but to a vast space of possible laws. I called this the landscape of theories, taking the language from population genetics, whose practitioners work with fitness landscapes.

"Over the last decade, many string theorists have embraced the concept of a landscape of theories. As a result, the question of how the universe chooses which laws to follow has become especially urgent. This, I will argue, is one of the questions that can be answered only within a new framework for cosmology in which time is real and laws evolve.

"Laws, then, are not imposed on the universe from outside it. No external entity, whether divine or mathematical, specifies in advance what the laws of nature are to be. Nor do the laws of nature wait, mute, outside of time for the universe to begin. Rather the laws of nature emerge from inside the universe and evolve in time with the universe they describe. It is even possible that, just as in biology, novel laws of physics may arise as regularities of new phenomena that emerge during the universe's history" (Smolin, 2013)

For Smolin, reducing things down to their smallest parts is not the most critical of the tasks of the scientist; that is understanding the emergent relationships that exist between things. Things in the past that we have assumed are immutable - rocks, water - are not in fact fixed in space-time for ever and a day. We know rocks eventually change into other things, water into ice or mist, atoms re-arranging themselves in different ways in these examples as they emerge from one state to the next. This leads Smolin to ask this question: if things in space and space itself is emergent, why not time?

In fact, he needs to get time out of the timelessness of current physics for his research programme to have any chance of working as this would mean that even time, which we observe as very real, is not timeless and can emerge just like any other thing and not last forever. Time must evolve. There is a slight circularity in this as to evolve is to change with time, but that does not seem to concern Smolin at this juncture of his truly Promethean project. The terms of engagement in his project are as follows, and they are truly scientific only and very laudable indeed:

"Although we don't yet have the cosmological theory, we already know something about it, if the principles I've put forward are sound:

- *It should contain what we already know about nature, but as approximations.*
- *It should be scientific; that is, it has to make testable predictions for doable experiments.*
- *It should solve the Why these laws? problem.*
- *It should solve the initial-conditions problem.*
- *It will posit neither symmetries nor conservation laws.*
- *It should be causally and explanatorily closed. Nothing outside the universe should be required to explain anything inside the universe.*
- *It should satisfy the principle of sufficient reason, the principle of no unreciprocated action, and the principle of the identity of the indiscernibles.*
- *Its physical variables should describe evolving relationships be-tween dynamical entities. There should be no fixed-background structures, including fixed laws of nature. Hence the laws of nature evolve, which implies that time is real."* (Smolin, 2013)

His own theory of cosmological natural selection, needless to say, fits his brief. The hypothetical start point is that new universes are created out of black holes. The mechanism of their birth is based on the idea that quantum gravity does away with singularities, start and beginnings. According to Smolin, concerning quantum gravity dispensing with start points etc, there is a theoretical robustness that comes along with this so that I, for one, will have to defer to his expertise and accept as good knowledge. As there are a billion billion of these black holes, there us a large potential for this theory to work. Different sets of laws can emerge from different black holes on many different combinations, and the one perfect for life - for example our one - can then emerge out of this dismal hole. Now you may have to wait a second or zillions of years to observe this, but subject to testing and prediction, it surely is.

He introduces the concept of precedence being the method of selection of the laws of nature. In his own words:

"Not because they are following a law but because the only law is a principle of precedence. Such a principle would explain all the in-stances in which determinism by laws work but without forbidding new measurements to yield new outcomes, not predictable from knowledge of the past. There could be at least a small degree of freedom in the evolution of novel states without contradicting the application of laws to circumstances that were repeatedly produced in the past. Common law in the Anglo-Saxon tradition operates by a principle of precedence, whereby judges are constrained to rule as judges have in the past, when presented with similar cases. What I want to suggest is that something like this might well be operating in nature." (Smolin, 2013)

"If nature is like this, then the future is genuinely open. We would still have the benefit of reliable laws in cases with ample precedent, but without the stranglehold of determinism." (Smolin, 2013)

"You can test a pair of particles for an entangled property like contrary that is a property of neither particle separately. Second, there appears to be an element of genuine randomness in the response of quantum systems to their environments. Even if you know every-thing about the past of a quantum system, you cannot reliably predict what it will do when one of its properties is measured.

"These two features of quantum systems let us replace the postulation of timeless laws with the hypothesis that a principle of precedence acts in nature to ensure that the future resembles the past. This principle is sufficient to uphold determinism where it's needed but implies that nature, when faced with new properties, can evolve new laws to apply to them" (Smolin, 2013)

This contrasts with his anthropic scientist colleagues who suggest that the timeless laws, the cosmic constants, the just rightness of all of these parameters that make life perfect for us, are not capable of experiment and prediction/falsification and therefore are not true science. Surely he is right, then – as long we mean by science a strict adherence to the scientific method only. In fact, he attacks any anthropic argument in the following way which is revealing about his own absolute presuppositions that I think will, in the end, compromise his research project. Smolin asserts that the anthropic principle runs from premise to conclusion as follows:

"(1) Galaxies are necessary for life. Otherwise stars would not form, and without stars there is no carbon and no energy to promote the emergence of complex structures, including life, on the surfaces of planets.
(2) The universe is full of galaxies.
(3) But the cosmological constant has to be smaller than the critical value if galaxies are to form.
(4) Hence, the anthropic principle predicts that the cosmological constant must be smaller than the critical value.

"Can you see the fallacy? Point no. 1 is true, but it plays no role in the logic of the argument. The real argument starts with point no. 2. The fact that the universe is filled with galaxies is evident from observations; it is irrelevant whether or not life would be possible without them. So the first point can be dropped from the argument without weakening the conclusion. But point no. 1 is the only place life is mentioned - so once it's dropped, the anthropic principle plays no role. The correct conclusion is:

(4)   Hence, the observed fact that the universe is full of galaxies implies that the cosmological constant must be smaller than the critical value." (Smolin, 2013)

In my understanding, following Aristotle, a syllogism should start with a

118

premise, and by unpacking what is implied in this premise, we should obtain new knowledge in the conclusion - and when I say new, in reality, as we all know, it must already be implied in the premise; you have just revealed what was already there.

So Premises (1) We have observable Laws of Nature.
The Deduction (2) We could not have Galaxies, star formation, carbon formation , 'us' formation, without these.
Conclusion (3) We observe it was ever thus and only could be as one tick of the dial this way or that of the laws of physics and we are blasted into oblivion!

In this way, the anthropological argument is formally correct. What you could argue is that whilst it is being correct, it is an analytical proposition and like all wholly analytical propositions it is a tautology and tells me nothing about reality. This is popular in those philosophy departments who have embraced the analytical realism of 20th and 21st Century. Following Kant, I would say this anthropic cosmological principle is an analytical synthetic, *a priori* proposition that does have very much relevance to reality. I say this just as Euclid's geometry is *a priori*. However, I would not knowingly walk on a bridge, fly in the air by aeroplane, sit in a tall building not constructed in accordance with his great bit of abstract thinking! The anthropic cosmological principle gives meaning to the world we participate in, formally abstract that it is, as with Euclidian geometry, its empirical observations, the cosmological constants, appear as fundamental absolutes and certainly I would not want to, let alone *could*, live in a world where these did not exist!

I agree with Smolin that one of the thrusts of his book and research programme is to make these laws subject to empirical observation and move them to be structured synthetically only. He provides a very neatly thought out and sign-posted way to this end, and this is the scientific method par excellence. I am sceptical about what truth it can reveal. The two ways of gaining knowledge - empirical and deductive - are as far apart as chalk and cheese and when people blur the two great confusion arises. Nevertheless, both paths can yield truth. If the anthropic syllogism is correct, as I believe it is, well, it's just that - as correct as any of our well thought out mathematical equations. If it is not only correct but also very much relevant to reality, i.e., we can't do without it, it's a rare Kantian synthetic *a priori* (the foundations of evolution and economics are examples of this, which we have shown in the above Chapters 5 & 8) and should be treated seriously. It is also just as valid a way of looking at this part of reality in his emergent way.

Smolin's project is an argument of science, which must have the potential to be proved wrong via experimentation/induction etc. The anthropic method is one of formal *a priori* deduction; it is formally right as syllogisms go, but unprovable by any other non-analytical (i.e., empirical) measures. Scientists attempting to cross over the divide will potentially generate much confusion.

Smolin's project is cutting edge science, fantastically ambitious and empirically based, as true science should be. If I am wrong about that, then all the rest won't apply. Smolin would appear to fail in his own words as this empirical and emergent universe he proposes, in the final analysis, needs to evoke a 'meta law', a great big elephant in the room of an analytical start point, not testable by his empirics. He acknowledges that this is an infinite-regress situation when one law needing to be explained by another can only be terminated by a meta law to which you just simply don't ask the 'what caused that' question, or, if you are true to yourself, you keep on asking and asking into infinity and beyond! I would go further and say if his project is to retain the concept of materiality, which these laws only work in and on, he requires a prior physical causes for all physical things. This also brings you into an infinite regress, going on and on *ad infinitum*, but it violates the law of causality as you are faced with suggesting the causeless (nonsensical) first bit of physicality which violates the understanding of materiality. To square his circle, he will not follow what logic dictates: an immaterial first cause as proposed by the centuries old Cosmological Argument: in the common man's language - God - as this does not suit his scientific mind. Smolin is stuck in a vicious circle of unreasoning that makes all that he holds dear, a material real reality, based on a contradiction. So his meta law would appear to be spiked by this horny dilemma. In fact, Smolin's project is skewered on whichever horn of destruction he picks. That said, I wish his project well and that it will continue towards great discoveries on the way to its destruction, as this is indeed the path to gaining all discoveries in science. The ever shifting gospel of science moves and changes, ever onwards, to reveal new pockets of truth hitherto un discovered by man.

Smolin would be better off with a solution to this dilemma by proposing the meta law (or call it the First Causeless Cause, The Prime Mover, Tao, Brahmin, Demiurge or, dare I say, God) as an absolute presupposition as it is test-less, neither right nor wrong , but gets you a start point to deduce/induce from. This is the start of his metaphysics proper, be it known or unknown to him. The rest that follows is science proper, as it is all about propositions that can be tested. Setting it up like this, he will thus advance the case of science much further than those before him. I salute him for that, and a true pioneer is he.

Before we move on from Smolin, I note that he makes another absolute presupposition which I believe he is unaware of: that of the law of precedence which, if I have understood it correctly, is the law of induction restated. Here we observe fundamental cosmological constant X. Take your choice. Call it potentially induced so it holds by virtue of it holding before. Make it not a given, timeless law dispatched from the Platonic heaven, to grace us with the pleasure of its divine rulership, but emerging from the universe itself, and then we can watch and observe things grow from it and rid us of the deterministic paradigm we are stuck in and open up genuine causality and an area of free will. Again, the limiting factor of free will is the goal post erected around the quantum world, where probability, within this predetermined framework, well, works, to produce the outcomes we observe.

I have no problem with absolute presuppositions since you cannot hope to try to describe the world in which we live, let alone the whole cosmos, without them. We need rationally thought out placeholders to generate any thoughts, and these are such, writ large. That is why, to be coherent, I believe you must fail in trying to explain the universe in one great big equation or series of them. But you can become fully coherent if you accept the fact that you are going to have to plug one or two absolute presuppositions in at the start of it all. Conversely, if you create a couple of pseudo metaphysical presuppositions, then they deserve to be exposed as propositions and treated to the laser logic of inspecting and exposing the deductive errors contained within. If it is empirical, test and expose away, and find where the truth lies - that's the scientist's game. So the trick in all of this is to adopt the right start point.

Concerning the question of why the universe exists, in fairness to Smolin he holds his hand up and accepts that he has no idea, and says:

"it is beyond the scope of the principle of sufficient reason."

He is compelled in his new schema to accept a cause for everything other than the universe itself. Until he evokes the meta law. In fact, in the final analysis the anthropic and the non-anthropic scientist are both very close together in their start points, it's just that the anthropic scientist's meta law is God whilst Smolin's is just the meta law. What's in a name anyway?

Einstein and his followers take time as being the illusion. For Smolin, space is the illusion, not time. Time is the everyday real thing that we experience in terms of past, present and future, despite its contradictions. Space is always relational, with laws emerging as described above and precedence governing the outcome of which laws stick and which don't, which move on to emerge into something else and which cease to be. The quantum wonderland provides the goal posts for the potential futures, or new nows, that will emerge. All of this approach, despite my critique of parts of it has, I believe, alot going for it.

The One Man Heavy Metal Rock Band of Science: Lawrence Krauss

Krauss, in his book "Why There is Something Rather than Nothing" (Krauss, 2012) openly rejects the traditional line of questioning that suggests the 'why' of the universe is unanswerable if a greater creative force is evoked, and his book is his attempt to answer the why question:

> *"These arguments always remind me of the famous story of an expert giving a lecture on the origins of the universe (sometimes identified as Bertrand Russell and sometimes William James), who is challenged by a woman who believes that the world is held up by a gigantic turtle, who is then held up by another turtle, and then another .... with further turtles "all the way down!" An infinite regress of some creative force that begets itself, even some imagined force that is greater than turtles, doesn't get us any closer to what it is that gives rise to the universe. Nonetheless, this metaphor of an infinite regression may actually be closer to the real process by which the Universe came to be than a single creator would explain."*

His fellow scientist and atheist commentator, Richard Dawkins, certainly thinks *he* has answered the 'why' question. This pope and high priest of atheism states this in his "Afterword" to "A Universe from Nothing", by Krauss, and we have the following part-hagiography about his new atheist saint:

> *"If you ask religious believers why they believe, you may find a few "sophisticated" theologians who will talk about God as the "Ground of all Isness," or as "a metaphor for interpersonal fellowship" or some such evasion. But the majority of believer leap, more honestly and vulnerably, to a version of the argument from design or the argument from first cause. Philosophers of the calibre of David Hume didn't need to rise from their arm-chairs to demonstrate the fatal weakness of all such arguments: they beg the question of the Creator's origin. But it took Charles Darwin, out in the real world on HMS Beagle, to discover the brilliantly simple — and non-question-begging — alternative to design. In the field of biology, that is. Biology was always the favourite hunting ground for natural theologians until Darwin- not deliberately, for he was the kindest and gentlest of men — chased them off. They fled to the rarefied pastures of*

> physics and the origins of the universe, only to find Lawrence Krauss and his predecessors waiting for them." (Krauss, 2012)

After those words, we can only expect something spectacular. However, I now feel impelled to pick up the suggestion that Hume dispensed with all arguments of first cause, and I will also touch on his arguments from design, as biology is mentioned as a refuting factor in the debate about God as creator of everything, before we look at Krauss' work.

A Digression on Hume and Kant

You will see in Book Two of the Against Atheism series in the "Controversies in Scripture" sections that the claims of Dawkins concerning scripture show little scholarship and are challenged by the evidence, and therefore I believe them conclusively refuted. But you will have to take my word for it until you reach this point. For now, in the above passage he chooses to evoke the ghost of Hume to suggest that the First Cause or Cosmological Argument, and the Design Argument, were deftly disposed of whilst sitting in his armchair. I take the latter as a rhetorical flutter, but now I will show how Hume is conclusively refuted.

In his Dialogues Concerning Natural Religion, Hume places words in the mouth of Dema, one of his key characters in the conversation, and masterfully outlines the Cosmological Argument. It can be summarized as follows[29]:

---

[29] I summarise David Conway's notes summarizing Dema here in his book that Flew attributed to converting him away from the atheist world view, 'The Rediscovery of Wisdom, From Here to Antiquity in the Quest of Sophia' (Conway).

I knew Flew and I know Conway. Flew was the 20th Century's most famous Atheist. This is what he wrote about this book (Flew, 2007):

"As for my position on the classical philosophical debates about God, in this area I was persuaded above all by the philosopher David Conway's argument for God's existence in his book "The Rediscovery of Wisdom: From Here to Antiquity in the Quest of Sophia. Conway is a distinguished

1. Everything that exists must have a cause or reason for existing.
2. Everything that exists must either exist necessarily in and of itself or not so exist.
3. If a thing does not exist in and of itself it must have been caused to exist by something else, which either exists necessarily or in and of itself and so on, ad infinitum.
4. This also applies to the whole universe.
5. If we are to apply this idea of a series of prior causes, the universe has no cause.
6. If you accept points 1 and 5, you can only conclude it can't be a beginning less series.
7. If you accept points 4 and 6, you must conclude that in the absence of the universe being necessary, its cause can only be something that is necessary in and of itself.
8. There is nothing to make you believe the physical universe is necessary.
9. Points 7 and 8 then tell you that the physical universe must be caused by something that necessarily exits in and of itself. This something is commonly called God.

Hume's Objections to the Cosmological Argument

Objection to Point 1

Hume argues (Hume, "Treatise of Human Nature", 1978) that you can spontaneously think of one thought, then another completely unconnected thought where no apparent cause is implied. Therefore you don't need a prior cause.

British Philosopher at Middlesex University who is equally at home with classical and modern philosophy."

"But in David Conway's The Rediscovery of Wisdom and the 2004 edition of Richard Swinburne's The Existence of God. I found especially effective responses to the Human (and Kantian) critique of the cosmological argument."

Refutation One

In reality, we must observe that such an abstraction takes place in his mind, and that his mind is the causality. We then must apply this in reality, and we can see even in the examples Krauss will give in his book, particles popping in and out of existence, in a quantum vacuum, resting in the bedrock of a quantum field from which the causality is emerging. They also rest in time, and if there was no time from which these things popped out of spontaneously, his schematic could not have happened. I digress – but more on that later.

Second Objection to Point 1

In his Dialogues (Hume, "Dialogues Concerning Natural Religion, 1778) he argues that you could assume the universe is eternal, therefore it would not need a cause.

Refutation

If we are to accept materiality of physical things, by definition of materiality, then a thing, anything, must have a cause. If you object and make it a causeless cause and assert that this bit of physicality or the whole of physicality is uncaused, you can't assert it as being material, since to be material it must have a cause. If you wish to run this argument, you choose between being destroyed on one of two horns of the dilemma. If you assert a causeless material universe, then the universe can't be physical at all as each and every bit of physicality is permanently linked to a prior causality. If you propose no causality for the material universe, you have no physicality. You are forced to only endorse the conclusions of the Cosmological Argument: that there is an immaterial first cause of all physicality.

Objection to Point Two

You can think of anything as non-existing without contradiction, and this applies to the deity.

Refutation

In Chapter 8 it will be established as part of our discussion of the Ontological Argument that the only thing that you can think of existing necessarily is the most perfect being whose non-existence would not be perfect, therefore you can't think if it as non-existent; so it must be necessary, by definition. The Cosmological Argument actually never argues that the perfect being exists, but concludes a necessary being that just is, in and of itself.

Objection to the Inference of Premise of point Four from Premise of point 3

The universe is the only instance of itself; it is, in effect, an effect from nothing and only the mass of finite things need causal explanations from something else.

Refutation

Scientists tell us the Big Bang was the cause of the universe and Krauss states the case very eloquently for inflationary cosmology. A 'something' did happen from a 'something' at that moment that was finite and happening in a specific time and place. Granted it was unique, but this point alone does not absolve it from any need of a causal explanation.

Objection to Point 5

Here, Hume skilfully argues that the cause of all the infinite finite things does not go beyond the sum of them, so if you can supply the causes to all the finite things of the universe you are not warranted to ask for an explanation of the whole as you have already explained it from within - bottom up, if you like, and not top down.

Refutation

What leaps up in front of me is that when you get back to that last cause in his finite series you must presuppose its prior existence, uncaused, so you are back into a contradiction: you have a material thing in need of its causal explanation in order to remain a material thing, otherwise it evaporates into a contradiction.

Objection to Point 8

Hume argues that in maths there are some things that are necessary and if you are a good mathematician, you may know that this is so. If you are an ordinary member of the public, you may not know it is so as you don't understand it. The analogy is that, like the maths, the universe may well be necessary but we have not worked it out yet.

Refutation

It's a nice bit of sophistry, but that elusive physical necessary thing, by definition, must possess the nature of necessity, and this, on its own, is not going to explain why the so called necessary thing pops into existence. It can't explain itself, by itself. Also, I would be wary of using a mental abstraction, albeit a very coherent one, for example maths, to apply to the real world of physicality of the first cause.

I will now add in to the same schematic the Kantian position on the Cosmological Argument.

Kant's Objections to the Cosmological Argument

Kant was a religious man. Yet his arguments against the proofs of God are now classically used to deny the existence of God. In his "Critique of Pure Reason" 1781 he writes that he had:

> *" ... found it necessary to deny knowledge of God in order to make room for faith."*

His rejection of the Cosmological Argument is addressed also in his "Critique of Pure Reason".

Objection to Point 1

He says that nature is a series of causes that we can observe and we can never know what the original cause(s) are. He says that we can find specific causes, but it is a "transcendental deduction" that there is a permanent physical substrate from which these changes take place. We adopt this stance to think about the world. This is what he calls a category or principle from which we can't but operate by. He further reasons that if we did not have this transcendental deduction, things popping into and out of existence would disturb the unity of the world we do observe and thus make it nonsensical (Krauss please take note) - which it is not. Change presupposes a prior physical thing to change into: there could never be a time before time. Physicality, as we know it, must be permanent.

Refutation of Point 1

The above may well be all well and good, but you can't assume that the physical process is nothing but contingent. Therefore it is warranted to ask the 'why does it exist' question. Physicality is not necessary, so it requires explanation.

Objection to Point 2

Kant deals with this objection by saying absolute necessity can only be found in thought alone. Nothing can be thought in the physical world to exist in and of itself, as necessary. God can be thought of not to exist.

Refutation of Point 2

If we assume physicality only, this must have a prior cause to it which assumes another physical thing. So it we just have physicality and existence. Just existing, we have something that has refuted the law of causality as it has no cause and therefore can't be something physical and all the seeming coherence of materiality falls apart. You descend into a vortex of hopeless contradiction if you hold this line of reasoning, like Kant.

Objection to Point 8

He posits that we can only suppose *a priori* that the physical universe is not necessary and that this is no good for assessing the physical world. The hypocrisy of this line of thinking leaps up at you as he uses an *a priori* argument to say nothing can be thought of as not existing. No doubt this line of argument gets quietly put in the secular diplomatic bag of immunity when debating these matters, as he uses an *a priori* to move to a matter of empirical fact. Leaving that aside, the thrust of his argument continues that just because everything is contingent, once again the physical substance via which all change takes place gives us no grounds for assuming it is anything but permanent.

Refutation of Point 8

This is the same as it was to point 2, so I will not repeat it.

Hume's Objections to the Design Argument

Cleanthes is Hume's voice in the Dialogues[30]

1. Nature looks like it is designed. Things in nature resemble the things we design. Each in nature is designed almost perfectly to fit its role and we can't help but admiring its perfection regarding our own contrivances.
2. Just as we design things that resemble nature, it is therefore probable that their causes are similar.
3. Whatever the cause of the things in nature will more than likely resemble the cause of the man made things, ie, simply put, a creator.
4. With man-made machines it is man that is the cause.

---

[30] Again, I adapt Conway's useful summary of Cleanthes with my own additions and subtractions.

5. It is likely that the nature of what caused the thing is a non-human intelligence.
6. It is highly likely that this intelligence exists.

Objection to Point One

Hume argues that the universe does not resemble any of our man made contrivances. Even the humble vegetable has not been brought forth into existence by man's intelligent design, let alone anything close to it, so it is hard to believe that the universe could have been created, or planned by, a man-like super being.

Refutation

Perhaps Hume could have been forgiven for not knowing what we know today about fundamental cosmological constants, for with one move on the dial one way or the other the whole of what we know is blown away into oblivion. Hume, at the time, would have been fully rejecting the Newtonian mechanical predictability of all things. That being said, just the sheer regularity, the certainty that X thing/event always happens after Y suggests some notion of great planning.

Kant accepts the Design Argument in part, only if the Cosmological Argument which, as we have seen, he rejects, holds. He maintains that even if it did hold true, all that it can allow the Design Argument to do is suggest an architect for Being, and not the God of the Abrahamic Faiths. You have to have faith for that, and that Kant did.

What are the Cosmic Fundamental Constants?

Scientists tell us that there are fundamental constants of nature, or of the universe. Change the constant slightly and the whole of what we observe will be eliminated or compromised, to the extent that at best our existence is seriously threatened.

What exactly are these?

From this link in Wiki[31] , I deduce the following;

Speed of light in a vacuum.
Newtonian constant of gravitation.
Planck constant.
Reduced Planck constant.

There are 12 electromagnetic constants listed. There are 12 atomic and nuclear constants listed, with 13 physico-chemical constants.

I don't know if this is a comprehensive list, but there are enough to be going on with.

What is more, the universe seems to have exploded into existence with all these dials set.

>Barrow and Tipler:
>
>'There has grown up, even amongst many educated persons, a view that everything in Nature, every fabrication of its laws, is determined by the local environment in which it was nurtured—that natural selection and the Darwinian revolution have advanced to the boundaries of every scientific discipline. Yet, in reality, this is far from the truth. Twentieth-century physics has discovered that there exist invariant properties of the natural world and its elementary components which render inevitable the gross size and structure of almost all its composite objects. The size of bodies like stars, planets, and even people is neither random nor the result of any progressive selection process, but simply manifestations of the different strengths of the various forces of Nature. They are examples of possible equilibrium states be-tween competing forces of attraction and repulsion.' (Barrow, 2009)
>
>"What this means is that the various structural parameters of our universe did not gradually evolve by a trial-and-error process of selection before they were able to find the right life-supporting

---

[31] http://en.wikipedia.org/wiki/Physical_constant

values. Instead, they emerged from the Big Bang with the right values already programmed in. This is what the term "invariant" means—it means that these structural values were never otherwise, which itself can only mean that these structural parameters emerged from the Big Bang in precisely the right format to promote the existence of life several billion years later."
(Corey, 2007)

And Roger Penrose, in his own words (Penrose, 1989):

> "This now tells how precise the Creator's aim must have been, namely to an accuracy of one part in 10 to the 10^{123}rd power. This is an extraordinary figure. One could not possibly even write the number down in full in the ordinary denary notation: it would be 1 followed by 10^{123} successive 0's." Even if we were to write a 0 on each separate proton and on each separate neutron in the entire universe- and we could throw in all the other particles for good measure- we would fall far short of writing down the figure needed."

If there was such a thing as infinity in the finite world, an infinity would allow for such an event as a random chance creation. As there is no infinity in a finite world, the conclusion is, to all intents and purposes, impossible, unless by some purposeful act of creation.

Second Objection to Point 1

Hume asserts that there is too much natural evil in the world for there to be any intelligence in design and, indeed, it would be incongruous to a loving designer. He says:

a) All animals suffer pain.
b) Nature should not display the regularity that it does if a benevolent designer needed to interfere all the time to stop pain.
c) If there was a benevolent designer, you would expect to see far more happiness around.
d) There are lots of natural disasters that would not be there in the eventuality of a loving designer.

Refutation

I will take these as a whole. If you have what Hume would see as a more lovingly created world, you would have a God (Good) Shepherd managing each and every minute detail of nature and every moment of our lives. Since over 4000 years BC - if you believe anything in Genesis - God's promise to Noah (Genesis 9:12-17) was never to interfere by making terrible natural disasters.

> 'And God said: "This is the sign of the covenant which I make between Me and you, and every living creature that is with you, for perpetual generations: I set My rainbow in the cloud, and it shall be for the sign of the covenant between Me and the earth. It shall be, when I bring a cloud over the earth, that the rainbow shall be seen in the cloud; and I will remember My covenant which is between Me and you and every living creature of all flesh; the waters shall never again become a flood to destroy all flesh. The rainbow shall be in the cloud, and I will look on it to remember the everlasting covenant between God and every living creature of all flesh that is on the earth." And God said to Noah, "This is the sign of the covenant which I have established between Me and all flesh that is on the earth."

Religious followers of the Abrahamic faiths have never suggested that the world should be more happy as being God created; they know that if an earthquake occurs, it is to thank God if anyone survives, and not to curse Him because the world is not perfect. Hume makes a claim that has misunderstood what religious people have long ago known: humankind has its own affairs to run, which implies a God not running a perfect world for us.

If you did not understand this at the time of Noah, before the 4th Century BC you were reminded again by the greatest of the Old Testament Prophets, Isaiah 54:9-10 in the 8th to 7th Century BC:

> "For this is like the waters of Noah to Me; For as I have sworn That the waters of Noah would no longer cover the earth, So have I sworn That I would not be angry with you, nor rebuke you. For the mountains shall depart And the hills be removed, But My kindness shall not depart from you, Nor shall My covenant of peace be removed," Says the Lord, who has mercy on you."

If there was a human, perfectly postulated world, the regularity of the fundamental cosmological constants would be dispensed with. If there is endless happiness, you are not in a position to really know happiness. To know anything you need to know what distinguishes it from other things ie, you must also know un-happiness. The pleasure of finding out something you did not know, discovering wisdom, is undoubtedly fulfilling and much more so than being unaware you are in a permanent state of bliss. It would seem pain can offer us good signposts to avoid on-going pain and experience greater pleasure.

In fact, the picture Hume is painting is that of a world where nothing can actually exist as we know it. Our Earth provides us with wonderful vistas with wide, varied geology, biology and diversified life forms. If we wanted to experience this Platonic heaven of Hume, a *la la* land of perfect abundance and love for all, we would need to postulate a non-scarce world, where the natural distribution of resources around the planet is exactly uniform, so that in each and every place a human being resides she/he has exactly the same as the next, with all enjoying abundant resources. Also, each and every human being must then possess perfect knowledge concerning how to use these resources in order to obtain the perfect amount of things they yield in the most perfect way. He/she must also to be permanently happy knowing who to trade with, with perfect knowledge of all prices everywhere at all points in time to be happy. Logically, this would mean there actually would be no trade as it is a situation of abundance for all in each and every measure; in effect, scarcity is abolished. This is not a world we recognize, it is not a human world. His objection can only amount to a feeble, wishful plea for more happiness to be spread about, and would we not have to assume a benevolent God would have dished up more of this goodness? Well yes, I agree in some respects: you can never say no to more good things, but cast out all of what he calls natural evil and we cease to have the world we want to live in at all as it is a non-human world. Of course we would all like a bit less of natural evil and a bit more happiness, more sunshine and lashings of strawberry jam without any calorific downside. Wraith like, we would exist in a permanent state of bliss in this world, *not knowing we are in a permanent state of bliss.* Unfortunately, a certain degree of 'natural evil' is warranted for us to exist, as painful as this is to us. I believe anyone really thinking about what Hume is saying will weigh up the experiences we have and think, yes, we would all like more happiness, but we would all reject the Platonic la la land of perfection as that is not living at all.

The central problem of 'why do the righteous suffer?' is addressed first by the Book of Job for believers of the Abrahamic faiths. The answer comes in the end: if you have trusted God you will be vindicated via your trust. Suffering for innocents can come from sin, for the need of strengthening, and to give opportunity to see a brighter future and to recognise His Grace. And sometimes we just have plain no idea why and it does seem odd and cruel to us. Now, this may sound feeble and a hard thing to tell a mother of a child of five years old suffering from terminal cancer, but this is what the Abrahamic faiths, and before Abraham (as Job pre dates Abraham), have always said.

Secondly, The New Testament addresses this matter slightly differently:

Luke 13:1-5

> *"There were present at that season some who told Him about the Galileans whose blood Pilate had mingled with their sacrifices. And Jesus answered and said to them, "Do you suppose that these Galileans were worse sinners than all other Galileans, because they suffered such things? I tell you, no; but unless you repent you will all likewise perish. Or those eighteen on whom the tower in Siloam fell and killed them, do you think that they were worse sinners than all other men who dwelt in Jerusalem? I tell you, no; but unless you repent you will all likewise perish."*

Pilate executed some pious people in their act of dedication. Whilst Christ does not deny the connectivity between sin and disaster, he does not positively affirm it either. The message is clear: now is the time to repent, as at any point in time disaster could strike you. No observer of either the act of Pilate or an act of random natural disaster should feel morally superior, as their time could be any time. Indeed, AD 70, the destruction of the Temple and the near extermination of the Jewish race, would be a sad but timely reminder of this teaching. When a person asked about the status of those who witnessed the tower collapse killing 18 people, suggesting the former must have been superior, again Christ neither affirms nor denies the connection, but reminds all they must repent.

Luke 13:22-30

> And He went through the cities and villages, teaching, and journeying toward Jerusalem. Then one said to Him, "Lord, are there few who are saved?"
> And He said to them, "Strive to enter through the narrow gate, for many, I say to you, will seek to enter and will not be able. When once the Master of the house has risen up and shut the door, and you begin to stand outside and knock at the door, saying, 'Lord, Lord, open for us,' and He will answer and say to you, 'I do not know you, where you are from,' then you will begin to say, 'We ate and drank in Your presence, and You taught in our streets.' But He will say, 'I tell you I do not know you, where you are from. Depart from Me, all you workers of iniquity.' There will be weeping and gnashing of teeth, when you see Abraham and Isaac and Jacob and all the prophets in the kingdom of God, and yourselves thrust out. They will come from the east and the west, from the north and the south, and sit down in the kingdom of God. And indeed there are last who will be first, and there are first who will be last."

Access to heaven is though a narrow door. Only those who know the owner of the house, God, will gain access. A sinner never will. A repentant sinner might. Anyone, not just the Jews, would be included in the heavenly banquet. Now there you have it: the heavenly banquet is our absence of evil. It is a place not of this world. To try to make it is place of this world, whilst admirable, will be impossible. The message from the Old Testament, shown by the rainbow passage, clearly states that God has made a covenant with man: not to get involved with natural disasters. The message in the New Testament is: don't equate natural disasters with sin or sinful acts with disaster, but get your affairs always in order, repent and believe, as you don't know when your time will be.

Non-believers and agnostics like Hume don't accept this line of teaching. However, those of faith don't accept the foundation of his questioning as the answer was provided thousands of years ago.

Objection to Premise 2

Hume asks: why assume one designer and not a multiplicity? He also asserts that blind necessity is the driver for change.

Refutation

It is always best to reduce to the simplest plausible explanation rather than multiplying your need for other causes, as per Ockham's Razor. This is the same refutation that applies to all the multi-universe theories that carry currency now, which we addressed when discussing the 'Many Worlds Interpretation' of the quantum world, so I won't repeat them here. Also, as we do observe such unique harmony with the cosmic laws, on the balance of probability, this would infer one entity doing the designing.

Post Darwin, for certain we have a very plausible methodology of change with time. We have seen King Solomon observing this 3,000 years ago, and various Greeks 2,500 years ago. Darwin provided the theory with its intellectual legs and with evidence, but this does not explain creation, it explains only the method of how, post-creation, things move though the passage of time. It does not explain the leap from non-living matter to living matter. There are wild speculations about matter in the primordial soup coming together in the right combinations to get a living cell up and running, so that it can not only self-select, but self-replicate. If the odds of the cosmic constants being as they are incapable of being written number by number on all the known particles of matter in the entire universe, then I wonder what the odds are of a single self-replicating, self-selecting cell coming randomly into existence?

Let's just think of that most humble of the building blocks of life, the cell, and ponder its chances of developing out of lumps of other matter, on its own, even over a billion of years or so. In the words of Michael Denton (himself no theist patsy, but an agnostic scientist):

> "To grasp the reality of life as it has been revealed by molecular biology, we must magnify a cell a thousand million times until it is twenty kilometres in diameter and resembles a giant airship large enough to cover a great city like London or New York. What we would then see would be an object of unparalleled complexity and adaptive design. On the surface of the cell we would see millions of openings, like the port holes of a vast space ship, opening and closing to allow a continual stream of materials to flow in and out. If we were to enter one of these openings we would find ourselves in a world of supreme technology and bewildering complexity. We would see endless highly organized corridors and conduits branching in every direction away from the perimeter of the cell, some leading to the central memory bank in the nucleus and others to assembly plants and processing units. . . . We would wonder at the level of control implicit in the movement of so many objects down so many seemingly endless conduits, all in perfect unison. We would see all around us . . . all sorts of robot-like ma-chines. We would notice that the simplest of the functional components of the cell, the protein molecules, were astonishingly complex pieces of molecular machinery, each one consisting of about three thousand atoms arranged in highly organized 3-D spatial conformation. We would wonder even more as we watched the strangely purposeful activities of these weird molecular machines, particularly when we realized that, despite all our accumulated knowledge of physics and chemistry, the task of designing one such molecular machine . . . would be completely beyond our capacity at present and will probably not be achieved until at least the beginning of the next century.
>
> What we would be witnessing would be an object resembling an immense auto-mated factory, a factory larger than a city and carrying out almost as many unique functions as all the manufacturing activities of man on earth. However, it would be a factory which would have one capacity not equalled in any of our most advanced machines, for it would be capable of replicating its entire structure within a matter of a few hours. To witness such an act at a magnification of one thousand million times would be an awe-inspiring spectacle." (Denton, 1986)

You are pulling my leg if you think I can imagine, even over a long period of time, the chances of this happening. Anyway, Harold Morowitz (an atheist scientist) was asked by NASA to make the calculation for life by chance. If you get to 1/1015 of a chance, you need more than the 15 billion years of the universe to allow it to happen. After studying the protein molecule, he calculated 1/10236. This takes into account all the known atoms of the universe coming together to just form one molecule:

> *"The universe would have to be trillions of years older, and trillions of times larger, for a protein molecule to have occurred by random chance."* (Denton, 1986)

The Fallacy of Circular Reasoning

His atheistic faith leads him to presuppose some more laws we are yet to discover to help get around these staggering odds, taking more time than the universe many times over to produce the most simple basic life form , let alone the human consciousness and the concept of 'I'. The fall-back position for someone arguing from the blind chance of self-replicating things – if, like me, you do not accept the odds of this - is to presuppose the existence of the cosmic settings of the constants as a 'given', a 'brute fact' or something that's just 'immediate'. So this, of course, means faith and not fact in these givens. Actually, if you just presuppose the prior existence of all the physical laws, and thus all the biocentric laws, to arrive at the conclusion of a biocentric universe, then you have actually just performed a spectacular performance of circular reasoning where your premises are your conclusion and your conclusion is the premise. This would not be acceptable in any branch of academia - other than in science, whose high priests seem to have a large diplomatic bag of immunity in which to place their get out of jail manoeuvres to achieve the conclusions they are after. To summarise: the scientist allows himself wild speculation when constructing his theories, whist prohibiting such license to any other discipline, including theology and philosophy. Another fall-back position for a pro-chance advocate is to just presuppose the eternity of the universe, and that as it is eternal, by definition it needs no explanation. The swapping of the aseity of God for the Universe has a problem because, almost certainly, we do know it had a beginning .

Back to Hume, Dawkins and Krauss

Dawkins makes light once again with the so-called ability of Hume to dispense effortlessly with theistic arguments. I, for one, find no evidence that Hume has refuted anything. So, once more, where Dawkins departs from his area of expertise, we must proceed with caution.

We now continue with the Dawkins Afterword:

> "Do the laws and constants of physics look like a finely tuned put-up job, designed to bring us into existence? Do you think some agent must have caused everything to start? Read Victor Stenger if you can't see what's wrong with arguments like that. Read Steven Weinberg, Peter Atkins, Martin Rees, Stephen Hawking. And now we can read Lawrence Krauss for what looks to me like the knockout blow. Even the last remaining trump card of the theologian, "Why is there something rather than nothing?" shrivels up before your eyes as you read these pages. If On the Origin of Species was biology's deadliest blow to supernaturalism, we may come to see A Universe from Nothing as the equivalent from cosmology. The title means exactly what it says. And what it says is devastating." (Krauss, 2012)

The 'why anything?' answer, then, would indeed seem to be answered by Dawkins: there *is* no why, it just happened, and that is just it. However, notwithstanding the futility of turtles all the way down, Krauss does acknowledge that the end point of his book will prove that the universe gets going out of nothing and needs to, if you accept his definition of nothing. His method of acquiring knowledge is only empirical and scientifically based, for certainly *a priori*, or synthetic *a priori* are anathema to him:

> "If we wish to draw philosophical conclusions about our own existence, our significance, and the significance of the universe itself, our conclusions should be based on empirical knowledge. A truly open mind means forcing our imaginations to conform to the evidence of reality, and not vice versa, whether or not we like the implications."

Krauss' mind is in fact closed to other methods of acquiring knowledge. His appeal to having an open mind is just rhetorical balderdash.

His 'nothing' is the absence of space and time. We might refer to empty space as nothing, and when our ancestors did so they would almost certainly have meant empty space meaning no-thing in it. We in the modern period consider empty spaces as actually filled up with force fields[32] and now also dark matter/dark energy that we can't identify, but by the process of deduction assume is there. The trust of the book then gives the latest evidence of particles seemingly randomly popping in and out of existence all the time in empty space, or space occupied by what we would formally have called nothing. Interestingly, his atheist colleague A C Grayling dismisses the notion of nothing-ness and says that we can only ever think of something. I think Grayling is correct.

In his chapter "Existence" (Grayling, Thinking of Answers , 2010)Grayling asks

"Why is there something rather than nothing?"

Grayling says since we don't know, the suggestions that a supernatural agency must have created it is question-begging and must be "dismissed immediately." Why? As it begs the question what created that supernatural agency, and so on - back we go for ever and ever never terminating in an answer.

He accepts there is something, but it is just one of his 'brute facts' and that it is more interesting to ask what the something is actually about, as the original question is actually unanswerable. He qualifies this by the suggestion

---

[32] It is now claimed that the universe (everywhere and in everything) is filled by the Higgs Field, and with some precision as it would seem the experiments at CERN confirm this. This means, we have a master force field, of zero value, that occupies the entire universe that gives us mass. Every time we spin around, we feel this as we experience pressure pulling us outwards. So we don't move relative to Newton's absolute space, but move on spacetime bathed in a field of Higgs which gives us our very mass. This would seem to explain why we and everything else with does not float off into the four corners of space and indeed move at the speed of light.

that we can only ask why there is nothing, if there was something before anyway. Thus:

> "When all the chocolates are eaten there is nothing in the box because there was something there before; you cannot introduce nothing ('nothingness'?) to a box other than by not putting something in it , or by taking everything out . So the primitive condition is that there is something, and we only understand 'nothing relatively and locally by its absence." (Grayling, Thinking of Answers , 2010)

Personally, I cannot conceive of nothingness. Even if I think of a totally empty space, as stated in abstraction, then fine, I can, but the concept of space is incoherent as Bradley has shown us, when pondered a little more deeply. As I understand theism: there is something, it is God, and He creates all of the something we call the material world, out of nothing physical, since he remains eternal and unchanged, and the something is all new creation. For materiality to stack up, as discussed before, He must be assumed as an immaterial first cause, so truly it always boils down to something from something .

When Krauss is opining on nothing, he really does mean something – it is just something that we have a tentative suggestion of, but something nevertheless:

> "Indeed, the immediate motivation for writing this book now is a profound discovery about the universe that has driven my own scientific research for most of the past three decades and that has resulted in the startling conclusion that most of the energy in the universe resides in some mysterious, now inexplicable form permeating all of empty space. It is not an understatement to say that this discovery has changed the playing field of modern cosmology.

> "We have discovered that 99 percent of the universe is actually invisible to us, comprising dark matter that is most likely some new form of elementary particle, and even more dark energy, whose origin remains a complete mystery at the present time.

> *And after all of this, it may be that physics will become an "environmental science." The fundamental constants of nature, so long assumed to take on special importance, may just be environmental accidents."* (Krauss, 2012)

Krauss and his Heavy Metal

It would seem that the atheist religion would not be complete without its zealot:

> *"I have challenged several theologians to provide evidence contradicting the premise that theology has made no contribution to knowledge in the past five hundred years at least, since the dawn of science. So far no one has provided a counterexample. The most I have ever gotten back was the query, "What do you mean by knowledge?" From an epistemological perspective this may be a thorny issue, but I maintain that, if there were a better alternative, someone would have presented it. Had I presented the same challenge to biologists, or psychologist, or historians, or astronomers, none of them would have been so flummoxed."* (Krauss, 2012)

The answer to his question is truly zero - if you mean scientific knowledge - as, funnily enough, theology and religion don't do science, just as science does not (should not) do theology or religion. Confused participants in either sphere may attempt to blur the lines, but they should be resisted and politely advised to remain in their own speciality. As we have seen, there are many scientist theologians who have made great contributions to the scientific endeavour, but they are doing science and not theology at the time. If a theologian says his theology is in the nature of the physical sciences, he is a witch doctor and should be exposed as such, and vice versa for a scientist.

This does not say that theology provides no knowledge - it provides plenty. The modified ontological argument of Anselm (see Chapter 8), or what I call the ontological deduction to necessary reality, provides strong grounds for a rational proof of the existence of God. This rests on a bedrock of faith in the workings of logic, our ability to reason, and predictability in the universe, just as the very science of Krauss uses this benign set of circumstances to give us new scientific knowledge. The Cosmological Argument and Design Argument have certainly not been refuted, as we have seen, and give us more reason to believe in a creator of the universe. This, to me, would seem to be a fairly important bit of knowledge to grasp. You can go through life with no knowledge whatsoever of the fact that there is a creator of the universe, that I don't doubt, but I suspect most people crave to know something about the origins of life and why on earth they are here at all! We should not forget as well, that having the knowledge to be diligently following in the footsteps of Christ, which Christians attempt to do, without a shadow of doubt is knowledge of the good life and is enormously beneficial to mankind.

What is more, based on the various 'proofs' of God, the aim of *theoria* in classical Greek philosophy, was, historically, and is now, to bring us closer to the ultimate cause of everything. Once you have gone beyond the physical, which can only help you answer the 'how' questions and not the 'why' question, truly you only have contemplation or theoria, which is well past the point at which Krauss is prepared to go, if you are at this highest level seeking to answer the 'why' question. Theoria, or Theology, was, and still is the queen of the sciences. Anything that is, or that can be, subjected to testing and verification which could shed light on the 'how' question, should be directed to science with immediate effect. Anything that can't - those over-lapping forms, soon to be mentioned in Chapter 7 concerning "On Being" which are impossible to fully define on their own - remain the realm of philosophy. Theoria, or contemplation, is of those absolute presuppositions in metaphysics proper: the true, original aim of theology, or understanding God. Knowledge about this gives us a much fuller understanding of the world in which we live.

Undeniably, organized religion then pours forth from *theoria* as it seeks to bring you to a practical life in the closest union you can have with the fundamental ground for being, and to live with it and all that surrounds you in peace and harmony. Now, much as Krauss thinks religion is the cause of most terrible things in the world and would rather rid all of humanity of its alleged malignant effects, the fact is that this is a very small minority view. Since the dawn of mankind billions, if not tens of billions of people have adopted religious ways that all seem to enshrine core beliefs urging respect for fellow humans and peaceful co-operation. The Decalogue of the monotheistic faiths is a good example of this, the Golden Rule another. So knowledge of the good life, the practices of billions of people, the template, if you like, of their practical existence, is governed by faith that comes out of theoria via religion; this is more about establishing a predictable pattern in people's lives and ethics which provides parameters within which you can practically work during your day-to-day life. I don't doubt that this knowledge, or aspects of it, can be found in a godless way by some, but not even someone like Krauss could deny the extraordinarily positive and often silent effect that religion has had on mankind, if he were to really spend more than a few minutes thinking about it. Religion gives people the knowledge about how to live in accordance with rhythm and predictability, and in accordance with a set of religious rules to aspire to and enjoy what its adherents believe is a fulfilling and prosperous, well-lived and worthwhile life.

The conversion of the whole of the West into the Judeo-Christian way of life must not be taken for granted by Krauss. He sits bathed in this tradition, with the respect for the individual at the heart of the political constitution of USA, from which he writes and opines. He should remember that it was the church courts which put the sanctity of the individual at the heart of the matter, as opposed to the secular prince-run courts of the feudal era where the Krausses of many generations back would have been considered the property of their local baron. Yes, they found cause to burn some heretics in their time, and each live wasted is a tragedy, but really, they pale into insignificance compared with the secular killings of the time.

Krauss should also remember the constitution of the monasteries as separate legal entities led to the endowing of the universities to with their own distinct legal framework. On this basis was the foundation of the modern corporation - a thoroughly religious genesis. His academic freedom today is a direct result of this religious invention.

The fact that this sowed the seeds for the development of double-entry accounting, and the eventual invention of the joint stock company and the ability to allow mass specialisation in the division of labour should not be overlooked. This is the very foundation of the modern capitalist system. Krauss, as we all do, benefits enormously today from our religious antecedents. So theology won't make me a GPS system - but it has, over millennia, provided the very architecture to support all of what we know as science today. He should be grateful for Judeo-Christian theology and its dangerous idea of putting the individual at the heart of our thinking. Theology provides us with a history over thousands of years of knowledge and know how.

The Science of Krauss

I think he can successfully establish (until the next Krauss amends it or refutes it as is the nature of the ever moving Gospel of science, of course) that there is a universe from something, but not from nothing. To get his schematic up and running he needs time. Time is the ultimate limiting factor for Krauss that would seem to impale his thinking, fatally. All events happen in time so the possibility of a random quantum fluctuation triggering staggering cosmological inflation needs time. As there is no time for any probabilities to play out if you are truly in nothingness, it would seem an impossible starting point for Krauss's scheme to get up and running. If he assumed a something, he could get it up and running. So not only does the quantum field – pre-existing and therefore in time and post Big Bang - have to exist or be presupposed to exist, time has to exist which is a post Big Bang event. It would seem he is fatally impaled on two counts. As discussed above, a theologian should argue the case for the fundamental ground for being, or God: this is a something indeed, not a nothing to get this cosmological inflation going. From this being came something. Krauss' quantum fields, from which particles pop in and out of existence, is from something, some *being*. If he seeks not to get a better understanding of that being, and just considers it a brute fact, then I believe he is doing a great disservice to his inquiring mind.

Maybe 35 centuries ago or 40 centuries ago (we don't quite know when Genesis was written) from that great non-scientific book we have the great scientific fact, that in Genesis 1:1

"In the beginning God created the heavens and the earth."

The beginning is the creation of time, the heavens is the creation of space and the earth is symbolic of the creation of material matter. This is the space-time of our 20th/21st century scientists. As a causeless physical cause can't be; we call its creator the immaterial cause of the Godhead. From this background emerges the popping in and out of existence of quantum things, but not from nothing.

As we can see, the Gospel of Science is ever changing. As a discipline, the fundamentals of theology are fairly predictable and virtually changeless over time. If science sticks to the 'how', along the way of its many changes, it will continue to deliver spectacular benefits to mankind. If theology is left to thinking about the ultimate 'why', and if religions bring us closer to union with the ultimate ground of being, it will continue to be massively beneficial. Cross over into each other's territory and cease to live side by side while knowing what each should be doing, always ends in tears.

Part 3 On Religion and Philosophy

Chapter 7 On Being

The Oneness of Reality

"For a long time now particle physicists have been dreaming of a grand unification. They have increasingly come to realise that apparently very different phenomena are often aspects of the same thing.

"For example, after the experiments of Michael Faraday and others back in the 19th Century, it was soon realised that electricity and magnetism are unified. More than that, the same unification also explained the nature of light.

"The idea of unification gathered momentum in the second half of the last century, when it was realised that all of the known forces in nature are, in a sense, copies of this electromagnetic prototype.

"The electromagnetic force, the string force, which binds together atomic nuclei, and the weak force, responsible for the burning of the sun, seem under reasonable assumptions , to fuse together into a single force if the energies are high enough.

"In other words, the forces of nature appear distinct only because we have been studying them at to low an energy. It is intriguing that the unification energy is so close to the energy governing the exploding universe, as inferred from the Bicep2 data."[33]

In a recent Legatum Leadership Forum[34] meeting, I was asked to participate in trying to define what 'prosperity' meant. This is an impossible task, I thought. Person after person did their best, but not much new fruit was

---

[33] Professor in Particle Physics, Brian Cox, and Jeff Forshaw of Manchester University, Sunday Times, New and Review Section , Page 2 23/03/2014 writing about their forthcoming book and in strong support of primordial gravitational waves & the hypothetical X (not their words) Dark Energy driving the initial inflation of the Universe.

[34] April 27th to 30th 2014 , Dubai

plucked from the tree. This is because it is impossible to get an exact definition from the word itself, as it is a philosophical concept that will, frustratingly, like all philosophical concepts, be truly elusive if you try to look at it as capable of offering a singular definition. This contrasts with a non-philosophical concept, such as, say, a number, which is a hypothetical construct and is definitive by the very understanding of what it is to be to a figure that represents, say, a one, or a two, relative to something which you can look at in this binary fashion. Alas, it is not for any philosophical concept. It became apparent that even if I could look at two apparent opposites: 'The Good' and 'Evil,' much overlapping (and indeed all such concepts) are absorbed into the wider concept of what I call *the oneness of reality*.

After writing the preceding science section, you can see that our scientist predecessors viewed there to be one reality to explore, and it was God's universe we were exploring. I am now more than ever convinced that both science and philosophy point to there being a oneness to our reality, and that while we perceive specific anatomised bits of reality as distinct and real, at the end of the day they are fully part of, and absorbed into, the one nature of all reality. We see that there are force fields that we are bathed in - the Higgs field being the newest - that give us mass when they vibrate, instantiating certain particles - such as us! The reductionist, materialist world view seems ever more impossible to maintain in science and in philosophy. And just as science points towards a unification in all things, so does philosophy. The philosopher may declare his subject matter pure being, yet it is the same pure being as that of the scientist.

For now, I will explore our understanding of what amounts to a philosophical concept and see whether it *does* lead to an underlying unity.

The quest to understand philosophical concepts in the Western world starts 2,500 years ago in Greece. Socrates, via Plato, bursts into the world to give us our earliest illustration of this problem in the end of book VI of the Republic (Plato, Plato Complete Works, 1997). To summarise: whilst maths and dialectics are thought-based, maths moves always from hypothesis to conclusion. Its hypothetical premise will always yield from it, so long as you apply the laws of reason - a correct conclusion. In maths you can't ask: 'is this assumption true?' (that, say, 2+2=4), 'let us see what would follow if it were not.' It is a way of thinking, certainly, but also a way of *not* thinking. Maths is therefore thought compromised. This contrasts sharply with a philosophical proposition, which will always run to a non-hypothetical conclusion. However, hypotheses are the stepping stones of the principles of everything - we have nothing else, according to Plato. Using the dialectic method, we are free to cancel the hypothesis, or assume the opposite and see if this brings further knowledge, as did Socrates. Philosophy is pure and unconstrained, unless restricted by the laws of thought it creates itself: logic for example. In my discussion with colleagues at Legatum, our placeholder at the end of the conversation was that prosperity was holistic flourishing. I say placeholder as we could not conclude a definitive set of words that could cater for every occasion, as we could go on and on to another investigation into what *that* really means. In actual fact, we committed the fallacy of identical coincidence, which we will come to shortly.

The Scale of Forms: Success and Failure, Prosperity and Poverty, Profit and Loss, Good and Evil , Some Philosophical Concepts Explored

R G Collingwood developed a method for looking at philosophical concepts (Collingwood R. , 1933) by noting that science is concerned with elucidating a series of universal truths. Philosophy, historically, has sought to discover what it calls universals. Whether this is possible or not I will not address here, but I will look a little more closely at what a philosopher's 'universal' is.

Step 1: This is when there is a plurality of individual instances that unites all into one class, called the plurality of instances. For example, all the colour reds can be united within a class. In this sense it is generic. The concept 'colour' is universal. Like the universal laws sought by scientists and constructed by mathematicians, so the philosopher seeks out his universals.

Step 2: Then, if you look a bit closer at the colour analogy in step 1, you will see that there is a plurality of *differentiation* in the various colours, red, green, blue, where all are united by something but different in all other respects, because all colours are united in the *class* of colours, though all are different in appearance. So they are formed into a *genus* of colour, in which they are each a *species* of colours.

With this in mind, if we now look a little further afield we can investigate whether this example helps us see what is common, and what differentiates. When we think of a song, for example, is it a work, or art, a poem or a piece of music or just a single work or art containing two specific forms? Or is it a bit of everything? I guess if there were five people to ask, we would all get slightly different answers. The wonderful thing about inanimate material studied in natural and empirical science is that this classification system works, as things are mutually exclusive. Quarks, protons, atoms, particles, waves, individual chemical compositions, a man not an ape; in fact, science is all about classification in the first instance. In maths, too, the classification, or identification, is not a problem as *a priori*, the matter is sorted out before you commence. With the specific classes of philosophical genus there is almost always an overlap, unlike the sciences.

Aristotle showed us in the 6th chapter of the first book of Nicomachean Ethics that *judgment* can overlap in a multiplicity of classes:

> "That it is raining is a judgment; that it is raining because I can hear it is an inference. Of these two statements, one includes the other; and it is therefore clear that the specific classes overlap: a judgment may also be an inference, an inference may also be a judgment". (Aristotle, 1995)

Judgments can be both affirmative and negative at the same time, which would not accord with the classifications that logic requires in either the sciences or maths. If I say, "this computer has stopped working", I can positively confirm this computer is not working and that it is (negatively) not in motion. In science, I can't say this is an atom and not an atom.

> *"I am making one statement, not two, and that statement is both the affirmation of one thing and the denial of its opposite."* (Collingwood R., 1933)

No methodology can be adopted in philosophy that apes the natural sciences and maths where the classification must be mutually exclusive. So in philosophy, we are presented with the idea of overlapping classes. Those who attempt otherwise, Collingwood warns:

> *"All such inquiries are vitiated by a fallacy, which may be called the fallacy of precarious margins."* (Collingwood R., 1933)

Any attempt to mitigate the overlap leads to potential disaster. You will then fall into the fallacy of 'identical coincidence'. This is where you recognize the overlap - then pronounce both identical. Collingwood uses the example that being happy requires often dutiful acts. Some could conclude a dutiful act causes happiness, therefore duty is happiness, for instance. If, for example, when we identified prosperity with holistic flourishing we concluded they must be the same, we would be committing the fallacy of identical coincidence. We must celebrate their overlapping nature and also that when we affirm, we also exemplify the negative. So: before Legatum sets up 1300 speed schools in one year to educate those in Ethiopia who have missed out on key schooling, there is absence of the prosperous life, as these children were uneducated. But now they are educated, they can have more chance of leading a more prosperous life. With an understanding of prosperity, we are committed to understanding the absence of it or poverty. The two can't be separated. The journey of Legatum in exploring prosperity must also explore poverty, as this is actually the opposite of prosperity and impossible to separate from it. Their forms over-lap, and are not mutually exclusive, as with the sciences, and they can never be separated. This characteristic is familiar to all philosophical concepts.

Collingwood said:

> "I call this the fallacy of false disjunction, because it consists in the disjunctive proposition that any instance of a generic concept must fall either in one or in another of its specific classes; and this is false because, since they overlap, it may fall in both. Applied positively, this yields the fallacy of precarious margins: namely that, since there admittedly is a distinction between two concepts, there must be a difference between their instances. Applied negatively, it yields the fallacy of identified co-incidents: namely that, since the instances can admittedly not be separated, there is no distinguishing the concepts."
> (Collingwood R., 1933)

The first rule of philosophy is to always be aware of these false disjunctions. The overlap must always be there. The two concepts may be the same as in the case where one exemplifies the other, but their being is not the same. Think of the dutiful-and-happiness example above, and the prosperity-and-flourishing example mentioned. I am often asked about failure and success in entrepreneurship. It is impossible to think of total failure, as this would mean ceasing to exist so, as such, it is a meaningless concept. Failure is actually embedded in the concept of success. Success can be identified. When in business, you know when staff, customers and suppliers are happy, which is one part of the measure of success. You know when your bottom line is richer. However, with both, you also know the customers, suppliers, staff etc you could have done even better with. Therefore, we have had partial success and partial failure, but never fully one of each - only scales of success, with areas of failure taking up more of the success, depending upon their intensity. Using philosophical language, it is impossible to think of the concept of universal failure - only in the abstract can you think of it. It collapses into so many contradictions when dwelt upon overly. That you cease to exist is the ultimate failure, so it is as meaningless as a universal as at the moment of not existing and it has fallen into non-existence. With the concept of total success, due to our human life always existing in space-time with only uncertain knowledge of the future, we move forward in our earthly endeavours and have *degrees* of success. Embedded within that success are degrees of failure. This, R G Collingwood called the 'Scale of Forms'. What we can draw from this train of thought is that even if we can think in the abstract about a pure form of, say, a colour, or prosperity, success or failure, it will remain abstract when we turn to the existing world; it must always be a something and, more importantly, a part of something. Even if we met the most perfect saint representing perfect goodness, that saint would never be fully perfect as he is compromised by his finality, his death, if you like. This compromises him. So on the scale of all forms in our existent world, there is never a perfect extreme end representation of the pure form, just as there is never a perfect extreme negation of it.

> "*The result of this identification is that every form, so far as it is low on the scale, is to that extent an imperfect or inadequate specification of the generic essence, which is realized with progressive adequacy as the scale is ascended.*" (Collingwood R., 1933)

The lower elements of the scale would hardly appear to be a species of that genus, but they cling to the genus even in the most tangential of cases. Sounds like a logician's nightmare, right? - I hear you cry. How could failure be an integral part of success? How can the African lady who used to use an open-cast fire in her hut (giving her cancer from the fumes) who has now been given an enclosed charcoal/wood burning fire with a flue, but is still living in poverty be described as living prosperously? Well, she has more of a prosperous existence than she did before. On the scale of forms, she is a little bit more prosperous and a little less poor. Poverty is an integral part of the concept of prosperity. Understanding just the degrees and the opposites is the key to unlocking the concept of prosperity further. Opposites exist on the same scale of forms. The thing to note is that if there is no opposition, no tension, you have no philosophical concept to discuss. There is always a tension implied in all philosophical concepts.

Right at the very start of this book, when I explored the common usages of faith and reason, with a little bit of probing I discovered that reason can't exist without faith, and that in fact reason is faith's handmaiden. This implies that a part of reason is contained in the concept of faith. This overlap is lost on many people; nevertheless, it is there, right under our noses, as the most obvious things often are.

Profit is often defined in financial terms as the surplus of money left over after all deductions are made during the course of the accounting period of an enterprise. Profit is thus a part of prosperity. A profit from something is also measured in a non-monetary way. For example, when I feel my soul enriched as I stare at the magnificence of the sunset from a wonderful aspect of my home, my holistic flourishing increases because of it. The university students I and my wife have helped financially to get their degrees have moved, hopefully, into better jobs and are doing greater things than that they wound have done had we not become involved in supporting them. Some, for certain, have been lifted out of drug-dependant families, allowing them to make a more positive contribution to their communities. This is creating a more prosperous life. So, to have a prosperous life, you must also have a profitable life. This could be enjoying the wonders of nature as opposed to being chained to a desk. It could be the rewarding pleasure you get from helping others. It could be the stimulation you get from free thought following its fancy, and many, many more things. Profit is poorly defined if it is only monetary benefits we focus upon.

Enter Satan into our Thoughts on the Matter of Pure Evil

Pure evil, like total failure, ends up being an untenable concept. Note that in all the 'good-guy-bad-guy' stories, the evil villain usually has an apprentice, or a tight group of confidantes. These he never fully trusts as he expects they may also have evil running though their veins, just like himself. One thing leads to another and eventually a mutual bloodbath occurs. If one of them is left standing, he can't be fully evil unless he destroys himself - as presumably being purely evil would make you hate yourself. Thus, pure evil is a nonsense. You only have goodness, which we can observe flourishing with degrees of badness or evil embedded in it, always in tension. Later, I will try to show how there is one exception to the scale of the forms, and this is the conception of pure goodness, which you *can* think of without contradiction. In the meantime, let's have a look at the Devil!

If God created all things, it stands to reason that He also created Satan, the nearest manifestation or image of pure evil we have. However, we must remember that as a created, existent being of some sort, he (or it) can't be totally evil as this falls away into contradiction. In a number of places in the Bible this same Satan is doing God's bidding, as Judas would do later on in the Bible events that relate to Jesus. For example:

> ***Job 1:6-12*** *Now there was a day when the sons of God came to present themselves before the Lord, and Satan also came among them. And the Lord said to Satan, "From where do you come?" So Satan answered the Lord and said, "From going to and fro on the earth, and from walking back and forth on it." Then the Lord said to Satan, "Have you considered My servant Job, that there is none like him on the earth, a blameless and upright man, one who fears God and shuns evil?" So Satan answered the Lord and said, "Does Job fear God for nothing? Have You not made a hedge around him, around his household, and around all that he has on every side? You have blessed the work of his hands, and his possessions have increased in the land. But now, stretch out Your hand and touch all that he has, and he will surely curse You to Your face!"*
> *And the Lord said to Satan, "Behold, all that he has is in your power; only do not lay a hand on his person. So Satan went out from the presence of the Lord."*

Evil is therefore the opposite of good, certainly, but it also is contained in the very manifestation of the form of good - only in varying degrees. In this opposition, this tension, we have one of the greatest philosophical pairings. When you say a man is bad, you say he does not do good acts with the frequency that you would expect a man to be doing in order to be called a good man. You also are saying very positively that he does bad acts, more so than would be required to call him a good man. So bad is both a distinction and an opposite. The bad man, however, is never 100% bad: this is an abstract concept, impossible to imagine in reality, remember; whilst we can imagine such a person in, say, a novel, it is always just that - a fiction created in the mind of its author, and never ontologically real. The evil man always stands in the shadow of goodness. So, too, the scale of forms, the spectrum of good and evil. In this case, it is both one of distinction and opposition to varying degrees. All that is higher up the scale will affirm the lower. For example, dutiful actions are always expedient, not just at the margins. But you can have a non-dutiful, expedient act. Duty is the higher on the scale. The higher up the scale always more perfectly embodies the lower down the scale; this is not only an overlap of extension, but also of intention.

When you are asked to define something, you often just focus on getting rid of ambiguities and arriving at what you already know better. In science and maths, definitions are absolute. Two properties must be present: the essence must be capable of absolute definition, and there must be an ability to know and to not know it. Neither are fulfilled in philosophical concepts like prosperity, good and evil. Poverty, as discussed, may seem the obverse of prosperity, but it is also implied in the genus of prosperity, with differentiation all the way up and down the scale.

On the Matter of Pure Goodness

I have thought about the concept of pure evil and rejected it as an abstraction in thought only, but could consider it in opposition, and in tension with the concept of good. We could also see that 'evil' represents the degree of an absence of goodness on the scale of over lapping forms. So I turn my mind to the thought of pure goodness. Now, I will propose something controversial as I conclude that all philosophical concepts are absorbed into this proposition and you can think of pure goodness as real and with nothing over lapping it in one instance and one instance only: when you are thinking about God as containing all the perfect predicates. First of all, to establish this, we need to consider how we know anything at all.

The absolute distinction between an ability to know and not know something can be displayed when you teach a person a geometrical shape of X sides so that now they know it, when they did not know of it before. This is a very black and white distinction. In philosophy we are never absolutely ignorant of the matter at hand or as totally complete in our knowledge as we are with a simple geometrical shape: this was revealed sharply when we tried to discuss what prosperity, good or evil actually are.

As exact science, we have categorical statements: eg the patient's temperature was X, the observation of Y symptoms happened at such and such a time and so on. In philosophy, we have categorical propositions so there is nothing hypothetical left. Plato, in 'The Republic', discusses the difference between the dialectic and mathematical approaches and shows how the dialectic demands for itself a non-hypothetical starting point. Plato had long ago laid down that to be, and to be knowable, are the same (Republic. 476 E) (Plato, Plato Complete Works, 1997):

"And he who, having a sense of beautiful things has no sense of absolute beauty, or who, if another lead him to a knowledge of that beauty is unable to follow–of such an one I ask, Is he awake or in a dream only? Reflect: is not the dreamer, sleeping or waking, one who likens dissimilar things, who puts the copy in the place of the real object?

"I should certainly say that such a one was dreaming.

"But take the case of the other, who recognises the existence of absolute beauty and is able to distinguish the idea from the objects which participate in the idea, neither putting the objects in the place of the idea nor the idea in the place of the objects–is he a dreamer, or is he awake?

"He is wide awake.

"And may we not say that the mind of the one who knows has knowledge, and that the mind of the other, who opines only, has opinion?

"Certainly.

"But suppose that the latter should quarrel with us and dispute our statement, can we administer any soothing cordial or advice to him, without revealing to him that there is

sad disorder in his wits?

"We must certainly offer him some good advice, he replied.

"Come, then, and let us think of something to say to him. Shall we begin by assuring him that he is welcome to any knowledge which he may have, and that we are rejoiced at his having it? But we should like to ask him a question: Does he who has knowledge know something or nothing? (You must answer for him.)

"I answer that he knows something. Something that is or is not? Something that is; for how can that which is not ever be known?

"And are we assured, after looking at the matter from many points of view, that absolute being is or may be absolutely known, but that the utterly non-existent is utterly unknown?

"Nothing can be more certain." (Plato, Plato Complete Works, 1997)

Plato in Parmanides (132 B)

"But may not the ideas, asked Socrates, be thoughts only, and have no proper existence except in our minds, Parmenides? For in that case each idea may still be one, and not experience this infinite multiplication.

"And can there be individual thoughts which are thoughts of nothing?

"Impossible, he said. The thought must be of something? Yes. Of something which is or which is not? Of something which is. Must it not be of a single something, which the thought recognizes as attaching to all, being a single form or nature?

"Yes.

"And will not the something which is apprehended as one and the same in all, be an idea?

"From that, again, there is no escape." (Plato, Plato Complete Works, 1997)

And happily this thought must be thought of something real. I know when I am thinking of something *unreal*, like a unicorn. In reality, they are just two real concepts put together, a horse and a horn. I can conjure up in my mind the most perfect island but in reality, again, these are just two words put together to make an imaginary thing, as what on earth could define what a perfect island is? Each and every person will have their own take on it. Our thoughts, when we think of real things, are clearly distinguishing what is real and what is not real. In mathematics, we know what we think of as the number two is an abstraction and not real, in the sense that this table I rest my computer on to write this is. When you think of the overlapping forms, as with all philosophical concepts, you are committed to thinking of something real. When we think of all those philosophical over-lapping forms, and keep in mind the most extreme opposition - that of good and that of evil - and if you conclude, with me, that evil is a lack of degree of goodness, then you can start to realistically think that all forms in some way fit up and down on this meta scale of form. They are all parts of reality. Justice, fairness, duty, altruism will all fit within the scale of the good at some point on it and it will overlap with other forms still contained within the over-all form of goodness. When we think of a 'good life' and further reflect on the 'perfectly good life' we might arrive at what it would mean to be a perfect being who could live a perfectly good life. This does not break down into contradictions as does the concept of perfect evil (ie it would hate itself so much it would self-destruct). The perfect being of God with all the perfect predicates in it – yes, including evil - must exist **necessarily** to be perfectly good, as to not exist would compromise it. From this substrate, all the overlapping forms pour forth as part of pure goodness, pure being, or as part of God. Any time we reflect on goodness, or one of the sub-species that form part of the genus, we are affirming God and asserting His existence; or the existence of pure being, that is, if you don't like to use the word God. This is the proof of the Ontological Argument, which we will explore in depth in the next chapter. If you hold that this is so, you are committed to recognise the wholeness of pure being and your own small, differentiated, but completely absorbed part of it. Collingwood adds:

> *"Reflection on the history of the Ontological Proof thus offers us a view of philosophy as a form of thought in which essence and existence, however clearly distinguished , are conceived as inseparable . On this view, unlike mathematics or empirical science , philosophy stands committed to maintaining that its subject-matter is not mere hypothesis, but something actually existing."* (Collingwood R. , 1933)[35]

If you are not yet convinced, it is worth noting that it is impossible to study logic or ethics without thinking you are studying something real. Logic is concerned with thought as its subject matter: both how we actually think and how we ought to think. In logic, the subject-matter is propositional; in science it is propositions about propositions. Logic is also about itself i.e., its rules must accord to anything on which it pronounces. Logic is never indifferent to itself, as are maths or science. Logic, unlike maths, is about an existing subject matter. The essence of this thought regarding the subject matter of thought itself must also imply its existence, otherwise it would be illogical:

> "Logic, therefore, stands committed to the principle of the Ontological Proof. Its subject-matter, namely thought, affords an instance of something which cannot be conceived except as actual, something whose essence involves existence." (Collingwood R., 1933)

So to be really clear, when we conceive the concept of pure being, we are conceiving something that is uniquely real. Of course, if this concept can be pulled apart by logic itself, if it can be shown to be contradictory, then it is not real. If it satisfies all the criteria of logic, then it is real. This I will explore in more detail the next chapter dealing with the Ontological Argument. Suffice it to say, I can think of perfect goodness with all the positive predicates that are contained within it, and I don't believe I contradict myself. This is the one and, I believe, only instance of a philosophical concept with no opposition in it, as it is indeed encompassing all that is real. So when we think of the good life or a life well lived and we identify this as good, we are identifying part of that supreme being and unpacking some of our understanding of God. We then position ourselves one step closer to God and understanding God, or pure being.

Postscript to Pure Being

Taking this further, I can see that if God contains all the positive predicates He contains everything. Therefore, we are all ultimately part of the concept of God. The concept of God implies the positive concept of being infinite, and if we try to make him finite He ceases to be. We occupy our particular spot in Him in the physical world He has created. Our scientist friends are actually stepping back and seeing the unity of reality more and more. Some may not acknowledge this, some may. Cox and Forshaw are seeing a unity in the pure being they study. If they acknowledge it as such - I don't know - but either way they are committed to studying it and see to be recognising they are studying it. Science and philosophy started to be taught as separate subjects some 2,500 years ago. I believe that we are seeing a coming together of them, suggesting that all the academy of thinkers will someday be drinking well, and in unison, at the Inn at the World's End.

This recognition of our oneness has a long uninterrupted history in the Judeo-Christian tradition and indeed is actually exemplified in the classical conception of Hellenistic philosophy at its best. St Paul's talk to the Athenians exemplifies this in Acts 17 22:31, as he addresses the Areopagus:[36]

> *"Then Paul stood in the midst of the Areopagus and said, "Men of Athens, I perceive that in all things you are very religious; for as I was passing through and considering the objects of your worship, I even found an altar with this inscription:*
> TO THE UNKNOWN GOD.
> *Therefore, the One whom you worship without knowing, Him I proclaim to you: "God, who made the world and everything in it, since He is Lord of heaven and earth, does not dwell in temples made with hands. Nor is He worshiped with men's hands, as though He needed anything, since He gives to all life, breath, and all things. And He has made from one blood every nation of men to dwell on all the face of the earth, and has determined their pre-appointed times and the boundaries of their dwellings, so that they should seek the Lord, in the hope that they might grope for Him and find Him, though He is not far from each one of us; for in Him we live and move and have our being, as also some of your own poets have said, 'For we are also His offspring.' Therefore, since we are the offspring of God, we ought not to think that the Divine Nature is like gold or silver or stone, something shaped by art and man's devising. Truly, these times of ignorance God*

---

[36] Prior to this, Paul had been accused of being a $\sigma \pi \varepsilon \rho \mu o \lambda ó \gamma o \varsigma$ or "seed-picker," translated to us as a "babbler." This is the charge that led to the execution of Athens' most famous and wisest son, Socrates. I find a profound symbolism here.

164

> *overlooked, but now commands all men everywhere to repent, because He has appointed a day on which He will judge the world in righteousness by the Man whom He has ordained. He has given assurance of this to all by raising Him from the dead."*

I find this report of Luke on his colleague Paul's speech fascinating, as our atheist friends would lead you to believe that the religious mind always perceives God as being a bigger man or grandfather like figure, living variously in a temple, up a mountain, above the clouds, and being progressively pushed back further from our reach as each time we look at said temple, mountain, clouds and on into the Cosmos, as we can't find the God (or gods) we are looking for because it/(they) move beyond time and become ever more mysterious:

> *"But as practical knowledge and understanding of nature increased, these agencies were thought of in more and more remote terms – they were shifted off mountain tops, into the sun, into the sky, finally beyond space and time itself."* Thus says A C Grayling. (Grayling, To Set Prometheus Free, 2009)

Paul gave the following speech just under 2000 years ago. He lays it on thickly that God can't be contained in any man-made edifice. He cites the more ancient Jewish tradition in 1 Kings 8:27, written in the 6th Century BC:

> *"But will God indeed dwell on the earth? Behold, heaven and the heaven of heavens cannot contain You. How much less this temple which I have built!"*

And again in 1 Chronicles 29:14:

> *But who am I, and who are my people, that we should be able to offer so willingly as this? For all things come from You, And of Your own we have given You."*

That God needs nothing from man and, indeed, that all creation is His, was taught in King David's time, some 1000 years prior to this speech. This is reflected in Psalm 50:9-12:

> *"I will not take a bull from your house,*
> *Nor goats out of your folds.*

> *For every beast of the forest is Mine,*
> *And the cattle on a thousand hills.*
>
> *I know all the birds of the mountains,*
> *And the wild beasts of the field are Mine.*
>
> *If I were hungry, I would not tell you;*
> *For the world is Mine, and all its fullness."*

Indeed, the Jews were teaching between 100 BC and 200 BC that God needed nothing from man in 2 Maccabees 14:35:

> *"O Lord of all, though you have need of nothing, you were pleased that there should be a temple for your habitation among us;"* NRSV

And in 3 Maccabees 2:9:

> *"You, O King, when you had created the boundless and immeasurable earth, chose this city and sanctified this place for your name, though you have no need of anything; and when you had glorified it by your magnificent manifestation, you made it a firm foundation for the glory of your great and honored name."* NRSV

God needs nothing from His creatures as He is not a finite thing, but is, rather, *everything*, and *we are part of that oneness*. And what is more, Paul reminds his audience that deep down in their traditions, this, too is actually what was believed by many Athenians. He quotes the 7th Century BC Cretean poet, Epimenides, from the Cretica:

> *"They fashioned a tomb for you, holy and high one, Cretans, always liars, evil beasts, idle bellies. But you are not dead: you live and abide forever, For in you we live and move and have our being."*

And Aratus, in *Phaenomena* 1–5[37]:

---

[37] http://spindleworks.com/library/rfaber/aratus.htm

> "Let us begin with Zeus, whom we mortals never leave unspoken. For every street, every market-place is full of Zeus. Even the sea and the harbour are full of this deity. Everywhere everyone is indebted to Zeus. For we are indeed his offspring ..."

Also, Cleanthes, in his Hymn to Zeus [38]:

> "Most glorious of the immortals, invoked by many names, ever all-powerful, Zeus, the First Cause of Nature, who rules all things with Law, Hail! It is right for mortals to call upon you, since from you we have our being, we whose lot it is to be God's image, we alone of all mortal creatures that live and move upon the earth. Accordingly, I will praise you with my hymn and ever sing of your might."

So. If you are a modern scientist observing that the universe and everything in it is just a lot of vibrating force fields, all producing what we observe as material things in our universe although deep down, it is all one great big chain of inter connectedness - then this observation is approximately 3,000 years old and has a tradition: it is the oneness of reality, in Jewish, Greek and Christian thought. If you are just doing science, you will leave it there, as it is not for you - according to your discipline and its methodology - to report on the non-finite. If you are a philosopher contemplating *theoria*, or theology, as with those before you, you are more than likely to reach the conclusion that there *is* oneness of reality. When you think of all those over-lapping forms, and everything ultimately being contained in the one master form of Goodness, or when you think of all physical connectedness, you can escape from concluding the oneness of reality and thinking of things, as being 'out there' presents a conforming appearance - but not a reality. The atheist straw man of a God located inside a temple, as finite as you and I, is just that: a straw-man whom they can blow down as much as they like. But, without doubt, they cannot blow down the totality of reality and our little bit of it in His creation. It is as robust as it was then, and is now.

---

[38] https://www.utexas.edu/courses/citylife/readings/cleanthes_hymn.html

Chapter 8 Anselm's Reflective Prayer

That Old Chestnut Again : Unpacking the Ontological Argument and the Great Debate in Mind , Collingwood v Ryle

> "Thanks be to you, my good Lord, thanks be to you. For what I once believed through your grace, I now understand through your illumination, so that even if I did not want to believe that you exist, I could not fail to understand that you exist." (Anselm)

> "Since, then, it is so readily clear to a rational mind that You exist most greatly of all, why did the Fool say in his heart that God does not exist?1— why [indeed] except because [he is] foolish and a fool! (Anselm, 2001)

> " And I thank Christ Jesus our Lord who has enabled me, because He counted me faithful, putting me into the ministry, although I was formerly a blasphemer, a persecutor, and an insolent man; but I obtained mercy because I did it ignorantly in unbelief. And the grace of our Lord was exceedingly abundant, with faith and love which are in Christ Jesus. This is a faithful saying and worthy of all acceptance, that Christ Jesus came into the world to save sinners, of whom I am chief. However, for this reason I obtained mercy, that in me first Jesus Christ might show all longsuffering, as a pattern to those who are going to believe on Him for everlasting life. Now to the King eternal, immortal, invisible, to God who alone is wise, be honor and glory forever and ever. Amen." 1 Timothy 12-17

St Paul, before his conversion, was recognised as one of the most zealous persecutors of the new Christians. In modern times, there is none more vocal than Richard Dawkins, a new version of Saul, perhaps. Tongue-in-cheekily I dropped the above biblical quote into this section, although I don't expect a conversion soon! The second quote taken from Anselm's Proslogion is also somewhat tongue in cheek, as Dawkins is without doubt no fool, but I do believe he should give serious consideration to this matter before he reissues his God Delusion book again, as I will seek to expose his ignorance on certain matters which I hope will blunt the thrust of his arguments.

Dawkins best represents a familiar lay person's view of the Ontological Argument. Here, too, he spectacularly misses the point. If he understood the argument and why it still stands today, we may well see a conversion of our modern day Saul. Far-fetched as that may sound, these militants do have a habit of changing their minds. Being scientists, as we will see, they are encouraged all the time to do so in the face of new evidence. In the meantime, we need to cover some basics before we get into the Ontological Argument proper.

Preliminaries

Before we start, may I just clarify some of the terms I use here in this section:

Ontology: the study of existence, and the nature of existence, or being, and how they relate to each other.

Empirical Judgment: this is reached when a proposition is formed, a proposition is tested, observations are made and the proposition is either confirmed, modified or denied on the basis of the observations. The classical example to give is any thought-out experiment and its result.

A Priori Judgments: mental reasoning that gives us truths which don't need any empirical observation to validate them. The classic example is any mathematical trail of reasoning: you don't need to have a pair of twosomes in front of your eyes to know the addition of them will equal four, etc. In all judgments of this type the predicate – or, if you like the part after 'is' - is found in the subject, thus: with 'my wife is a woman' the nature of being a woman is contained in the word wife.

A Synthetic Judgment: when the predicate is not found in the subject: 'my computer is on the desk' is one such judgment. The concept of a desk is not held in that of a computer, but I am telling you a thing I have observed about my reality in front of me.

Synthetic A Priori Judgement: an *a priori* judgment is initially just plain thought in which the predicate is in the subject. However, crucially, it gives us knowledge of something about the physical world we live in. These we will illustrate at the end of this section.

Part 1. The Delusion of Dawkins

Augustine in "On the Trinity": "faith seeks, but understanding finds."

In Dawkins' book, "The "God Delusion", Chapter 2 is entitled: "The God Hypothesis" (Dawkins). This is where he discusses attempts there have been at proving the existence of God. So bearing in mind what we have said in Chapter 3 concerning metaphysics and pseudo metaphysics, we should be warned straight away that he does not start out with a correct metaphysic of God, or pure being. He is putting his God up as a straw man, as a pseudo metaphysical proposition which he can then shoot down. Now, in fairness, many of our muddle-headed ancestors have actually contributed to trying to sustain the straw man God Dawkins attacks. To this effect, he does theologians a great service by helping religion rid itself of childish superstition. No apostle, no Father of the church or major theologian ever believed this 'straw man' view of God. Scripture never presents God in the light Dawkins does. Moreover, Dawkins's book is thus worth a good read for the service it does, via his own polemical words, in tearing down his faulty view of God. However, not being aware that this is what he is actually doing, he attempts rather childishly to attack some of the wiser views about God, or Pure Being, as well, and exposes his lack of knowledge on the matter; he actually fails to hit the real target of God, or the fundamental ground for being, quite spectacularly. In fact, his target gets off very lightly indeed and in the end remains completely intact.

We will explore his understanding of the argument of Anselm in that part of his (Dawkins, The God Delusion, 2006) Chapter 3 called: "The Ontological Argument and Other A Priori Arguments" [39]

> *"An odd aspect of Anselm's argument is that it was originally addressed not to humans but to God himself, in a form of a prayer (you'd think that any entity capable of listening to a prayer would need no convincing of his own existence)."* (Dawkins, The God Delusion, 2006)

---

[39] In 2007, I had a closer look at his attempted disposal of the cosmological argument, which again I thought missed the mark due to faulty logical reasoning on his part.
http://tobybaxendale.com/the-richard-dawkins-delusion/

It is often the case that two people can read the same thing and interpret it differently. You can see where Dawkins has read the prologue to the Proslogion, when Anselm discusses two works:

> "I named the first Monologion, which means a speech made to oneself, and the second Proslogion, which means a speech made to another." (Anselm, 2001)

One can start to see where this opening confusion may lie. So who *is* the other person? The Proslogion is a prayer, certainly, to God, but it is also Anselm's awakening to an understanding of God that he expounds in this prayer; it may even be considered a personal confession - not anything designed to make God believe in His existence! All prayers are from one being directed to another.

A brief history of this argument shows us that it actually has its antecedents in two key thoughts in philosophy - one outlined by Plato in "The Republic" who, according to Collingwood: "long ago laid it down that to be, and to be knowable, are the same." (Collingwood, Philosophical Method) The relevant section of the Republic is 476 where he says:

> "Tell us, does the person who knows know something or nothing?" You answer for him. He knows something. Something that is something or something that is not? Something that is for how could something that is not be known?" (Plato, 1997)

And the neoplatonic thought of God expressed in "De Trinitate" by Botheius, is a being who is:

> "that which is beautiful and stable," (est id pulcherrimum fortissimumque)

... a unity of existence and essence, or a perfect being *(nihil deo melius excogitari queat)*; better than God, nothing can be imagined, this lays out the metaphysical conception of the absolute perfect being. Add these two streams of thought together and you can see when we really use reason to its most challenging and exact state, and come to an idea of thought, for surely it is a thought of something real. Anlsem added this thought, that which is beautiful and stable, to that of the Platonic perfect oneness of forms, from which all plurality pours, and we have an understanding of the perfectness of absolute reality.

To avoid further confusion, and in case readers have not read Anselm, I will put down now what I think are his central arguments. Chapter 2 (Anselm, 2001) is the main forum in for his argument, as follows:

> *"Now we believe that you are something than which nothing greater can be thought. So can it be that no such being exists, since "The fool has said in his heart, 'There is no God'"? (Psalm 14:1: 53:1) But when this same fool[40] hears me say "something than which nothing greater can be thought ," he surely understands what he hears; and what he understands exists in his understanding, even if he does not understand that it exists [in reality]. For it is one thing for an object to exist in the understanding and quite another to understand that the object exists [in reality]."* (Anselm)

> *"So even the fool must admit that something than that which nothing greater can be thought exists at least in his understanding, since he understand this when he hears it, and whatever is understood exists in the understanding. And surely than that which is greater cannot be thought cannot exist only in the understanding. For if it exists only in the understanding, it can be thought to exist in reality as well, which is greater. So if that than which a greater cannot be thought exists only in the understanding, then that than which a greater cannot be thought is that than which a greater can be thought. But that is clearly impossible. Therefore, there is no doubt that something than which a greater cannot be thought exists both in the understanding and in reality."* (Anselm)

So, in short, if you understand the concept you cannot deny it; if you do, you are the fool. I think anyone can understand this concept if they reflect upon it. It would probably be a more fruitful debate to question: "OK, I understand the concept of a supreme perfect being existing in reality, in fact it is the ground of being, I can't deny it, but what does it actually *mean*?" Also, in the

---

[40] The Psalm written 1000 years BC, by King David should be compared to a Proverb 1:7 written by his son, King Solomon *"The fear of the Lord is the beginning of knowledge, But fools despise wisdom and instruction."* The 2000 year gap between this and Anselm's use of a similar Psalm shows that 1000 year post Anselm , the fundamental ground for knowing anything is still in dispute.

172

case of Anselm: "Why should it mean the God of Christianity?" I believe these are legitimate questions which flow from understanding, but to deny it, well, maybe it is harsh to say you are a fool, but you could certainly be called remiss!

The third chapter of Proslogion[41] is often overlooked in terms of much analysis I read regarding the Ontological Argument, but it is critical to follow it as it refutes the attack of Kant on the Ontological Argument. Kant argues that existence is not a predicate. This indeed, on its own, is an empty concept that tells us very little. It's a bit like claiming you know the essence of the statement: 'black is black', then declaring it as proof of blackness! Chapter 3 of the Proslogion allows us to move beyond this, and it establishes the actual necessity of His existence. In this necessity, this fundamental ground for being, our being, we can then start to reflect upon what such a truly existing, necessary concept of pure being could mean to us:

> "This [being] exists so truly that it cannot be thought not to exist. For it is possible to think that something exits that cannot be thought not to exist, and such a being is greater than one that can be thought not to exist. Therefore, if that than which a greater cannot be thought can be thought not to exist, then that than which greater cannot be thought is not than that which a greater cannot be thought; and this is a contradiction. So that than which a greater cannot be thought exists so truly that it cannot be thought not to exist.
>
> "Indeed, everything that exists, except for you alone, can be thought not to exist. So you alone among all things have existence most truly, and therefore most greatly. Whatever else exists has existence less truly, and therefore less greatly." (Anselm, 2001)

In summary, this, Anselm's 'necessity' argument, puts something very real into the concept of empty existence on its own. We can think of everything not existing - with the exception of being. To think of being as not existing is a contradiction. If you try to argue against this, you are presumably asserting

---

[41] I am grateful for the Process Theologian (The School of Alfred Whitehead and Charles Hartshonre, here God is not an absolute, but processing (changing) through space-time as we do) , Daniel Dombrowski and his book on Rethinking the Ontological Argument (Dombrowski, 2006) for so eloquently banging the drum of this very point and bringing it fully to my attention.

173

your being as part of the greater being and thus contradicting yourself; it is a performative contradiction to do so, therefore His necessity, or the pure ground for being, must be true. Here, the very essence of existence and existence itself are un-separable. The genus and the specific are one and the same. It would seem to me the case for God, or pure being, is looking pretty water-tight. In my opinion, just as the absolute presuppositions of all of science are water-tight, so the uniformity of the universe and the laws that allow us to access the secrets of the universe are unquestionable; and so is Anselm's argument. This is one argument that won't go away because it has legs to stand on. A later Scholastic, St Thomas Aquinas, would not question the soundness of the logic contained in the argument, but being for ever Aristotlean, he preferred to reason God via the senses, or *a posteriori,* as the abstract nature of the thought still did not flesh out a full understanding of God. His preferred route would be the Fourth Way of his Five Ways to God, which is the Argument from Degrees and Perfection. Here, you can look at any sentient object, such as a statute, and compare it with another; there will be differences in degrees of beauty, perfection, form. From this, you can grade, in degrees of perfection, all things, right up to the most perfect standard. So whether you come to God from a top down perspective, or up to God from a bottom up perspective, what is important is that you can still get there.

Hume objected to the Ontological Argument in the "Dialogues Concerning Natural Religion". Here, Hume believes he disposes of the Ontological Argument by saying that evidence of evil in the world means the omnipotent and perfect power is compromised, therefore[42] He can't exist. So we have Hume not denying necessary existence of God, but saying, via empirics, that he can't possibly exist, as empirics can never wholly affirm anything. As I believe we all have good grounds to deduce things from analytical proofs - such as the truths of geometry, economics and evolution,

---

[42] Natural evil as a seeming problem to the existence of God is dealt with in my refutations of Hume in Chapter 6 in the Krauss science section.

then I can't agree with Hume. These proofs will be shown in the next section. In the meantime, I agree with the following:

> "One of the features of the Ontological argument that continues to make it interesting is that, even if Hume is correct that one cannot prove the existence of something a priori unless the contrary implies a contradiction,[43] he has still not thereby disproved the argument. This is because, according to the defenders of the argument, the denial of God's necessary existence does imply a contradiction. Thus Hume's criticisms do not in themselves destroy the modalized version of the argument." (Dombrowski, 2006)

Here is a great observation from the current leading process theologian, Dombrowski:

> "There are statements regarding existence whose negation it is impossible to conceive, contra Hume. For example, there is the statement that "Something exists." There seems to be no experienceable alternative to the existence of something in that the very experience of the alternative would exist." (Dombrowski, 2006)

Leaving aside the classical case against the Ontological Argument, and its refutation by the likes of Dombrowski, I will offer some more subtle points Anselm is making in his other chapters to add to the discussion, as they say much about what he actually thinks God is and is not, before we look at Dawkins's attack in detail.

In chapter 13 of the Proslogion, we have a commitment to an immaterial God that is not bounded by time or place:

> "Everything that is at all enclosed in a place or a time is less than that which is subject to no law of place or time. Therefore, since nothing is greater than you, you are not confined to any place or time; you exist everywhere and always."

---

[43] Later, I will put forward the case that you can prove something *a priori* from a notion of its existence, when we look at the foundation of economics, geometry and evolutionary biology, which are all grounded on the a *priori* axioms that do very much have meaning in reality. They are Kantian elusive synthetic *a priori* judgments, as we will shall come to see.

Created spirits can exist unbounded, in the sense that they can be everywhere, but as they always manifest themselves in one place they can appear bounded, but are not. Only the Lord is uniquely unbounded. He is the oneness of reality.

In chapter 16 God is the "inaccessible light where he dwells": to really understand God is not a truly possible act as it is like looking at the direct light of the sun: the Lord's light becomes blinding.

In Chapter 18, Anselm asserts that you can't chop the Lord up into parts in order to try to understand him. Why not? That would diminish His perfection. There was no straw man-god, the god of the atheists, a personification up on a mountain or in the sky somewhere; for this saint:

> "Instead you exist as a whole in every place, and your eternity exists as a whole always."

If He becomes finite, then he ceases to be the perfect ground for being. This would imply that all experience of anything is part of Him.

This assertion is further supported in chapters 19 & 21:

> "So it is not the case that yesterday you were and tomorrow you will be; rather, yesterday, today and tomorrow you are. In fact, it is not even the case that yesterday, today and tomorrow you are ; rather , you are simply outside time altogether . Yesterday, today, and tomorrow are merely in time. But you, although nothing exists without you, do not exist in a place or a time; rather, all things exist in you. For nothing contains you, but you contain all things."

> "So is this "the age of the age" or the age of the ages"? For just as an age of time contains all temporal things, so your eternity contains the very ages of time. This eternity is indeed "an age" because of its indivisible unity, but it is "ages" because of its boundless greatness. And although you are so great, Lord, that all things are full of you and are in you, nonetheless you have no special extension, so that there is no middle or half or any other part in you."

It is worth nothing that the Monk Gaunilo offered a "Reply on Behalf of the Fool." Gaunilo will either establish his case against his fellow clergyman or he will lay the case for the fool teaching the wise-man something. At this juncture, a quote from that most sophisticated high priest of atheism, A C Grayling, comes to mind, from his "Book of Wisdom" (Chapter 4):

> 12. No one came to be wise who did not know how to revise an opinion.
> 13. The wise change their minds when facts and experience so demand. The fool either does not hear or does not heed.
> 14. But the wise man knows that even a fool can speak truth. (Grayling, The Good Book, 2011)

Gaunilo said he could understand a lot of false things, and this does not make them real. For Anselm's proposition to stand up to scrutiny, he must show that:

> "Unless perhaps it is established that this being is such that it cannot be had in thought in the same way that any false or doubtful thing can, and so I am not said to think of what I have heard or to have thought, but to understand it and to have it in my understanding, since I cannot think of it in any other way except by understanding it,," (Anselm, 2001)

For Gaunilo, this argument or proof is only for someone who already believes in the existence of God.

He continues:

> "And one can seldom or never think of any truth solely on the basis of a word. For thinking of something solely on the basis of a word, one does not think so much of the word itself (which is at least a real thing: the sound of letters or syllables) as of the meaning of the word that is heard." (Anselm, 2001)

Gaunilo is searching for a fact, in reality:

> "First I must become certain that this thing truly exists somewhere, and only then will the fact that it is greater than everything else show clearly that it also subsists in itself."

We see now a veering away from the tight path Anselm suggested. In trying to make God a finite being - in sum, a chopped up fact – He, for sure, ceases to exist. They are now talking cross purposes in their debate. The God of Anselm is not a big man in the sky or up some mountain, but pure being itself, indeed the ground for our existence and everything finite in experience. This is the pure being assumed by scientists when today they assume laws of its uniformity to even commence their science. *This is the oneness of reality*:

> *"For example, there are those who say that somewhere in the ocean is an island, which because of the difficulty – or rather, impossibility – of finding what does not exist, some call 'the Lost Island.' This island (so the story goes) is more plentifully endowed than even the Isles of the Blessed with an indescribable abundance of all sorts of riches and delights. And because it has neither owner or inhabitant, it is everywhere superior in its abundant riches to all other lands that human beings inhabit. Suppose that someone tells me this. The story is easily told and involves no difficulty, and so I understand it. But if this person went on to draw a conclusion, and say, 'You cannot any longer doubt that this island, more excellent than all others on earth, truly exists somewhere in reality. For you do not doubt that this island exists in your understanding, and since it is more excellent to exist not merely in the understanding, but also in reality, this island must exist in reality. For if it did not, any land that exists in reality would be greater than it. And so this excellent thing that you have understood would not in fact be more excellent.' – If, I say, he should try to convince me by this argument that I should no longer doubt whether the island truly exits, either I would think he was joking, or I would not know whom I ought to think more foolish: myself, if I grant him his conclusion, or him, if he thinks he can establish the existence of that island with any degree of certainty, without first showing that its excellence exists in my understanding as a thing that truly and undoubtedly exists and not in any way like something false or uncertain."* (Anselm, 2001)

Anselm's Reply to Gaunilo:

Anselm seems very much aware that if he is right being aware that the perfect being, to be perfect, must also be necessary:

> *"But I say with certainty that if it can be so much as thought to exist, it must necessarily exist."* (Anselm, 2001)

Understanding the words said by Anselm, he reiterates you must be a fool if you don't then except what is suggested. Gaunilo suggests that you can understand the words and symbols expressed, but this does not necessarily mean you have understood the words. Anselm points out the contradiction in this: if you understand, you understand. The "Lost Island" point by Gaunilo is masterfully dealt with by way of pointing out that this unique thought of perfection is the only thought that this argument for God can apply to, and nothing else:

> "*But you say, that this is just the same as if someone were to claim that it cannot be doubted that a certain island in the ocean, surpassing all other lands in fertility (which, from the difficulty-or rather impossibility of finding what does not exist, is called "the Lost Island"), exists in reality, because someone can easily understand it when it is described to him in words. I say quite confidently that if anyone can find for me something existing either in reality or only in thought to which he can apply this inference in my argument, besides that than which a greater cannot be thought, I will find and give to him that Lost Island, never to be lost again.*" (Anselm, 2001)

Like the monk Gaunilo, Dawkins is well aware he can think of such a concept as the perfect being, and that it exists in his mind, but for Dawkins it is "infantile" word play and such "logomachist trickery" that it offends him aesthetically. We may understand the word "Lost Island," most perfect and "surpassing all others," but put them together and think about them and you tie yourself up into contradiction after contradiction. Is the Most Perfect Island a random shape, any shape? Does it have all the resources of the world, or some? If some, which ones? Does what it excludes make it less perfect? Could there therefore be a more perfect one? Being finite, it ends up as a hopeless contradiction - it is mere words.

Dawkins seems aware that Kant and Hume offered the most impressive attacks on the argument of Anselm, but he chooses not to cite these. In the following section we will examine much more closely the Kantian argument against the Ontological Proof and Hegel's refutation of it and give it the attention it deserves. Dawkins draws to his readers' attention to an "ironic proof" by the Australian philosopher Douglas Gasking that "God does not exist" adding that:

"Anselm's contemporary Gaunilo had suggested a somewhat similar reduction" (Dawkins, The God Delusion, 2006)

I, myself, cannot find this in Gaunilo's work at all, however Dawkins continues to quote as follows

"1 The creation of the world is the most marvellous achievement imaginable.

2. The merit of the achievement is the product of (a) it intrinsic quality, and (b) the ability of its creator .

3. The greater the disability (or handicap) of the creator , the more impressive the achievement."

4. The most formidable handicap for a creator would be non-existence.

5. Therefore if we suppose that the universe is the product of an existent creator we can conceive a greater being – namely, one who created everything while not existing.

6. An existing God therefore would not be a being greater than which a greater cannot be conceived because an even more formidable and incredible creator would be a God which did not exist.

Ergo:

7. God does not exist." (Dawkins, The God Delusion, 2006)

I find this *reductio* quite absurd, as 4 would put an end to creation; 5 is contradictory, as something non-existent can't create anything at all; 6 is illogical, and 7 therefore can't follow.

He also draws to our attention as web site called http://www.godlessgeeks.com/LINKS/GodProof.htm which is the height of infantile discussion on what is the most important question to confront us: "Is there a God?" It is surprising that such an eminent scientist should be prepared to endorse such a site when he knows that for twenty-five centuries the debate still rolls on amongst of the most stellar minds of philosophy. For these great minds to be put on the same level as this web site? Really, Dawkins is scraping the bottom of the barrel.

Part 2.   The Collingwood v Ryle Debate

The great philosopher Gilbert Ryle was successor to his interlocutor, R G Collingwood, and like him held the Waynflete Chair of Metaphysical Philosophy at Oxford. Also, like Collingwood, he wrote extensively on the Ontological Argument. Ryle launched a scathing attack on the latter most notably in the journal "Mind" in the mid-1930s. Another noted philosopher, Harris, rebutted Ryle and a final word on the matter then came from Ryle. Collingwood remained silent in this journal. "Mr Collingwood and the Ontological Argument" (Ryle, Mr Collingwood and the Ontological Argument) is the title of the article. In his own words, this journal article is "destructive only." Why? He needs to refute Collingwood's views stated in this book the "Essay on Philosophical Method" with special reference to his chapter VI: Philosophy as Categorical Thinking," where he suggests:

> " .... *that philosophical propositions are in a peculiarly close way connected with what exits; in a way, indeed, in which the empirical sciences are remoter from what exists than philosophy is. And a part of his theory is that philosophy can by the Ontological Argument establish the existence of a very important somewhat and that philosophy in general aims at discovering – and not other sort of enquiry can discover – the nature of the somewhat. So that, if Mr Collingwood is right, constructive metaphysics is the proper*

> business of philosophy , and Hume and Kant were wrong in so far as they maintained that a priori arguments cannot establish particular matters of fact."

Collingwood, like Plato and Kant before him, would argue that philosophy cannot start with hypotheticals; hypotheticals are the nature of the empirical world of fact that can be tested and verified. Philosophy is in the business of its own suicide as it identifies lots of things in it which, if it can then define, it can jettison and have that set up as its own science. For example, economics spun out from the study of the political economy, that came out of the study of politic,s that came out of the study of political philosophy, that came out of philosophy and so on. You track this trend of subdivision, then more subdivision, again and again, in all matter of empirically orientated knowledge. So, starting with an absolute presupposition, such as 'the universe has uniform laws', or 'pure being' or 'God is that than which nothing greater can be thought' would pose no problems as a start point for Collingwood.

Incidentally, I can prove a matter of fact from an *a priori* argument concerning the whole discipline of economics and Euclidian geometry. I have written[44] on this before and in the next section I repeat the core argument with some modification. To prove something like this calls into question the Kantian denial that from an *a priori* thought you can't deduce a matter of fact. Ryle attacks Collingwood's position on the Ontological Argument, thinking he just needs to evoke the ghost of Kant. But Collingwood is saying something much more subtle which, again, we will explore in more detail shortly. For now, we must establish the whole body of economics from an *a priori* proposition - just to show that it can also be done in the far lesser matter of economics than the matter of God's existence!

The Ontological Deduction

First of all, what is an *a priori*, correct reasoning that Ryle is referring to

---

[44] http://tobybaxendale.com/the-richard-dawkins-delusion/

from which you can't derive an empirical fact? How do you correctly reason, using the a priori method as opposed to the induction method of the scientists?

Aristotle worked out that there were three Laws of Logic and the formal explanation is as follows:

1. A=A: The Law of Identity. A table is a table because it just is so.
2. Not (A and not A): The Law of Non-Contradiction, if I am being boring, then it is not the case that this book is not boring
3. A or not A: The Law of the Excluded Middle, if you have two contradictory properties i.e. green and not green, all things are either one of the two, green or not green, and certainly not both.

Any argument that contradicts the above needs to be discarded.

A great example of how you can use logic to reason correctly is in maths. For example, we all know that if 2 x X = 20, X must be 10; if you tried to argue it any other way, you would be in conflict with the laws of Logic. However, any which way you manipulate the equation, as far as a logical argument is concerned it will always lead to a truthful answer, as the premise is correct.

The Synthetic *A priori* : Economics, Geometry , Logic , Rational Thought and the Whole Collection of Facts that Make a Whole Underlying Reality

This is very powerful because we can establish truthful propositions in logic that can only be refuted should their premise or the deductions from them fall foul of one of Aristotle's *a priori* laws of logic. Not only are the truths of mathematics rooted in the *a priori*, so also are the truths of the human sciences. For example: the Austrian polymath Ludwig von Mises shows in his masterful book "Human Action" (1949)[45] how all the laws of economics can be deduced from the axiom that *humans act purposefully*. As Mises shows, in order to be, we act purposefully. Not being, we would not act, indeed we would not

---

[45] http://store.mises.org/Human-Action-The-Scholars-Edition-P119C0.aspx

exist. We act upon satisfying our most urgent needs first, then our second most urgent needs, and so on a so forth. Ranking preferences, with the most urgent needs/demands being satisfied first and the least urgent the furthest away in time. From this hierarchy we derive the law of demand, the downward sloping demand curve, the law of diminishing marginal utility (see here for a good illustration)[46] and so it goes from this axiom which is an illustration of how you can unpack the whole laws of economics. Lord Lionel Robbins, in a commanding 1932 book, The Nature and Significance of Economic Science"[47] shows in very clear terms how all the laws of economics are derived from the *a priori* thought process. No data of experience is needed to establish that a demand curve is always downward sloping. This has real meaning in life, and impacts upon how man acts in society. This is what Kant called a synthetic *a priori* proposition. Experience cannot refute these laws, although many modern economists will produce sets of statistical data that seem to contradict some of the laws of economics, whereas in reality they have come to whatever they are trying to correlate wrongly. *A priori* knowledge, for economics and for mathematics itself, contains real truths that are not just meaningless tautologies.

Try to refute it and you cannot, as you act purposefully in order to to do so. Just as Pythagoras's Theorem is implied via the concept of a right angle triangle - and we knew about the concept of the right angle triangle before Pythagoras 'discovered' his theorem - so, too, do the laws of economics flow from the one irrefutable axiom that humans act purposefully. It is a bit like saying Darwin 'discovered' the Theory of Evolution, when what he actually did was to articulate it and find very plausible data sets to help explain it to the skeptical mind. Evolution was always there.

If Euclidian geometry is tautological, as a positivist would argue, it can tell us nothing useful about the world we experience. For example,

---

[46] http://www.mises.org/humanaction/chap7sec1.asp

[47] http://store.mises.org/Essay-on-the-Nature-and-Significance-of-Economic-Science-An-P372.aspx

in engineering, the laws of Euclidian geometry are applied to the construction industry. The fact that you would not want to knowingly walk on a bridge not constructed within the confines of the laws of Euclidian geometry - as it would fall down - implies that these laws have a great benefit to our understanding of the world and are not mere tautological propositions that can deliver up no knowledge capable of being acted upon. So, contra Ryle, I submit that this is established as a matter of fact from an *a priori* set of reasoning. What is more, economics is a permanent feature of man's interaction in the empirical world. He is never in a situation where there is totally certainty facing him, which would require no action; man is always propelled to rank his choices and do the most urgent and pressing thing first.

Collingwood says:

> "thought when it follows its own bent most completely and sets itself the task of thinking out the idea of an object that shall completely satisfy the demands of reason may appear to be constructing a mere ens rations, but in fact is never devoid of objective or ontological reference." (Ryle, Mr Collingwood and the Ontological Argument, 1935)

For Collingwood, the Ontological Argument of Anselm fails because you still need to have faith to hold it, as you do with all absolute presuppositions:

> "but the substance of his thought survives all objections ...." (Ryle, Mr Collingwood and the Ontological Argument, 1935)

The Ontological Argument states that the essence involves existence in the one case concerning the ultimate being. The 'perfectness' of it involves existence. There is a contradiction in denying it as it would not be perfect or necessary, as we have discussed before. Ryle passionately disagrees:

> "There is no way of arguing validly to the existence of something of a certain description from the non-empirical premises, namely from premises about the characters combination of which is symbolised by the description. There is no way of demonstrating a priori particular matter of fact. Inferences to the existence of something, if there are any, must be causal inferences and inferences form the existence of something else. Nor

> *are there any 'demand of reason' which can make us accept as proofs of existence combinations of propositions which contain an overt fallacy."* (Ryle, Mr Collingwood and the Ontological Argument, 1935)

I can't see how Ryle's position holds in the light of the proof from the case of economics, and from geometry: that you can very much take a thought, in all its *a priori* glory, and apply it to reality in all times and all places. I have also demonstrated that this is also the same for the evolutionary algorithm, a splendid thought that has direct application to reality. Collingwood, as we have seen in my discussion of what I call the oneness of reality, shows how philosophy ends up totally committed to the fundamental ground of being, that which a theologian would call 'God', and a philosopher 'being'. It is also unqualified by anything finite; the finite is absorbed into it in accordance with the reasoning of Anselm as laid out in the Proslogion that we have touched upon. Ryle then denies that the role of philosophy is to eject all propositions that can be subjected to testing to the other sciences or create new ones, thus all you should be left with is the study of those hard matters for which there is no proof either way. Take away your commitment to being and, if you are a philosopher, you will be like the Road Runner Wile E Coyote in the cartoon who runs always of the end of a cliff edge, carries on running with his legs spinning wildly, then pauses to realise he is running on air only, following which he drops out of the sky! Anyway, Ryle disagrees, but does not give his reasons, other than to say:

> *"I see no force in the argument that philosophy would have no subject matter unless it had access to a special entity, I do not find myself alarmed by this threat."* (Ryle, Mr Collingwood and the Ontological Argument, 1935)

A year later, in the same journal, "Mind", E E Harris[48] defends the Collingwood version of the Ontological Argument and traces it to Hegel's refutation of Kant on the matter. Harris says Ryle misses the point of Hegel's

---

[48] 20 Century South African born philosophy professor whose teaching was done in RSA, UK and USA.

Ontological Argument[49]. This all rests on the Kantian observation that Existence cannot be made a 'predicate'. This supposes existence is not part of the character of the subject which is asserted to exist.[50] Harris also repeats what Ryle asked: "How can particular matters of fact be deduced from *a priori* or non-empirical premises?" And concludes, as we did with the establishment of economics, that yes, you can derive a matter of fact from *a priori* premises.

Concerning the first, Harris says:

> *"I should be unwilling to agree that it is entirely and finally true, but so much may be admitted to say,, in bare abstraction, that X exists adds nothing to our conception of X. Hence Hegel is led to remark, "if we look at the thought it holds, nothing can be more insignificant than being."* Encyclopoedie. (Harris, 1936)

This simply says that the proof of God's existence is of no philosophical importance, just that it is a bare/empty concept. Many a theologian, I suspect, is minded to accept this line of argument of Hegel's. Alternatively, they would spell out revelation and the evidence of scripture as giving us an understanding of God. I would not disagree, but say the two are in fact inseparable, as the Ontological Argument gives you a rational argument as to why you should hold

---

[49] I have not read sufficient Hegel to know if this is a correct rendition of his Ontological Argument, so only know of Hegel's refutation via Harris.

[50] The view of Harris that I am influenced by here is about as popular in the philosophical world – and, indeed, the theological world - as being a gay in a Welsh village in the 1950s. Even noted philosopher-theologians, like Richard Swinburne (a leading Christian apologist) say: "It is not incoherent to claim that God does not exist. Contra the ontological argument the word, "God" and "exist" do not suggest a true proposition by just what they say. "What makes it true, if it is true, is something else, 'how things are'" (Swinburne, 1977) Also, my personal friend the noted philosopher and theologian David Conway says: 'I do not regard the Ontological Argument as being anywhere near as formidable an argument for God as , so I shall argue, are each of the two other arguments for God on which proponents of the classical conception of philosophy have always been principally reliant.' (Conway) (the two being the Cosmological and Design arguments)

your beliefs, while the argument from scripture is evidential. Both play their role and are not mutually exclusive.

As we have shown, Ryle says "matters of fact" can't be deduced from "non empirical" premises. To which Harris says:

> "I shall assume , therefore (I hope without doing violence to his view) that Mr Ryle is prepared to admit to a proper proof of existence the sort of premises which states a fact given in sense-perception." (Harris, 1936)

Harris asks you to ponder the existence of the pen he is writing with. You can feel it, you can see the marks on the paper and so on and so forth. None of these factors prove the existence of the pen on their own, only when taken together as a whole:

> "The fact of the existence of the pen is proved by the mutual corroboration of several perceptions which together provide a body of evidence.
>
> "The establishment of a fact, then, depends first on a body of evidence, and secondly on the ordered system of the experienced world. To prove the existence of a thing we must show on sufficient evidence that the thing is a part of the system of things in space and time. The evidence is sufficient when to deny the conclusion to which it leads would disorganize the system." (Harris, 1936)

A point he attributes to the philosopher Bernard Bosanquet in "Implications and Linear Inference" is this:

> "The necessity of the inference is due to the system, and lies ultimately in the impossibility of rejecting the system in its entirety."

Harris continues:

> "(1) Mere sense-perception cannot prove the existence of anything other than momentary consciousness.

> *(2) No judgment of perception by itself can prove a matter of fact; nor can any number of such judgments, except by demonstrating a body of evidence from which we can infer to the fact question.*
>
> *(3) This is true even when the matter to be proved is the existence of something at the time present to the senses."* (Harris, 1936)

So it is *not* the empirical character of the premises:

> *"but the systematic character of the evidence which they contain."* (Harris, 1936)

When you are faced with choosing this fact or nothing, you commit "intellectual suicide":

> *"In other words, whatever particular facts we may deny or doubt, what we cannot possibly deny or doubt is the whole world of fact, for upon it any denial must depend for its validity and any doubt for its justification."* (Harris, 1936)

Hegelians maintain the absolute whole of reality encompasses material things which are part of the whole of reality, an aspect of or an appearance only. And denying a finite part of a whole is one thing, but denying the whole is a serious matter. This is the crux of the Ontological Argument. If God is the most perfect being, He is the whole of Reality .....

> *"and the existence of that whole our intellect demands as the logical condition of intelligibility of all our experience."* (Harris, 1936)

The essence of God is a total all-inclusiveness. There can be no denial of the existence of God:

> *"for there is nothing on which such a denial could rest."* (Harris, 1936)

Ryle may counter: just because the intellect demands a complete system does not mean there *is* a complete system, but then you would only have a system of incoherent chaos:

> *"our intellect demands an absolutely whole system of reality and if the satisfactions of this demand is the sine qua non of the validity of all arguments, including proofs of existence of finite things, then the absolutely complete system of reality must be."* (Harris, 1936)

Harris is arguing much like Collingwood and Anselm (but is not understood by Gaunilo, Kant and Dawkins): that if we conceive of God in finite terms, then yes, Ryle's claim will have plausibility. However, the conception of the whole is a reality whose existence cannot be doubted. This is a truth Kant overlooked in his 'hundred Taler' argument and Ryle overlooks it as well.

> Hegel: *"Existence is ....a term too low for the Absolute Idea, and unworthy of God."* (Harris, 1936)

Harris concludes, much as Anselm did, with:

> *"God is not in existence so much as existence is in God."* (Harris, 1936)

A year later, once more in "Mind", Ryle rather feebly responds (Ryle, "Back to the Ontological Argument").

Here, Ryle accepts he was attacking a version of the ontological argument that was not Collingwood's and indeed was the same attack launched by Kant and off the mark. He claims that Harris is actually saying that Collingwood is arguing "a variant of the Cosmological Argument or the argument *a contigentia mundi*.:"

> *"The difference is that the Cosmological Argument is not a scientist's argument but a philosophical argument. And, as Kant saw, it presupposes the Ontological Argument (in the form which I tried to refute it). True, it covers its tracks by reassuringly introducing an empirical premises about the whole world of fact or the world of finite experience. But this enters into the argument only in this way, that there is now alleged to be a contradiction not just in the denial of the existence of the Absolute but in the conjunction of this denial with the affirmation of the existence of our world of fact logically implies*

190

> the existence of the Absolute. The former is a part, or an aspect, or an appearance of the latter." (Ryle, Back to the Ontological Argument, 1937)

Ryle says:

> " ... existence propositions are synthetic, and are never logically necessary. So no existence-proposition is philosophically intelligible, if this is what it means to call something philosophically intelligible ." (Ryle, Back to the Ontological Argument, 1937)

That which Harris calls philosophically intelligible - *"no matter what it is, it will have to be consistent with the admission that no existence-proposition can be logically necessary or demonstrable from a priori premises or such that its denial involves a contradiction"* - I believe shows that this counter-argument from Ryle can't hold as manifestly since something so empirical and matter-of-fact as economics is deduced from the axiom of action. It is a true synthetic *a priori*. Ryle is clearly not aware of this, so he continues:

> "There can be no proof from a priori premises that there exists something of which the world of finite experience is an aspect, part or appearance."

> "To summarize: A philosophical argument for the existence or reality of something must be one of two forms.
> (1) Either it argues that there is a contradiction in the denial of existence or reality of such things, which is the Ontological Argument proper.
> (2) Or it argues that something is empirically known to exist but that it is logically impossible for anything to exist unless either its existence is logically necessary or its existence logically implies that something else exists of logical necessity.
> Neither holds water if 'there exists a so and so' is a synthetic proposition or one the negation of which contains no contradiction and so is logically possible.

> "If I were to succeed in making only one contribution to this debate, it would be to establish the point that what is at stake in it, as indeed in every debate about nay subject matter other than logic and mathematics, is not knowledge but rationality, and that 'proof' outside formal systems of logic and mathematics means 'test'; so that they only proposition we are entitled to accept as premises for action and further thought are those that it is rational to accept because they have passed the test for reason or observation or both." (Ryle, Back to the Ontological Argument, 1937)

At the end of the day, perhaps Ryle was not aware of the use of geometry in engineering, the foundations of economics being *a priori*, and the basis of the evolutionary dynamic - to move from an *a priori* to fact.

The Great Debate has not Moved on

Our most impressive academic high priest of atheism, A C Grayling, opines in a similar tone (Grayling, Thinking of Answers , 2010). theists say you can't prove a negative, therefore there is a chance of God. Proof is described by Grayling as the formal deductive proof of the syllogism

> *"Demonstrative proof, as just explained, is watertight and conclusive. It is a mechanical matter; computers do it best. Change the rules or axioms of a formal system, and you change the results. Such proof is only to be found in mathematics and logic.*

> *"Proof in all other spheres of reasoning consists in adducing evidence of the kind and in the quantity that makes it irrational, absurd, irresponsible or even lunatic to reject the conclusion thus being supported."*

Again, (Grayling, To Set Prometheus Free, 2009): [quote marks around title, again]

> *"Demonstrative proof is watertight and conclusive. It is a mechanical matter; computers do it best. Change the rules or axioms of a formal system,, and you change the results. Such proof is only to be found in mathematics and logic.*
> *Proof in all other spheres of reasoning, and paradigmatically in science, consists in adducing evidence of the kind and in the quantity that makes it irrational , absurd, irresponsible or even a mark of insanity to reject the conclusion thus being supported."*

Then, enter the great Straw Man analogy:

> *"For a simple case of proving a negative, by the way, consider how you prove the absence of pennies in a piggy-bank. You break it open and look inside: it is empty. On what grounds would you assert nevertheless that there might possibly still be pennies in there, only you cannot see or hear or feel or spend them?"* (Grayling, To Set Prometheus Free, 2009)

At this point, the committed atheist will trot out this little vignette from Carl Sagan written in "The Demon-Haunted World: Science as a Candle in the Dark", Ballantine: New York, 1996[51]:

> *"A fire-breathing dragon lives in my garage." Suppose (I'm following a group therapy approach by the psychologist Richard Franklin) I seriously make such an assertion to you. Surely you'd want to check it out, see for yourself. There have been innumerable stories of dragons over the centuries, but no real evidence. What an opportunity!*
>
> *"Show me," you say. I lead you to my garage. You look inside and see a ladder, empty paint cans, an old tricycle--but no dragon.*
>
> *"Where's the dragon?" you ask.*
>
> *"Oh, she's right here," I reply, waving vaguely. "I neglected to mention that she's an invisible dragon."*
>
> *You propose spreading flour on the floor of the garage to capture the dragon's footprints.*
>
> *"Good idea," I say, "but this dragon floats in the air."*
>
> *Then you'll use an infrared sensor to detect the invisible fire.*
>
> *"Good idea, but the invisible fire is also heatless."*
>
> *You'll spray-paint the dragon and make her visible.*
>
> *"Good idea, but she's an incorporeal dragon and the paint won't stick." And so on. I counter every physical test you propose with a special explanation of why it won't work.*
>
> *Now, what's the difference between an invisible, incorporeal, floating dragon who spits heatless fire and no dragon at all? If there's no way to disprove my contention, no conceivable experiment that would count against it, what does it mean to say that my dragon exists? Your inability to invalidate my hypothesis is not at all the same thing as*

---

[51] I quote form the "rationalwiki" page which lists it , http://rationalwiki.org/wiki/The_Dragon_in_My_Garage#cite_note-3

> *proving it true. Claims that cannot be tested, assertions immune to disproof are veridically worthless, whatever value they may have in inspiring us or in exciting our sense of wonder. What I'm asking you to do comes down to believing, in the absence of evidence, on my say-so.'*

The Dragon is God, for the purposes of his illustration, the garage owner the ignorant theist, and the questioner the great rational atheist, champion of reason. As we can see from the exposition of the Ontological Argument above, even if you totally strip it of all its religious and theological connotations, Sagan is committed to the Ontological Argument. The orderliness of his whole world of fact he presupposes to be able to even concoct his Dragon in the Garage story. The underlying, fundamental ground for being that he is part of and can't remove himself from is not taken into account in this allegory. The God he should be looking for is not found in some finite place like a garage, but is the undeniable fundamental ground for being that gives coherence to the world. Theologians of the monotheistic religions have never presented God as a finite thing like a dragon in a garage. When Christians have written about Jesus being both man and God, this can be put to empirical test; for us, in Book Two of the Against Atheism series in the "Controversies in Scripture" sections where some of these empirical manifestations will be explored. However, for a number of monotheists, God is an *a priori* thought whose demonstration is born out by the very thought of it itself, as we have discussed - just as the foundations of economics, geometry and the evolutionary process is itself. The Cosmological and Design Arguments are more empirical in their arguments and are explored below in the Krauss section in Chapter 6, "The Current Cannon of Science". Sagan should be focusing on these if he is looking for empirical proofs or not-proofs, I suggest, rather than postulating mythical dragons to prove they are mythical on all tests of demonstrative proof that you can apply to a finite thing. This is a classic straw man argument that does not advance the debate further at a serious level concerning the cause of the creation of the universe.

Here is another straw man diversion from the Dawkins/Grayling "Camp Quest" he calls "the great unicorn hunt."

> "Astronomy, critical thinking, philosophy and pseudo-science are covered at Camp Quest. One of the most popular exercises is the invisible unicorn challenge. The children are told there are two invisible unicorns who live at Camp Quest but that they cannot be seen, heard, felt or smelt, and do not leave a trace. A book about them has been handed down through the ages but it is too precious for anyone to see.
>
> All counsellors – as the adults are called – are said to be staunch believers in these unicorns.
>
> Any child who can successfully prove that the invisible unicorns do not exist is rewarded with a prize: a £10 note with a picture of Charles Darwin on it signed by **Richard Dawkins**, or a "godless" $100 bill, printed before 1957 when "In God We Trust" was added to paper currency in the US.
>
> Since this challenge began in 1996, the prize has been unclaimed.
>
> The camp's director, Samantha Stein, said that the exercise had elicited all sorts of interesting responses from the children about the burden of proof. One child had insisted that it was up to the counsellors to prove the unicorns did exist. Another said it was just impossible to prove.
>
> Stein said that the exercise was not about trying to bash the idea of God – just to make the children think critically and rationally[52].

I submit that you should apply the Sagan 'Dragon in the Garage' approach of demonstrative proof to your mythical and finite unicorn, which proves absolutely that there is no dragon there known in any finite way, so be done with it and pick up your prizes. I look forward to receiving mine, by the way.

Logic and maths are accorded quasi-sacred status with good reason, but why not philosophy? Rationality, for A C Grayling, is an all or nothing affair. The proposition 'god-exists', if it means anything, has a "gap left by the point-millions-of-zeros-one probability" to allow religious views to squeeze through, yet it must be black or white when reason is applied, not of probability. A C Grayling says those who argue religion is not testable essentially should accept that it is meaningless. This is Popper's falsification theory applied to the non-scientific arena which says that if it is not a potentially refutable proposition, it's not a meaningful proposition, for the purposes of good science. God is not studied via the tools of science, but via reason. God is untestable in that respect – yes - but the large body of evidence of the Bible stories, especially the

---

[52] http://www.theguardian.com/science/2009/jul/29/camp-quest-richard-dawkins

resurrection and the many hundreds of prophetic sayings contained in that book, some of which I explore Book Two of the Against Atheism series in the "Controversies in Scripture" sections can. These just can't be dismissed as being meaningless as they are eminently testable. I personally believe that, according to my reading, much of it would stack up as good evidence, good witness testimony, in any court. Whether you choose to believe it or not is down to you - that is the challenge of it - but it is totally empirically based, or just as testable as you get from any other slice of our history. The empirical testing of God is left to later. Meanwhile, the rational Ontological Argument, in my opinion, survives very much intact. I am satisfied that the debate in the journal "Mind" shows us that we can have a rationally thought out concept of the perfect being, and that it exists in both mind and in reality. What this is, is of course another question. The idea of God can be rationally obtained via the mind with the knowledge that He has reality in our experience of the world/universe around us. It can also be said with the same certainty that a scientist assumes conformity in the universe, and all of these are ultimately presupposed by reason, which as we know, you can only hold, in the final analysis, on faith. Like the action axiom, which is the foundation of economics, as with the ontological argument: you have a performative contradiction if you attempt to deny it.

So in the final analysis, when we are being most reasonable, we know deep down that we hold our views by reason, and what it discovers for us. We feel very secure in this happy state of awakening; however, this reason is not held on anything other than a thin thread of faith. Reason, when contemplative, even at its most mysterious and engaged in serious reflection, terminates in faith. Anselm had faith in order to understand. I thought I had reason in order to understand, but I now understand that it is faith that has given me reason to understand. As with all the so called 'proofs' of God, I prefer to phrase it differently and say that you can hold this God view with enough certainty, and be humble enough to accept your ignorance, and know it is held on faith which reason reassures you of. Like Aquinas and his "Five Ways" this is another way to God.

A C Grayling (Grayling, The God Argument , 2013) has an interesting perspective on the Ontological Argument. He says that the Argument needs to have a comparative element to it, so that its perfection can be assured to be the most perfect. If we go back to the core part of Anselm's proposition: "a being than that which no greater can be conceived," Grayling's view would seem to be that Anselm is inviting us to do the mental comparisons of things and rise up the ladder from where we stand to divine perfection - so which is more perfect? What compares with what? This is an attempt to understand perfection as a finite comparable. Grayling says the Anselm type of argument falls as it seeks degrees of perfectness, with God being the most perfect of potentially non-perfect things. There is, of course, nothing remarkable about being the most perfect of imperfect things. I believe Grayling is saying that in the case of the thought of absolute perfection, even if we did accept perfection as an absolute, with imperfection as its opposite, we only know degrees of imperfection. He then proceeds to dispose of the Anselm style arguments, noting that there is nothing in our world, even in our minds, that can make us observe an example of unqualified perfection. This is solely an empirical way of disposing of this argument.

As we have seen in my discussion of the Ontological Argument above, I think, unlike Grayling, that you *can* conceive of absolute perfection; it is a coherent analytical statement. If it also tells us something in addition to what is contained in its coherent concept, then it becomes a meaningful analytic/ synthetic proposition. Anselm never invokes the thought of comparing *this* level of perfection with *that*. For, as we have seen in Proslogion, an angel, as a created being, or a saint, assumed as created, is to be finite and thus limited in their perfection. The absolute standard of perfection has no limitations, it is perfect.

Grayling, for sure, will not hold this, as he feels there are contradictions in the term 'omnipotent':

> *"Could an omnipotent being eat itself"* (Grayling, The God Argument , 2013)

For example, it is never possible to do impossible things; this is not a restriction on omnipotence, but a function of reality. There is no qualification to omnipotence, just a better understanding of what that term contains: the ability to do anything possible, is by definition not an ability to do impossible things, as they are just that - impossible:

> *"A logically impossible action is not and action. It is what is described by a form of words which purport to describe an action, but do not describe anything which is coherent to suppose could be done."* (Swinburne, 1977)

Another atheists' favourite is the paradox of the stone analogy. The argument runs like this: if God makes the biggest stone that becomes too heavy to lift, his power is compromised by that and by the fact that he can't then make a bigger one.

The eminent philosopher and theologian, Swinburn answers:

> *"True, if an omnipotent being actually exercises (as opposed to merely possessing) his ability to bring about the existence of a stone too heavy for him subsequently to bring about its rising, then he will cease to be omnipotent .... But the omnipotence of a person at a certain time includes the ability to make himself no longer omnipotent, an ability which he may or may not choose to exercise. A person may remain omnipotent for ever because he never exercises his power to create stones too heavy to lift, forces too strong to resist, or universes too wayward to control."* (Swinburne, 1977)

I view this slightly differently. I would say He is immaterial, so He does not do lifting, and if you engage in trying to make God a physical human, with bulging muscles, you have missed the nature of God entirely. And what ever He makes, he can unmake as well as make: this is ultimate power. I also note that what laws He sets up in our reality, He can also change that reality. This is true omnipotence. Any being that can create the entire cosmos, with all its coherent struture, can truly do anything, any which way, over and over again, by changing His creation.

Grayling finishes his discussion of the Ontological Argument with a discussion of Platinga's conception of it, by saying 1) that the contention that theism is more consistent than atheism, as a orderly universe is assured by the latter and an un-orderly one assumed by the latter, is a bizarre view and that 2) Ockham's razor should be applied to this as the laws of conformity just *are*, and you don't need to insert a deity into the picture. So he would be perfectly happy to chop off the God part to assume the non-divine, by asserting Being, and just assume the external, mind-independent world, the laws of nature as immediate or just as they are. I find this ability to bin God, as it were, and insert some placeholders as just given, never questioning why they are there, to be positively mysterious for a rationalist like Grayling. These, then, become his Gods. To me, this would seem an intellectual surrender in order to avoid assuming God.

Part 4 Those Deeply Religious Men: The Atheists

Chapter 9 Richard Dawkins (Plus Others) and His Creedal Statements

In questioning those who suggest that evolution is God's preferred method, Dawkins writes:

> "This is a transparently feeble argument, indeed it is obviously self-defeating. Organized complexity is the thing we are having difficulty explaining. Once we are allowed to simply postulate organized complexity, if only the organized complexity of the DNA/protein replicating engine, it is relatively easy to invoke it as a generator of yet more organized complexity ... .But of course any God capable of intelligently designing something so complex as the DNA/protein replicating machine must have been at least as complex and organized as the machine itself." (Dawkins, The Blind Watch Maker, 1986)

> "One thing that makes evolution such a neat theory is that it explains how organized complexity can arise out of primeval simplicity." (Dawkins, The Blind Watch Maker, 1986)

In the first quote, 'postulate' should be exchanged with the word 'speculate' to be more accurate, and this is what we have when we realise that speculation about the primeval soup is his pseudo-metaphysics. His faith is based in his unquestioning belief in pseudo-metaphysics so, strictly speaking, it is of the unthinking, worst kind of religious thinking: the supposition of a presupposed, self-replicating DNA engine as just existing in the primordial soup – oh, lovely. Concerning the second of his quotes, relating the simplicity of the moment of creation to the complexity we observe today does not mean that the creation event was simplistic. As we have established, physical rationality means you can't sustain a world of physicality that then is created by a physical thing, as this would necessitate another explanation of another physical thing and so on and so forth. As we observe physical things every day and we believe they are real, in order to give them a rational grounding we can only assume a God who is an immaterial being. If we don't, we have causeless physical causes or cause which, since cause is a property of being physical, would mean it would be lacking its cause and therefore not physical at all, let alone being able of being physical. For that 'being' to create life as we know it, in that first cell, with all to come implied in it (the whole of life, past present and future), can be no mere conjuring tick: this is an event of immense complexity. As there is nothing in our intelligence that can explain this magnificent event in all its detail, the implication is that this creator is more intelligent than us and beyond our reach of explanation or even comprehension. Just as the limit of artificial intelligence is capped out by the intelligence level of its creators, ie, us (it can un-create what it created), so are we capped out at understanding anything in detail about this creator.

If he were to re-think his position, like another well-known professor from Oxford, A Flew, we may well yet see Dawkins abandoning his atheistic world-view as it has no rational grounding. Then he could answer his religious yearnings by going back to the religion of his youth, with the rhythm, the rituals, the comfort and the joy it clearly has given him in the past. "Richard Dawkins, the atheist scientist, admitted he is a 'secular Christian' because he hankers after the nostalgia and traditions of the church," reports the Daily Telegraphy of 26th May 2014. Dawkins himself adds:

> "I would describe myself as a secular Christian in the same sense as secular Jews have a feeling for nostalgia and ceremonies."

Daniel Dennett and His Bizarre Statements

Dennett is another of the high priests of atheism, often referred to as one of the 'Four Horsemen of the New Atheism' - one other of which is identified as Richard Dawkins, who we have referenced many times here. Like Dawkins, Dennett is fond of hyperbole and here are two great gems from him:

> "The philosopher Ronald de Sousa once memorably described philosophical theology as "intellectual tennis without a net," and I will readily allow that I have indeed been assuming without comment or question up to now that the net of rational judgment was up. We can lower it if you really want to. It's your serve. Whatever you serve, suppose I rudely return service as follows; "What you say implies that God is a ham sandwich wrapped in tin foil. That's not much of a God to worship!" (Dennett, 1996)

> "Before you appeal to faith when reason has you backed into a corner, think about whether you really want to abandon reason when reason is on your side.....Would you be willing to be operated on by a surgeon who tells you that whenever a little voice in him tells him to disregard his medical training, he listens to the little voice?" (Dennett, 1996)

That he holds his reason purely as a matter of faith, as we have discussed in this work, does not seem to register with him, despite being a philosopher of distinction (also a student of Ryle, mentioned above). When he and Ronald de Sousa figure this out, they may well find the tennis court to actually stand on so they can even being to start serving back their witticisms. The rational net of judgement will, surprisingly, catch most of the idiotic things he says. When he can transcend these pigmy moments, perhaps he will be worthwhile playing tennis with: raise your game, Dennett!

Dennett's assertion is that the God idea in humans is parasitic:

> "Now Lancet Flukes (Dicrocelium dendriticum), in order to complete their life cycle, have to get into the belly of a ruminant cow or sheep by commandeering a passing ant, climbing into its brain, a driving it up a blade of grass like all terrain vehicle, there the more likely to be eaten by a cow or a sheep. Incredibly smart. Of course the lancet fluke is stupid, but the strategy is brilliant. The lancet fluke doesn't even have a brain, really. It has the IQ of a carrot, roughly, I'd say. But the strategy that it engages in is very devious and very clever, and it's sort of spooky. Here we have a hijacker. We have a parasite that infects the brain and induces suicidal behaviour on behalf of a cause other than one's own genetic fitness. Spooky. Gee, I wonder if anything like that happens to us!" (McGrath, 2008)

We, of course, do this to all animals we cultivate to eat, all the time. Not exactly get into their brain, but cultivate in their brain the idea that when they are going down the tunnel to the stunning device, the captive bolt, the knife or electrical stimulation, they think they are going to be fed, rather than killed so as to ultimately be fed to us! Anyway, the implication is that there could be a god parasite/virus/gene/something that infects us with God. He does clarify, thankfully, that it is not a "worm" that infects us, but an idea, a meme jumping from infected human to another one, and so on. In a spectacular piece of pseudo metaphysics, he says:

> " ... wild memes of religion were fortunate to get themselves domesticated because they acquired stewards-people who were prepared to devote their lives to the health and spreading of those very ideas." (McGrath, 2008)

Religion, to Dennett might be metaphorically like the common cold. He suggests that just as you can get fit and rid yourself of the common cold, so you can the God idea, and you need to do so if you are going to objectively study this matter scientifically. No meme has ever been observed, to my knowledge. I may be wrong, but as far as I am aware this idea was floated by Dawkins in 1976 (Dawkins, The Selfish Gene, 1976), and has gained some traction as a way of expressing how an idea travels, but that is about it. It is puzzling that

Dennett wants to debate with the tennis net up because he often plays with it desperately low, and possibly nowhere near the tennis court of reason at all. This unobserved entity thus becomes a core component of atheistic, naturalist propositions. Like all propositions, it should be tested, and as it does not exist, it should be discarded. If it is just scientific jargon to say it's a word or series of words that can culturally take off and get widely accepted, I don't know why this is not just said instead of writing it up using scientific babble.

The Bible has a good session on faith that I think applies to Dennett. In Jeremiah 13:1-2, the symbol of the 'linen sash' depicted the wearer's the sash wrapped so close to their flesh - tightly upon it – to indicate the way he was meant to hold the covenant:

> *"Thus the Lord said to me: "Go and get yourself a linen sash, and put it around your waist, but do not put it in water." So I got a sash according to the word of the Lord, and put it around my waist."*

Jeremiah is then instructed to put this in water, which he does, and his Lord tells him that this sash will now not profit anyone and is an analogy for the benefit of his unfaithful Jewish audience. Dennett does not seem to know that he wears the covenant of faith which the creator of the universe supplies. He is prone to wading about in the murky water of what he thinks is objective reasoning, but falls so short of the mark. On this basis, the blind faith, the unreasoning faith in the atheistic meme is never discussed or explored as such: it is just assumed to be self-evidently true. Of course, Dennett believes he has objectively discovered this, unaffected by anything – he is the true dispassionate objective, reason-based observer.

Dennett, in an appeal to a fully and proper discussion on religion says:

> *"Don't play the faith card, but join the conversation."* (McGrath, 2008)

I really wonder whether he will actually ever seriously question his faith in his objective-rationality-only model of the world? He represents his religion at its worst, as unthinking, unquestioning and as blind faith that the things that are actually taken on faith require no understanding at all and are just a given, brute fact. Oh, how the (un)rationalist mind of Dennett lets himself down.

I can't depart from my thoughts on this professor without saying you may hear his name associated with the 'Bright' movement. This is a movement whereby you can sign up and become a 'Bright', a person who has accepted the naturalistic world view and therefore, by definition, has no residual supernatural views lurking in their minds. Those who do are called 'supers'. I often tell my children: less reading of fiction, read fact, it is much more fantastic, as often you feel you couldn't have made it up yourself! Well, with the Bright Movement, we have pretence and delusion on a massive scale. From its web page[53] we have the following:

"Why the international Brights movement?

- *Way too much supernatural hokum in society.*
(Brights usually spot it quickly.)
- *Prevalence of nonsensical ideas.*
(Brights care when we see absurdities given priority over reasonable real world facts.)
- *Unjust privileging in society of people who embrace or tout groundless beliefs*
(Brights are mindful of how institutions that have been organized around these beliefs, particularly in the name of religion, are given unwarranted advantage.)"

It is clear that Brights who advocate random chance turning lifeless matter into consciousness, universes popping into existence out of nothing, multiple universes, endless universes, points of singularity of no density with all density compacted within, to no space at all, infinite existence and so on, reserve a large bag of diplomatic immunity into which they can place all their pseudo-metaphysical supernatural mumbo-jumbo. Dennett, Dawkins and Grayling are all listed here as "Enthusiastic[54]" Brights.

---

[53] http://www.the-brights.net/movement/reasons.html
[54] http://www.the-brights.net/people/enthusiastic/index.html

No doubt they would reject this, but it seems their religion is a religion of naturalism which stands on shaky pseudo-metaphysical foundations, whose presuppositions they don't even realize, or are prepared to acknowledge, that they hold. Not only are they the ultimate mystics, they are the true 21st Century witch doctors. So much for the bright in Brights.

When they are not attacking the strawman 'super' there is actually much talk about the need for the Brights to aspire to an egalitarian 'civic vision'. Not much flesh is put on the bones of this, but I hope it is not the egalitarianism of their atheistic socialist fellow travellers, which has spectacularly unravelled into death on a massive scale, as we will see in the next chapter. Rather, I hope it is like all the good religions, based around a belief that the Golden Rule - to treat others as you wish to be treated - runs through the DNA of everything you do in any aspect of your life, private or public.

What inflammatory nonsense to call yourself a 'Bright', anyway, as though everyone else is not bright. This smacks of eugenics, social Darwinism, and general supremacist views, the implication being that from their loins and their loins only will a master race of enlightened people emerge. For all their positioning of civic equality, co-operation with 'supers' to obtain more understanding, I somehow fear this may rapidly not become the agenda. Both Grayling and Dawkins would have observed supremacy at work in the colonial countries of their childhoods and I hope they are not becoming the white master colonial equivalents of today with this (not so) Bright movement.

Much as I put no blame on Darwin himself for eugenics, he did say the following (Darwin C., 1896):

> "With savages, the weak in body or mind are soon eliminated; and those that survive commonly exhibit a vigorous state of health. We civilised men, on the other hand, do our utmost to check the process of elimination; we build asylums for the imbecile, the maimed, and the sick; we institute poor-laws; and our medical men exert their utmost skill to save the life of every one to the last moment. There is reason to believe that

vaccination has preserved thousands, who from a weak constitution would formerly have succumbed to small-pox. Thus the weak members of civilised societies propagate their kind. No one who has attended to the breeding of domestic animals will doubt that this must be highly injurious to the race of man. It is surprising how soon a want of care, or care wrongly directed, leads to the degeneration of a domestic race; but excepting in the case of man himself, hardly any one is so ignorant as to allow his worst animals to breed."

"The surgeon may harden himself whilst performing an operation, for he knows that he is acting for the good of his patient; but if we were intentionally to neglect the weak and helpless, it could only be for a contingent benefit, with a certain and great present evil. Hence we must bear without complaining the undoubtedly bad effects of the weak surviving and propagating their kind; but there appears to be at least one check in steady action, namely the weaker and inferior members of society not marrying so freely as the sound; and this check might be indefinitely increased, though this is more to be hoped for than expected, by the weak in body or mind refraining from marriage."

From Darwin's suggestion of stopping marriage between the weak and the inferior, you ultimately come to the perverse genetic experiments of Dr Mengele in Hitler's death camps and the ideology of a master race trying to cling to some scientific respectability. I hope the Bright movement does not contain any tragic consequences brewing up for generations to come, but the warning shots are there for all to see.

A C Grayling the Philosophical Atheist

For a philosopher of such calibre, Grayling tells us that in the absence of religion, we must subscribe to:

" ... a naturalistic world-view, that is, a view to the effect that what exists is the realm of nature, describable by natural law. This is accordingly a world-view premised on observation, reason and science, and excludes any kind of faith-loving element."
(Grayling, The God Argument , 2013)

He does not appear to consider that he holds all these matters as an article of blind, given, immediate faith as discussed concerning his friend and atheist collaborator, Daniel Dennett. He goes on to add:

> "By 'faith' this is meant belief held independently of whether there is testable evidence in its favour, or indeed even in the face of counter-evidence[55]. This latter is regarded as a virtue in most religion; in Christianity the case of Doubting Thomas is held out as illustrating the point." (Grayling, The God Argument , 2013)

Curiously, Grayling has his understanding of the story of Doubting Thomas wrong. That Thomas doubts is not in doubt. Jesus provides him with empirical evidence of his resurrection by presenting his physical body for inspection by Thomas, whose doubt ceases when such evidence is presented. May I suggest Grayling reads John 20:24-29 in order to establish this.

He holds a belief in the mind-independent world (by the way, which I also do, but I take it on faith alone), the fundamental constants of which (the orderly nature of the universe, rationality and logic itself are never testable - he is as religious as you can get, according to his own definition, and as faith-based as you can get. His moniker as 'high priest' of atheism is well deserved.

Throughout his works, he prefers to use 'g' as opposed to 'G' to signify God as he does not believe God exists but acknowledges 'it' as a sociological phenomenon. Substitute the word 'Fred' for 'God' and they have the same

---

[55] The passage of John 20:24-29 is as follows:

> "Now Thomas, called the Twin, one of the twelve, was not with them when Jesus came. The other disciples therefore said to him, "We have seen the Lord."
> So he said to them, "Unless I see in His hands the print of the nails, and put my finger into the print of the nails, and put my hand into His side, I will not believe."
> And after eight days His disciples were again inside, and Thomas with them. Jesus came, the doors being shut, and stood in the midst, and said, "Peace to you!" Then He said to Thomas, "Reach your finger here, and look at My hands; and reach your hand here, and put it into My side. Do not be unbelieving, but believing."
> And Thomas answered and said to Him, "My Lord and my God!"
> Jesus said to him, "Thomas, because you have seen Me, you have believed. Blessed are those who have not seen and yet have believed."

explanatory power, according to Grayling. Fred created the universe enters the same category as a Christian asserting that God created the universe.

The Good Book: Aping Religion in Literature

A C Grayling has created a secular bible (Grayling, The Good Book, 2011). It's a fantastic testimony to a lifetime's work and well worth a read. For this alone, he is the archbishop of atheism and its chief theologian. He comments as follows, concerning this book:

> *"Anyone who rises above his daily concerns in hope of finding and following truth, will discover it here."*

I agree with part of the above claim - there is a much in the way of truth packed in there, but as to following truth, I think that is too grand a claim. In parts, we can draw out some of his metaphysical propositions, which I think are flawed. Most occur in his first chapter.

His opening section - naturally, if somewhat plagiaristically, called Genesis - has no beginning moment as, for Grayling, there always was something, so no beginning is required. How this something came into being is just assumed as ... being. Wonderful! A spectacular bit of pseudo metaphysics. Newton is mentioned in verse 7 of Chapter 1 as the critical moment of advancement in humanity. I guess the 1687 (publication of ("Principia Mathematica") was the start of civilization (after those nasty Christians had destroyed it, perhaps?), following this trend! In Chapter 2 verse 1 he praises those courageous men of science, those religious men like Newton and all the others before him who we have mentioned here, as well as some since Newton. Somehow, I suspect his praise is not so generous for their religious sentiments. Verse 8 restates his view that nothing comes from nothing. In chapter 3 we do come across the nearest we shall get to a creation moment in verses 1-2, which indicate that he favours our life coming into being from the depths of the sea. 5 evokes the power of change through time, or evolution. In verse 7, nature mysteriously orders herself. Chapters 4 and 5 assume nature's laws are just a given. Chapter 5 always spins out a nice circle of life view of existence with no beginning or end, all very charming and quaint. The story unfolds in subsequent chapters where atoms are assumed to live by their own powers; from whence these came nobody cares: nature is her own God and she is empirical only. He holds it on faith and faith alone that nature needs no causes: this is particularly expressed in Chapters 11-13. He glorifies induction and the scientific method only, and the Gospel of Science is fully poured out in chapter 15.

The Wisdom and Parables chapters are excellent.

The final chapter (22):

> "9 And though you are not yet a Socrates, you ought to live as one desirous of becoming a Socrates, who said, 'The life most worth living is the life considered and chosen.'
> 10. The question to be asked at the end of each day is, 'How long will you delay to be wise?'
> 11. And the great lesson that the end of each day teaches is that wisdom and the freedom it brings must daily be won anew."

Great words.

On my favourite subject, one I call 'Informed' (or Learned) Ignorance, after Cardinal Cusa's book on the matter, Grayling writes as follows:

> Chapter 19
>
> "16 And if anyone tells you that you know nothing, and you are not angered by what he says, you may be sure that you have begun to be wise."

And:

> "12. To which the stranger replied, 'Exactly so; for Aristotle says, "He who says, I do not

211

know, has already attained the half of all knowledge."

The "Concord" section one could find little to disagree with and much to positively affirm. Lamentations was - well, no surprises, gloomy. Some areas covered were the insignificance of our individual lives. There is no magic and mystery in life and philosophers can supply this need. We are all fellow sufferers in life. And much more. This section contrasts for the most part with the Good News message of the Gospels, and much of the New Testament and forms a big part of the book that I suspect Grayling wishes to replace as a core book of guidance for the secular life.

His chapter on "Consolations" has the overriding purpose of showing that reason is your ally in getting out of situations of grief. Time heals all. Much is made of the fulfillment of life by getting old, and the awareness and active appreciation of culture, and how death is a most natural thing. A C Grayling is like a truly religious man: he does not fear death as it the final act of a natural life. Only in truly religious believers do you observe such a lack of fear.

There is no God of Abraham, Brahmin or Tao for Grayling, but nature herself. This is taken from Chapter 22:

"1. That end of life is the best, when, without the intellect or senses being impaired, nature herself takes to pieces her own handiwork which she also put together.

2. Just as the builder of a ship or a house can break them up more easily than anyone else, so nature, which knitted together the human frame, can also best unfasten it.

20. For nature puts a limit to living as to everything else,

21. And we are the sons and daughters of nature, and for us therefore the sleep of nature is nature's final kindness."

Shades of mysticism abound when his vision of the final earthly act is recorded in Chapter 26: "The Consolation of the End":

"25. It is a wonderful thing to learn thoroughly how to die. You may deem it superfluous to learn a text that can be used only once;

26. But that is just the reason why we ought to think on a thing.

> When we can never prove whether we really know a thing, we must always be learning it.

27. 'Think on death.' In saying this, we are bidding ourselves to think on freedom.
28. He who has learned to die has unlearned slavery;
29. He is beyond any external power, or, at any rate, he is it. What terrors has any experience of life for him?
30. This is the final consolation: that we will sleep at evening, and be free for ever."

Grayling knows that each of us needs a little bit the mystery of the unknowable to keep us moving forward through life, which is something all religions that survive the test of time tend to adhere to. His religion of atheism knows this. This is born out more thoroughly by the philosopher Alain de Botton, who we will discuss shortly.

Meanwhile, Grayling's chapter "Sages" is interesting. There is much advice regarding what is good, what is evil, what are right values to be practiced - but none are ever defined. I can only presume that is because the author views them to be self-evident. That said, all of it is relevant to all sentient beings who want to continuously improve their lives. He writes as if it is the master talking to his pupil. I would happily relate to my own children all of this section.

Fragments of poetry play their role in his "Songs" section, demonstrating Grayling's awareness of the human need to put the rational into the irrational of verse. No poet am I, but I have to say it did not move me as the Song of Songs in the Hebrew Bible did, which must count as one of the most beautiful poems every composed.

The "Histories" chapter would seem to be a heavily edited version of Herodotus's account of the Greco-Persian Wars. Best, I would think, to read them in the original rather than in a Grayling redacted version. Especially as Herodotus was the first historian to account for events in a systematic style that would pass as history, devoid of myth, today. Essentially it follows a West = Good, East = Bad plot line.

"Proverbs'" is organized into 145 Chapters, each with a single word heading, starting with "Action" and ending with "Youth" in which wise words are uttered on all subjects. "Reason" is covered, but there is nothing on its master: Faith. The subject of "Death" contains 47 verses and is the longest. "Evil" is covered, although nothing enlightens us as to its origin. There is nothing concerning 'good,' although the last section of the Good Book is 'The Good". There is a placeholder only called "Goodness" which, for someone of A C Grayling's stature, is wishy-washy in the extreme. I don't think any comparison can be made with The Book of Proverbs in the Bible.

The God of Nature is emphasised once more in this chapter:

"Chapter I08: Nature
1. To know nature, consult nature.
2. It cannot be nature, if it is not sense.
3- Nature is the true law.
4. Nature obeys necessity.
5. Nature pardons no mistakes.
6. To command nature one must obey it.
7. The volume of nature is the book of knowledge.
8. Wisdom and nature never say different things.
9. Nature always returns.
10 Nature does nothing in vain."

According to verse 10, it would appear that nature even has a mystical purpose.

Concerning Chapter 14 and "Truth" we see a bizarre verse 4 that asserts: "All great truths begin as blasphemies." His prejudice against God is so extreme that he claims all great truths develop from insults to God. Tell that to mankind's greatest who have discovered truths (many religious, and listed at the back of his book as source inspiration), that the genesis of the truth was made manifest in a moment of blasphemy. Come on, A C Grayling, you let yourself down here! But other than a few oddities, I came away from reading the "Proverbs" with a sense of deep satisfaction.

The "Lawgiver" chapter is where he sketches out a political philosophy that I would describe as natural rights based, promoting the great scope of human liberty. The source of the natural rights postulated is not discussed, other than to say that all who participate agreed to seed certain of their rights to the state to allow it to adjudicate peaceful cooperation, which in turn actually strengthens their natural right of freedom as they can live more free of fear this way. These sentiments we can locate within the social contract tradition. Maximum liberty is the aim, we read; all of the state should aim its policies at the good. But this is not defined. Democracy is the least imperfect and should be default position. There is the extensive use of the Greek preference for aged and wise leaders, and much which is descriptive of that happy state.

The "Acts" section is rather like the "Histories" section and both might be better read un-redacted, in their original classical sources. The "Epistles are based on "Chesterfield's Letters to His Son" and they are, on the whole, exceptional and very positive. Much is provided here about leading a wise and selfless life.

He finishes with his own Decalogue:

> *"Love well, seek the good in all things, harm no others, think for yourself, take responsibility, respect nature, do your utmost, be informed, be kind, be courageous: at least, sincerely try."*

Not much to disagree with there. Note, there is no compulsion from a God if you transgress, a key component of the Decalogue of Moses. Finally, he reveals the main authors from whom he has cribbed. I note that they are overwhelmingly theist writers, just like him, albeit his God is nature; they are followers of the whole pantheon of gods or God. For one man to write a Bible for his followers, he trumps any of the Four Horsemen of the new atheism. For my money, he is not only their Archbishop, but the founding priest, the Apostle Peter of atheism, on whom his church will be built, and the Paul-like teacher of the theology and doctrine of his new religion as well - actually a cross between Peter, Paul and John (the philosophical dimension) wrapped up in one person: A C Grayling.

The Extreme Intolerance of Atheism: On the Teaching or Not of Religion to Under 18 Year Olds

Despite his liberal political philosophy, if "The Good Book" is anything to go by, he is most illiberal in matters of how a parent should bring up a child of its own:

> "It would, though, be far better if religious doctrines and systems were not taught to people until they had attained maturity. If this were the case, how many would subscribe to a religion? Without being given a predisposition through childhood indoctrination to think there might be something in one of the many and conflicting religious beliefs on offer, the likely answer would surely be: not very many." (Grayling, The God Argument, 2013)

I paused, thinking to myself: is he advocating a ban, or suggesting it should be thought of as a serious proposal? Either way, although you can't conclusively pin the advocacy of an outright ban on A C Grayling, you can see that his thought is pushing you at best to consider this as a serious option. A C Grayling equates faith schools in Northern Ireland with conflict. Yes, they may be regarded by some as a polarizing fuse. The majority of that country's citizens want this separation (though it is not state mandated) and maybe very few who send their children to a faith school will have much of a clue as to the key differences in the doctrines and teaching of these two branches of the Christian faith: Anglican and Roman Catholic. The salient point running under all of this is, importantly, that one is associated with being the nationalist community's school and the other the loyalist: one Irish, one British in cultural outlook. This is the point. Under most 'religious' disputes, dig past the surface and you will find more human interest, such as how the various bit of economic cake are cut or not cut as the case may be.

If Grayling's religion gains traction, I wonder what we will teach children when they keep asking to know why the universe came into being. Do we trot out, "well, scientists say it was the Big Bang, caused when the seeming impossible happened ... there was a point of singularity that had both the infinite density stuffed into one volume. Yes, yes, it's one great bundle of contradiction, but we must believe it because it is the height of scientific rationality to do so." Or: "in the primeval soup, the complex building blocks of life happened to coincide all at once so they could then kick off evolution of all life as we know it and due to the long time span of a couple of billion years or so, we can expect this to happen." Or: "it just *is*, don't ask any more questions, something has always existed". Or: "for you to exist, the universe could only be this way because, as we know, one micro % of difference in this chemical structure here and one micro % of difference there just means that is the actual miracle of it - but it just *is*, as are the laws of nature, logic, math , reason. Have some faith - no, sorry, I mean just believe, as you must, it can't be any different. I know this is a spectacular example of circular reasoning, as I presume all the fundamental constants lead us to assume that only order of some kind can provide the right climate for our existence - but that goes into the accepted bag of diplomatic immunity. Now stop asking questions!" Or: "there are many universes - not that we have observed anything to tell us there are, but this is the cause behind this one of ours: it just goes on and on to infinity, despite the contradictory notion of infinity, but let's ignore that." Or: "just as our universe inflates, science tells us it will contract so we are to presume that at some point it will just auto kick off again. We don't have any evidence of this as well, but the best science tells us it is so, and it is intellectually respectable to believe it." That child would be quite rightly puzzled, indeed mystified at the incoherence of such adult mentors.

The elegance of a God, or fundamental ground of being, which reason tells us must be eternal, and that God kicking off the whole conception of the universe, may well be the ultimate Ockham's razor argument, as it is far more simple to absolutely presuppose the one immaterial cause that reason requires of us than all the great unfounded schemes of science. In fact, I think discouraging or banning the teaching of religion until post-18 or whenever someone is deemed 'rational' will, for young minds, just encourage more questions and more temptation to dare to know what their parents or the 'system' is trying to get them *not* to know! In China, an atheist state, there are now living almost more practicing Christians that in the whole of Western Europe, and soon they will exist in even greater numbers. Curiosity peaks when something is banned. No doubt Grayling will promote Humanism instead of a prime mover of the universe, but it has no special claim to warranting a first place in a people's belief system. I was hoping to read that liberal tolerance would necessitate the teaching of a whole raft of belief systems, always encouraging the enquiring mind and allowing people to come to their own conclusions, much as his Good Book advises (apart from when he advocates the avoidance of belief in a god or Gods). However, this can't be achieved if you are bent on banning the teaching and active promotion of belief systems held by billions of people on planet earth.

I maintain that Grayling is, in reality, fully faith based, and fully religious. His particular faith may be called un-reason, supported by nothing; it just is. He worships nature. He worships the material world with no beginning, despite this being incoherent, as we have discussed. His religion, at base, is thus one of the more primitive varieties knocking around, despite the great edifice he has presumed for it.

Alain de Botton and His Atheist Church

The philosopher de Botton recently wrote a book "Religion for Atheists" (de Botton, 2012). Please note that all quotes below referencing de Botton come from this book. He is under no illusion about the fact that he is seeking to create an alternative religion, albeit one based on a traditional theme, in the sense that it takes what he thinks is the best from the old religions while selectively applying it to his new, godless one. He is very confident that anyone holding a god-based religious view is unwarranted in doing so, and he enjoys debating and gaining pleasure out of some of the incoherence in many believers' views as they attempt to express them. For the record, I believe the atheist position is intellectually untenable, but I would not hold de Botton to be a simpleton or a maniac. However, it puzzles me deeply as to why this so-called atheist needs to use such hostile and dismissive language to attack believers in God:

> *"Attempting to prove the non-existence of God can be an entertaining activity for atheists. Tough-minded critics of religion have found much pleasure in laying bare the idiocy of believers in remorseless detail, finishing only when they felt they had shown up their enemies as thorough-going simpletons or maniacs."*

That said, he is very much in tune with the pulse of his theistic religious interlocutor and may well indeed understand what certain aspects of religion are about:

> *"The premise of this book is that it must be possible to remain a committed atheist and nevertheless find religions sporadically useful, interesting and consoling — and be curious as to the possibilities of importing certain of their ideas and practices into the secular realm. One can be left cold by the doctrines of the Christian Trinity and the Buddhist Eightfold Path and yet at the same time be interested in the ways in which religions deliver sermons, promote morality, engender a spirit of community, make use of art and architecture, inspire travels, train minds and encourage gratitude at the beauty of spring. In a world beset by fundamentalists of both believing and secular varieties, it must be possible to balance a rejection of religious faith with a selective/ reverence for religious rituals and concepts.*

> *"God may be dead, but the urgent issues which impelled us to make him up still stir and demand resolutions which do not go away when we have been nudged to perceive some scientific inaccuracies in the tale of the seven loaves ([56]) and fishes."*

---

[56] Matthew 14:17 And they said to Him, "We have here only five loaves and two fish." Most

God's dead! Well, that is news to billions of believers around the globe. Perhaps it's a rhetorical point, though I suspect he fully believes it:

> *"I recognized that my continuing resistance to theories of an afterlife or of heavenly residents was no justification for giving up on the music, buildings, prayers, rituals, feasts, shrines, pilgrimages, communal meals and illuminated manuscripts of the faiths)."*

> *"The challenge facing atheists is how to reverse the process of religious colonization: how to separate ideas and rituals from the religious institutions which have laid claim to them but don't truly own them."*

One thing he quickly homes in on is the coming together of the Christian service of Mass. This diffuses a sense of alone-ness, he suggests, that all possess. He recognises this coming together in worship allows believers to put aside their egoism and immerse themselves into the collective gathering at the Mass, entering the spirit of the family of the church and achieving that great sense of extended community; more importantly, it is a God-worshipping community inhabiting a 4,000 year continuous timeline, albeit with some changes in colour on the way. He is aware the Mass is the central framework of the church family for most Christian denominations. He is aware of the way it follows the Last Supper of Jesus through its invitation to re-enact the Christian commitment of breaking bread with each other, just as Jesus did with his apostles on that final occasion before his Passion. But his knowledge of Christian history regarding the Eucharistic feast is limited and questionable, shaky at best. He places himself alongside the same standard of scholarship on these matters as other atheists such as Dawkins and Grayling, so I guess one should not expect anything more when reading about a god-based religion that is, to all of them, bizarre at

---

choose the feeding of the 5,000 not the feeding of the 4,000 as an example. I assume the same *"scientific inaccuracies"* apply to the more famous cousin as well.

220

best and not requiring any need for scholarly accuracy. For example, he continues:

> "In honour of the most important Christian virtue, these gatherings hence became known as agape (meaning 'love' in Greek) feasts and were regularly held by Christian communities in the period between Jesus's death and the Council of Laodicea in AD 364. It was only complaints about the excessive exuberance of some of these meals that eventually led the early Church to the regrettable decision to ban agape feasts and suggest that the faithful should eat at home with their families instead — and only thereafter gather for the spiritual banquet that we know today as the Eucharist."

The Eucharist means 'thanksgiving' in Greek. By the 0050s AD, in the first Epistle of St Paul to the Corinthians, this had become a regular Christian practice and was spiritual in its effect. The historical backdrop is that gentiles were participating in various types of pagan worship at their altars and Paul wanted them to desist from this and adopt the correct practice that had been instituted some 20 or so years before by Jesus himself.

1 Corinthians 10:14-22:

> "Therefore, my beloved, flee from idolatry. I speak as to wise men; judge for yourselves what I say. The cup of blessing which we bless, is it not the communion of the blood of Christ? The bread which we break, is it not the communion of the body of Christ? For we, though many, are one bread and one body; for we all partake of that one bread. Observe Israel after the flesh: Are not those who eat of the sacrifices partakers of the altar? What am I saying then? That an idol is anything, or what is offered to idols is anything? Rather, that the things which the Gentiles sacrifice they sacrifice to demons and not to God, and I do not want you to have fellowship with demons. You cannot drink the cup of the Lord and the cup of demons; you cannot partake of the Lord's table and of the table of demons. Or do we provoke the Lord to jealousy? Are we stronger than He?"

In 1 Corinthians 11:23-27 Paul says:

> "For I received from the Lord that which I also delivered to you: that the Lord Jesus on the same night in which He was betrayed took bread; and when He had given thanks, He broke it and said, "Take, eat; this is My body which is broken for you; do this in remembrance of Me." In the same manner He also took the cup after supper, saying, "This cup is the new covenant in My blood. This do, as often as you drink it, in

> *remembrance of Me."*
>
> *For as often as you eat this bread and drink this cup, you proclaim the Lord's death till He comes."*

Clearly, Paul would have understood this from his travelling companion, Luke. At least, this from Luke's Gospel, where the Last Supper is reported in detail:

Luke 22:19-21:
> *"And He took bread, gave thanks and broke it, and gave it to them, saying, "This is My body which is given for you; do this in remembrance of Me." Likewise He also took the cup after supper, saying, "This cup is the new covenant in My blood, which is shed for you."*

You can also compare the texts of the other apostolic witnesses some 20-25 years previously who wrote in a similar vein (see Matthew 26:26-29 and Mark 22:17-20). The Gospel of John covers the Lord's Supper in Chapter 13, giving more detail of the events of that night, presumably as his fellow apostles had covered the Eucharistic ritual in detail already in pervious gospels. The great Servant passage and the betrayal of Judas are also added in by John to the Last Supper narrative. It is not unusual for John to add more than the others had already reported. Paul knew this tradition, and seeing it grossly abused in the name of Christianity sought to get it back on track and the abusers of this ritual out of the Church of Corinth.

For many ancient societies food was associated with spiritual matters. If you had adverse side effects from eating food, you might considered possessed by demons (in the form of stomach sounds, flatulence, vomiting, for example). Much as we wish to get rid of harmful bacteria, our ancestors wished to get rid of demons who possessed them, pure foods being associated with the divine.

The Eucharist as described by Paul is in the spiritually pure food like the ancient Israelites received in the wilderness, though by his time it is upgraded to become the spiritual representation of Christ's blood (wine) and his body (bread).

1 Corinthians 10:20:

> "Rather, that the things which the Gentiles sacrifice they sacrifice to demons and not to God, and I do not want you to have fellowship with demons."

Paul is very specific in distinguishing the historic association of demonic possession with bad food from the meaning of the Eucharist that we understand today.

From Paul, you can also participate in the true divine nature as opposed to the false nature of idols. The participants of the Eleusinian Mysteries believed they became one with Dionysus; Paul actually attested you became one spiritually with Christ.

It was clear in the first couple of centuries that there were some who still participated in these pagan practices who might have been called Christians, but they were not, as Justin Martyr who was only one generation removed from the last Apostle John, testifies:

Justin Martyr Apology 1 26[57]:

> "By the help of the demons he has made many in every race of men to blaspheme and to deny God the Maker of the universe, professing that there is another who is greater and has done greater things than he. As we said, all who derive [their opinions] from these men are called Christians, just as men who do not share the same teachings with the philosophers still have in common with them the name of philosophy, thus brought into disrepute. Whether they commit the shameful deeds about which stories are told—the upsetting of the lamp, promiscuous intercourse, and the meals of human flesh, we do not know; but we are sure that they are neither persecuted nor killed by you, on account of their teachings anyway. I have compiled and have on hand a treatise against all the heresies which have arisen, which I will give you if you would like to consult it."

---

[57] http://www.ccel.org/ccel/richardson/fathers.x.ii.iii.html (A reference to the charges of incest (facilitated by darkness) and cannibalism which other Apologists (Athenagoras, Tertullian, Minucius Felix) treat at length.)

However, the Acts of the Apostles was arguably compiled no later than AD 62, recording events following the death of Christ by Luke, as it does not report on Paul's death in Rome. This book is ordered in the canon directly after the Gospels. It also reports the Eucharist being an established tradition of the early church and also Sunday as the day it was performed, after the end of the day's work (with no restriction on keeping the Sabbath), to celebrate the resurrection and the start of the new understanding of Christ and thus the beginning of the Christian week.

Acts 2:42 , 2:47, 20:7 , 20:11 , 27:35:

> "And they continued steadfastly in the apostles' doctrine and fellowship, in the breaking of bread, and in prayers."

> "So continuing daily with one accord in the temple, and breaking bread from house to house, they ate their food with gladness and simplicity of heart"

> "Now on the first day of the week, when the disciples came together to break bread, Paul, ready to depart the next day, spoke to them and continued his message until midnight."

> "Now when he had come up, had broken bread and eaten, and talked a long while, even till daybreak, he departed."

> "And when he had said these things, he took bread and gave thanks to God in the presence of them all; and when he had broken it he began to eat."

Peter, in 2 Peter 13-16, notes "spots and blemishes" concerning certain people who feasted with the early Christians, as false teachers were infiltrating the Asia Minor church and this letter is his warning to remove such people. Following Jesus's resurrection Jude (Judas), the half-brother of Christ, was now a believer, and, as in Peter 1:12:

> "These are spots in your love feasts, while they feast with you without fear, serving only themselves. They are clouds without water, carried about by the winds; late autumn trees without fruit, twice dead, pulled up by the roots."

Sharing in the love of Christ in a feast, worshiping and receiving charity was one thing, but doing it with false prophets, fornicators and the generally bad, was quite another. The agape understanding or connection as described by de Botton is highly debatable. Fifty odd years later the Didache[58] (the teachings of the Apostles written in the early part of the first century or very early part of the second century during the latter years of John the Gospel writer and Apostle) mentioned the Eucharistic feast, as did Ignatius of Antioch[59] and Justin Martyr[60] in similar times as the traditional thanksgiving we know today. You can understand why I doubt de Botton's attempts at Christology. That said, the point he makes is that it is one of the most fulfilling aspects of organised religion is feasts on High days and Holydays, which are incredibly spiritually enriching moments of the year. This is not to deny agape feasts went on as he describes, and were duly proscribed, but the spiritual banquet that we know as the Eucharist was with us and practiced by the apostles and their followers right from the very dawn of Christianity - not from 364 AD, as suggested by de Botton. In fact, as it is Christ's Passover feast, we should actually recognise its fundamental roots in a 3,500 year history dating back to the actual Jewish Passover, modified by the followers of Christ shortly after he commanded it as remembrance for the ultimate Passover sacrifice of Himself in a one-off exchange for the forgiveness of our sins. And so it continues today, and even in this secular age many hundreds of millions, if not billions of people regularly, and with conviction, partake in this activity.

This leads de Botton to suggest the establishment of communal restaurants for atheists ('churches'?) where it is possible to *break bread* together just as the Christians and also the Jews, do via their respective religious celebrations. For restaurants enable people to gather together, they make for a social occasion. Co-owning restaurants myself at the moment, I can confirm that our communal tables make conversation happen between, for example, singles who are in town and need to eat, people who are looking for company. If I could be totally non-commercial and still survive, I would love to create a huge, communal restaurant as I am sure it would get people talking and

---

[58] http://www.paracletepress.com/didache.html (generally dated from AD 50 – AD 150).
[59] http://www.earlychristianwritings.com/text/ignatius-philadelphians-lightfoot.html (Chapter 4) He was Bishop of Antioch in AD 67 and a student of the Apostle John.
[60] http://www.newadvent.org/fathers/0126.htm Apology 1 Chapter 66

partaking in a whole host of things together, which may be a good thing. If de Botton is braver than I in this endeavour we may well see him not only set up his own church in this way (see more of that later) but get his own communal vibe going in the restaurant scene, and good luck to him. He will be practising what he preaches.

He is also aware of the inviting and friendly signalling that goes on in churches when the service invites the "sign of the peace.[61]" This follows Christ's command to come into His house, as the cornerstone of the Church, with all arguments either left outside the door, but better still forgiven, resolved and surpassed. For de Botton, his restaurants would embrace a slightly different practice, though one based on this sort of notion:

> *"Such a restaurant would have an open door, a modest entrance fee and an attractively designed interior. In its seating arrangements, the groups and ethnicities into which we commonly segregate ourselves would be broken up; family members and couples would be spaced apart, and kith favoured over kin. Everyone would be safe to approach and address, without fear of rebuff or reproach. By simple virtue of occupying the same space, guests would — as in a church — be signalling their allegiance to a spirit of community and friendship."*

Just as what happens in hundreds of thousands of churches across the world each week, in de Botton's restaurants we would observe the following:

> *"Thanks to the Agape Restaurant, our fear of strangers would recede. The poor would eat with the rich, the black with the white, the orthodox with the secular, the bipolar with the balanced, workers with managers, scientists with artists. The claustrophobic pressure to derive all of our satisfactions from our existing relationships would ease, as would our desire to gain status by accessing so-called elite circles."*

---

[61] Paul mentions this in Romans 16:16, 1 Corinthians 16:20, II Corinthians 13:12, 1 Thessalonians and Peter in 1 Peter 5:14

He posits figures of saints as "ideal friends" noting that Catholics draw great comfort, particularly in times of distress, from praying to these figures. In the de Botton religion, there would be no harm in creating your own, who you could reflect upon in times of trouble and apparently receive answers from. But in reality this would just be drawing out from you what you know anyway. The point is slightly missed, as the Catholic prays to the saint a) because it is held that saints exist in an immaterial spiritual world, and b) because their intervention in the material world may assist whatever cause the petitioner is bringing forward. Replacing traditional Christian saints with, I am glad to say, not only film stars and singers, but brave and generously spirited types, eg Lincoln, Whitman, Churchill, Stendhal, Warren Buffet or Paul Smith, will surely not evoke the same kind of reverence. Surely, his hard-headed atheist chums would consider a statute of Paul Smith (the fashion designer, I presume?) in the corner of the room to consult with in times of need, as quite batty.

De Botton's religious world view would seek to change our universities as well. Out go the old subjects, history and literature, to be replaced by valuable material that will "torment and attract our souls." In his own words:

> *"The redesigned universities of the future would draw upon the same rich catalogue of culture treated by their traditional counterparts, likewise promoting the study of novels, histories plays and paintings, but they would teach this material with a view to illuminating students' lives rather than merely prodding at academic goals. Anna Karenina and Madame Bovary I would thus be assigned in a course on understanding the tensions of marriage instead of in one focused on narrative trends in nineteenth-century fiction, just as the recommendations of Epicurus and Seneca would appear in the syllabus for a course about dying rather than in a survey of Hellenistic philosophy."*

One thing is for sure: de Botton is disruptive. I view this as potentially a good thing, and would welcome a shake-up in academia to make it more in line with some of the deeper needs of humanity rather than being, as it often is, a functional means to tick the boxes in order to get a pass, a certificate, a job. In reality, universities should be cultivating a life-long love of learning in all of us as their end product beyond the job whilst the job should be a by-product only. I fear the pendulum has swung too much in recent years towards functionality at the expense of learning and loving the free pursuit of knowledge of all kinds, and de Botton is right to seek to revolutionise this sector. De Botton has a slightly wider vision than I, though would view these institutions somewhat similarly as they are explored by lay elements of the church today, topics like:

> " ... being alone, reconsidering work, improving relationships with children, reconnecting with nature and facing illness. A university alive to the true responsibilities of cultural artefacts within a secular age would establish a Department for Relationships, an Institute of Dying a n d a Centre for Self-Knowledge"

The role of the preacher/teacher would then be very much like that of the "African-American Pentecostal Preachers," as he says in a great quote:

> "Secular education will never succeed in reaching its potential until humanities lecturers are sent to be trained by African-American Pentecostal preachers."

Maybe the atheist preachers could be equally engaging and animated, but one believes he is inspired by God, the other by nature worship, or the "fact" that we are randomly created assemblies of atoms. I don't see any atheist being driven to such heights by his world view. Of course, it is always possible, but I suspect de Botton is beating a dead horse here. He goes on to ape the metaphysical poet and one time Dean of St Pauls, John Donne.:

> "The preaching of John Donne, the Jacobean poet and dean of St Paul's Cathedral, was comparably persuasive, treating complex ideas with an impression/of effortless lucidity. Forestalling the possibility of boredom/during his sermons, Donne would pause every few paragraphs to sum up his thoughts in phrases designed to engrave them-selves on his listeners' skittish minds (`Age is a sicknesse, and youth is an ambush'). Like all compelling aphorists, he had a keen command of binary oppositions ('If you take away due fear, you take away true love'), in his case married to a lyrical sensibility which enabled him to soar along contrails of rare adjectives before bringing his congregation up short with a maxim of homespun simplicity ('Never send to know for whom ' the bell tolls; it tolls for thee'). "

The quote in the last line here issued from Donne's sick bed and not from a sermon, as far as I am aware. I get the point though: he wants his preachers to *move* his congregation.

But truly, de Botton, even in his distrust of the supernatural, has almost surely never read the Gospels. Take this quote:

> *"There is arguably as much wisdom to be found in the stories of Anton Chekhov as in the Gospels, but collections of the former are not bound with calendars reminding readers to schedule a regular review of their insights."*

Even if you strip the Gospels of any supernatural events, they are an outstanding testimony to wisdom, recording and sometimes explaining the parables Jesus used to teach, illustrating how to live a good life. Atheists might profit by reading the Gospels just for these teachings and get much good out of them, arguably far more than from reading Chekov. Just as people can, if religiously minded, read de Botton's colleague, A C Grayling's Secular Bible and get much good out of it as well. But as to his Church, or the new religion for atheists that he purports to be building, I suggest they would do better to stick to readings with key meanings, repeat key readings with key learning, get a rhythm going - then he might have a chance of having a flourishing religion: feed the needs of your congregation.

De Botton recognises the success of Benedictine monks and their monasteries focussing on a programme of care of the body, spirit and mind in contrast with the superficial modern spa with its emphasis on plush toiletries and massages, which are spiritually void places, despite their promises. But his religion for atheists would encourage another disruptive vocation - the re-orienting our some of our architects to build "Temples to Tenderness" where we could contemplate great works of art. This references once again universities:

> *"Like universities, museums promise to fill the gaps left by the ebbing of faith; they too stand to give us meaning without superstition. Just as secular books hold out a hope*

that they can replace the Gospels, so museums may be able to take over the aesthetic responsibilities of churches.

"Christianity, by contrast, never leaves us in any doubt about what art is for: it is a medium to remind us about what matters. It exists to guide us to what we should worship and revile if ₁ we wish to be sane, good people in possession of well-ordered souls. It is a mechanism whereby our memories are forcibly jogged about what we have to love and to be grateful for, as well as what we should draw away from and be afraid of.

"The challenge is to rewrite the agendas for our museums so that art can begin to serve the needs of psychology as effectively as, for centuries, it has served those of theology. Curators should dare to reinvent their spaces so that they can be more than dead libraries for the creations of the past. These curators should co-opt works of art to the direct task of helping us to live: to achieve self-knowledge, to remember forgiveness and love and to stay sensitive to the pains suffered by our ever troubled species and its urgently imperilled planet. Museums must be more than places for displaying beautiful objects. They should be places that use beautiful objects in order to try to make us good and wise. Only then will museums be able to claim that they have properly fulfilled the noble but still elusive ambition of becoming our new churches."

He is explosive with regard to museums, and I think his proposed changes have much to say for themselves.

So the 'School of Life' is his actual Church. Here is a man who does practice what he preaches and I take my hat off to him for that. An article by Daisy Waugh in the Sunday Times Magazine brought it to my attention. [62] She delightfully announces to the world that she is fully free from the last embraces of Catholicism and has fully taken up the atheist world view, or religion. At their Bloomsbury Sunday gathering, there is a sing-song saying, something uplifting, and a reading by someone preaching something morally meaningful/thought provoking. What puzzles me about this is that if you need the soothing rhythms of religion, why not get the real thing and get down to your local synagogue/church/mosque/temple? It seems to me it might be

---

[62] http://www.thesundaytimes.co.uk/sto/Magazine/Regulars/article1157431.ece

because while you reject the belief in any supernatural God or gods, doing away with such belief, you still get all of the things that Daisy went looking for and more in spades, bells and whistles, bling - at the places of the established religions. The 'School' also hosts links to The Philosophers' Mail [63] where you will find daily articles on moral issues and those that provide you with comfort, condolence, and support with much discussion about established religions and how one can learn from these movements how to live a better and more contented life - excluding God.

The 'School' is part of de Botton's alternative religion, and it clearly sets out to provide some people with the spiritual support that he knows all too well established religions provide. It will be very interesting to see how this develops in years to come. I hope for him that his movement gains more traction than the 30,000 member British Humanist Association, which has been promoting a 'no God' alternative for 120 years. A similar organisation called 'The Sunday Assembly' has also been recently established [64] - time will tell if this succeeds or not.

Whether or not, like Christianity, these atheist organisations can persuade billions of people to adopt their way of life and belief systems, I suspect that we, during our life time, will never know, particularly if they have the slow take up of something like the British Humanist Association. Whilst these new religions acknowledge the success of the older established ones in feeding superficial spiritual needs, I suspect that we will continue to prefer the significance of the bells and whistles of the older religions, God included.

The philosopher de Botton is a modern religious practitioner who has created his own 'church', then. Other than that, he is an atheist and does not think any of the arguments to God stack up. I don't know what his metaphysical or pseudo-metaphysical presuppositions are - they are not

---

[63] http://www.philosophersmail.com

[64] http://en.wikipedia.org/wiki/The_Sunday_Assembly

revealed in this book. No doubt he will say none of the above, preferring to believe that reason and reason alone is guiding him: this is my speculation.

Chapter 10 Secular v Religious Murder, a Silly Debate

"All wars are created by religious conflict"[65]

Atheists are very fond of vaguely putting the blame for wars and the practice of ritual murder on 'religion'. Here, I examine two cases involving Christianity before going on to scrutinize other major conflicts for which there is no evidence whatsoever of religious motivation, in order to question such misunderstandings.

Those Religious & Atheist Mass Murders

Without a doubt, if those who hold offices that come with a high degree of fiduciary responsibility to others - doctors, politicians, lawyers, all in receipt of public funds, policemen, judges, trustees, accountants, officers of companies, priests, social workers and so on and so forth - commit crimes, they should be held to a higher account than others, especially if the misdemeanour relates to those to whom that relationship appertains. In the case of the priest and, in general, the Church, we have the terrible and bloody episodes of the Crusades and the Inquisition to deal with.

The Crusades

What was that all about? I turned to the three-Volume Runciman (Runciman, 1990) history of the Crusades to see what the best of scholarship says on the matter in order to really understand what these 'religious' wars were about. I soon discovered all is not as it seems, and that rather than describe this 200 year series of events a religious war it could better be described as being *in the name of religion,* with all the usual human weaknesses of greed, envy , jealously pride and misunderstanding leading the charge.

---

[65] A standard quote trotted out by anyone truly ignorant on matters of history, politics and religion.

The Christian religion for its first three hundred years gains traction by a large scale conversion of Jews and Gentiles. These conversions were all voluntary and taken on in the face of much Roman persecution. What is more, if you were an active leader of the new Christian religion, you almost certainly faced persecution and, in notable circumstances, painful and horrible torture and death. The conversion of Emperor Constantine and the acceptance of the new religion helped mainstream it in the lands of the Roman Empire, which became, by default, Christian lands. This reflected the fact that the majority of the populations in these lands became that way inclined. The context is that from the mid-600s, all the Christian lands in what we call today the Middle East were under attack by the Muslims who had embarked on their unilateral Jihad to subject the whole known world to Islam. Of the five Pentarchies, Jerusalem, Antioch, Alexandria, Constantinople and Rome, all bar Rome fell to Islamic Jihad. Constantinople was the last, in 1453, while Jerusalem, Alexandria and Antioch, each a great and significant Christian city, had fallen to Islamic invasion all within the first 50 years of the creation of Islam. Once occupied, mass murder, forced conversions and heavy taxation were levied if native inhabitants chose to remain Christian – these strictures, we must remember, were an unequivocal instruction of the Qur'an, repeated many times, for Muslims to follow. The burning of Christian churches and the general suppression of people's ability to live a Christian life was the norm then, much as we see the so-called Islamic State today tearing down Christian and other non-Islamic religious monuments, forcing conversions, and killing Christians, unless they can be enslaved and made useful for the Muslim cause. Back then, The Jihad set about wiping Christianity out of its ancient ancestral lands in North Africa, with the exception of Ethiopia, reaching to the doors of Rome, occupying Sicily, Spain and small parts of France. In our more recent history of 100 years ago, the people of the first Christian nation, the Armenians, were subjected to an Islamic led genocide that killed 1.5 million Christians. This is no problem for Islam because, as I said before, a great many places in the Qur'an[66]

---

[66] You can take you pick from these 63 Ayats (Verses) and 19 Surah (Chapters) 2:190-191, 193-194, 216-218, Surah 3:56, 140-143, 151, Surah 4:74, 76, 89, 95 (exemptions from murder are given for certain Muslims), Surah 5:33, Surah 8:7, 12, 15, 39, 59-60, 65, 67, Surah 9:5, 14,

contain clear instruction to kill unbelievers (in Islam), as Allah will be preparing terrible things for them in Hell. Against the background of such a sustained pattern of intolerance towards Christians on the part of Islam, the Crusaders were to respond to a 400-year build-up of consistent oppression. What specifically triggered the first Crusade was that 3000 Christian inhabitants of the Holy Land had been massacred and the Eastern Christian Empire in Constantinople was also under attack from the Seljuk Muslims, so the then Pope, Urban II, requested a military campaign to be launched to assist the Eastern (Christian) Empire and reclaim the Holy Land for Christendom from whom, several hundred years earlier, it had been brutally taken. The Crusades, as they proceeded, had the effect of weakening the hereditary Caliphate as non-descendants of Muhammad came to the fore within it, notably Saladin and Nureddin. Much more co-operation between Muslim and Christian Scholars had previously taken place between Constantinople and the wider Muslim world but Frankish warlords caused the Crusades to come to a brutal end and diminished the current propensity for academic flourishing. Of course this was a failure for theocratic Islam as well. These quotes are taken from the Summary in the third volume of Runciman:

> "The harm done by the crusades to Islam was small in comparison with that done to them to Eastern Christendom. Pope Urban II had bidden the Crusades go forth that the Christians of the East might be helped and rescued. It was a strange rescue; for when the work was over, Eastern Christendom lay under infidel domination and the Crusaders themselves had done all they could to prevent its recovery. When they set themselves up in the East they treated their Christian subjects no better than the Caliph had done before them. Indeed, they were sterner, for they interfered in the religious practices of the local

---

20, 29, 33 (to call to make Islam superior to all religion end of story) 38-39 (if you were Muslin and did not kill willingly, then you will go to hell), 73, 111, 123, Surah 17:16 (ask if they want to covert 1st before "utter destruction," Surah 18:65-81, (parable of Moses re honor killings and killings for apostasy required) , Surah 22:39-40, Surah 24:53, Surah 25:52, Surah 33:18, 23, 25,26, 60-62, Surah 42:39, Surah 47:3-4, 20, 35 Surah 48:17 (Hell if you don't do Jihad), Surah 48:29, Surah 61:4, 9, 10-12, Surah 66:9. Surah 73:20, Surah 98:6. I discount ayats that urge the killing of Jews/Christian/Polytheists in self defense, otherwise most get the instructions to murder non Muslims up to well over 100 ayats.

churches. When they were ejected they left the local Christians unprotected to bear the wrath of the Moslem conquerors." (Runciman, 1990)

Today, in Syria, we still see the remnants of the on-going destruction of Christianity in that area playing itself out.[67] The intolerance of the Franks and their inability to understand their Christian brothers and sisters - little indeed to do with religion but rather on total non-acceptance or incomprehension that these people were different to them - led to the wipe-out of the last parts of the Roman Empire and its overthrow:

> *"Its was the Crusaders themselves who wilfully broke down the defense of Christendom and thus allowed the infidel to cross the Straits and penetrate into the heart of Europe. The true martyrs of the Crusade were not the gallant knights who fell fighting at the Horns of Hattin or before the towers of Acre, but the innocent Christians of the Balkans, as well as of Anatolia and Syria, who were handed over to persecution and slavery."*

(Runciman, 1990)

The Frankish princes, whilst originally motivated by faith, were soon overcome by more base human motives: "genuine faith was often combined with unashamed greed." Material advantages, and land and power grabs, enslavement of native Christians (whose traditions and practices they could not understand) soon started driving the motive for conquest:

> *"The triumphs of the Crusade were the triumphs of faith. But faith without wisdom is a dangerous thing. By the inexorable laws of history the whole world pays for the crimes and follies of each of its citizens. In the long sequence of interaction and fusion between Orient and Occident out of which our civilisation has grown, the Crusades were a tragic and destructive episode. The historian as he gazes back across the centuries at their gallant story must find his admiration overcast by sorrow at the witness that bears to the limitations of human nature. There was so much courage and so little honour, so much devotion and so little understanding. High ideals were besmirched by cruelty and greed, enterprise and endurance by a blind and narrow self-righteousness; and the Holy War*

---

[67] **Radical** Islam is certainly bad religion with bad men (in the main) prosecuting a death cult war, that cant be doubted, but their perversion of Islam should not allow us to aggregate all religions into the same pot.

itself was nothing more than a long act of intolerance in the name of God, which is the sin against the Holy Ghost." (Runciman, 1990)

What can we conclude from this? That God is not the problem: man was, and still is.

When trying to determine the exact numbers of the deaths caused in the 200 odd year period known as the Crusades and the 350 year period of the Spanish Inquisition, there is no hard and fast number to quote. I decided to conduct a web search and came across the web site called www.necrometrics.com . This is run by a librarian called Matthew White, who seems to have complied a comprehensive list of some of the most terrible things man has done to man. His survey of history puts the death toll of the 200 years of the Crusades at 3m. The overwhelming majority are the result of wars driven by desires to take territories and resources, with very little attributed specifically to religiously-driven wars. The popular refrain that we tend to hear - "all wars are religious wars," or variations of this theme - is simply not supported by the evidence. This is shown in the Appendix.

The Spanish Inquisition

This was the Spanish monarchs' way of enforcing the ongoing conversion (to Christianity) of those Muslims and Jews who were left once the Spanish had liberated their lands from these occupiers. It is considered one of the bloodiest moments in Christian history. We have estimates in the low thousands to several hundreds of thousands during this 350 history of Inquisition. The Appendix shows a list of key scholars and their estimates. That these deaths are a stain on the history of the Christian Church is not in doubt, but they are just a small fraction compared with incidents of secular blood-letting, which we will go on to explore. The Inquisition amounted to religious persecution over many three and a half centuries, but it pales into insignificance compared with man-on-man secular blood-letting.

The Atheist Wars

"Religious wars really are fought in the name of religion, and they have been horribly frequent in history. I cannot think of any war that has been fought in the name of atheism. Why should it? A war might be motivated by economic greed, by political ambition, by ethnic or racial prejudice, by deep grievance or revenge, or by patriotic belief in the destiny of a nation. Even more plausible as a motive for war is an unshakeable faith that one's own religion is the only true one, reinforced by a holy book that explicitly condemns all heretics and followers of rival religions to death, and explicitly promises that the soldiers of God will go straight to a martyrs' heaven. Sam Harris, as so often, hits the bullseye, in The End of Faith: The danger of religious faith is that it allows otherwise normal human beings to reap the fruits of madness and consider them holy. Because each new generation of children is taught that religious propositions need not be justified in the way that all others must, civilization is still besieged by the armies of the preposterous. We are, evennow, killing ourselves over ancient literature. Who would have thought something so tragically absurd could be possible? By contrast, why would anyone go to war for the sake of an absence of belief?" (Dawkins, The God Delusion, 2006)

I don't know any wars, as Dawkins suggests, which have been motivated by a purely atheistic world view. Having said that, although there are religious wars, these amount to but a small fraction of the extent of secular wars. Take the modern case of Northern Ireland. We are told it is all boils down to a case of Catholics v Protestants. Having spent some time in the North of the island of Ireland[68], I can absolutely say I have never heard anyone say they were doing their bombing to force people to believe in the Eucharist as an act of remembrance, or as the enactment of the real presence of Christ. To my knowledge, regarding the Christian West v the Christian East (a reconciliation

---

[68] The common language in Northern Ireland to discuss the "Troubles" is actually conducted in the form of Nationalist (pro Irish) v Loyalist (pro British) viewpoints . This is witnessed by the fact that many people who have the "Catholic" label added to them vote for parties labeled "Protestant" when in fact they are voting to remain economically tied to Britain rather than Ireland.

between those two branches of Christianity, still to my knowledge is not formally concluded, although peaceful for many centuries now) the battle cry had been 'kill these schismatics they don't believe the son proceeds from the father but that he follows from the father." When a suicide bomber from Islam chooses to end his life by including in his last message quotes from the Prophet Mohamed, he may be doing so because he feels that in his country his way of life is being oppressed to the extent that he can only have resort to an act of extreme desperation, for right or for wrong. Never do they say: "I am bombing you because you don't believe in the revelation given to Muhammad, end of.[69]". When you dig past the label of 'religious war' you begin to see that seems to be about not liking difference in others: their customs, their practices. Above all, it appears to be about territorial (economic) gain, and control. This is about man's intolerance towards his fellow man. So I would agree with the atheist when he says: don't do suicide missions (or at least not yet, we will need to see how this religion grows as there is a militant edge to it that could sow the seeds for extremism) - to promote atheist religion per se. But then neither does the man who is overtly religious, who understands his theology and the doctrinal issues contained within his religion.

That said, looking at historically recorded wars, the biggest in terms of human death by hundreds of millions are secular wars driven by the same motives of intolerance, contempt for other ways of life, economic and territorial control for enrichment of the conquerors and so on. I attest that atheism *is* a religion. I do not hold that it is free of belief. It has its pre-suppositions, some of which we have explored, just like any other system of beliefs. I do use the word atheist in the next section, tongue in cheek - more to make the point that just as the atheist can label all manner of wars religious, very few actually are, so a theist, on those same terms, can label many, many worse atrocities atheist. Although, granted, the motives of the three I look at

---

[69] http://www.huffingtonpost.co.uk/mehdi-hasan/jihadist-radicalisation-islam-for-dummies_b_5697160.html Enough said, religious warriors they certainly are not. I also suspect that vast majority of the IS gang know very little indeed about their creed.

(the wars caused by Hitler, Stalin and Mao) can't be placed in the same category as anything coming from Dawkins or Harris!

However, atheist secular socialists managed to kill over 140,000,000[70] people in the last century alone. The commonality in their ideology is their atheism - their belief in social Darwinism in the specific case of Hitler and Stalin, and a belief in the ownership of the means of production, distribution and exchange being owned by 'the people', communally, for the benefit of all, purportedly, although these are, of course, expressed this differently in each respective case. Alone among them, Hitler favoured the corporatist version of socialism, with a strongly nationalist bent. This meant you were still allowed to own private property, so long as it was exclusively working in the interest of the advancement of the racial goals or national goals of the state. For the others, it was common ownership by the state, driven by the state for the advancement of the state. For avoidance of doubt, both socialist variations - national or international - invariably indicate control by the particular gang of criminals who occupy the commanding positions of the apparatus of the state, despite the seeming laudable exhortations by the original founder's socialism.

Hitler

If there was any doubt about Hitler's views on religion, I would urge you to consult the Nuremberg Trial documents from the 6th of July 1945.[71] These are titled ANNEX 4: THE PERSECUTION OF THE CHRISTIAN CHURCHES

> *"Throughout the period of National Socialist rule, religious liberties in Germany and in the occupied areas were seriously impaired. The various Christian Churches were*

---

[70] Bullock in his Appendices (Bullock, 1991) puts the figure of losses caused by the atheist socialists during the Second World War at 40m in Europe and the USA, this is additional to the 100m specifically socialist caused wars mentioned by Courtois. Its is also worth mentioning that the First World War caused 7.7m deaths, the Russian Civil War 10m, the Spanish Civil War 600,000. The Chinese losses are estimates at anywhere between 10m and 22m deaths during the Second World War.

[71] http://www.leics.gov.uk/the_nazi_master_plan.pdf

systematically cut off from effective communication with the people. They were confined as far as possible to the performance of narrowly religious functions, and even within this narrow sphere were subjected to a many hindrances as the Nazis dared to impose. These results were accomplished partly by legal and partly by illegal and terroristic means.

"National Socialism by its very nature was hostile to Christianity and the Christian churches. The purpose of the National Socialist movement was to convert the German people into a homogeneous racial group united in all its energies for [the] prosecution of aggressive warfare.
"Innumerable indications of this fact are to be found in the speeches and writing[s] of Hitler and other responsible Nazi leaders..."

What is clear when you read this is that Hitler and his gang tolerated Christianity, but only under strict conditions. Then the screw was progressively turned, using legal restrictions, bans and active thuggery towards believers until he could engineer a total destruction of the churches. He was obsessed with his own religiously styled beliefs in "Providence[72]" driving both himself and the world inexorably to a Nazi 1000 year paradise of national socialist racial purity. Hitler was for the removal of all religious outlooks other than his own. The Jewish faith, needless to say, was the first to go. The Christian faith, so long as it could be controlled and marshaled in the interest of the Reich, could be lived with, for now, until all the churches could be destroyed. Himmler with his paganism, and Hess, with his astrology, were laughed at, by their National Socialist friends.

"On the other hand Hitler's own myth at least had to be protected, and this led him like Napoleon, to speak frequently of Providence, as a necessary if unconscious projection of his sense of destiny which provided him with both justification and absolution . 'The Russians', he remarked on one occasion[73], 'were entitled to attack their priests, but they

---

[72] I note that this belief in Providence is remarkably similar, but should not be confused to the atheist nature worship that we have explored with Dawkins and Grayling, the latter we have seen evokes mystery in the purpose of nature in his Good Book, tempting though it is , I expect Hitler's was a much more personal providential mysterious guidance as opposed to the more general guidance of the nature suggested by Grayling.

[73] Hitler's Table Talk http://vho.org/aaargh/fran/livres10/HTableTalk.pdf

> had no right to assail the idea of a supreme force . It's a fact that we're feeble creatures and that a creative force exists.'" (Bullock, 1991)

Hitler believed in the forces of nature he felt were propelling him. This should not be confused with the nature worship we see in Grayling's 'The Good Book'. The promotion of the myth of Hitler is well documented, with his use of film, using the acclaimed director Leni Riefenstahl, and architecture, via the work of Albert Speer. To the eternal shame of the German nation, the majority were fully behind this movement, but the earliest challenge to the indoctrination of all the German people came from the church:

> "Resistance took the form of a call for a Confessional Church 'independent of the state and the pressure of political power', led by two Berlin pastors Martin Niemoeller, a former U-boat captain, and the young Dietrich Bonhoeffer, with the backing of the leading Lutheran theologian Karl Barth.' (Bullock, 1991)

The Barmen Declaration of May 1934 rejected the false teaching by which the state is equated with the sole total order of human life. It also attacked persecution of the Jews, the cult of the Fuhrer and unlawful actions of the Gestapo.[74] However, it should be pointed out that there was a minority section of the church who formed the Nazi Movement of German Christians, who sought to abolish all church councils and, in true Nazi style, have one Reich Bishop, the army chaplain, Ledwig Muller, running the show for the advancement of the Reich. Such a state of affairs did not develop into anything serious and lasting.

> "There were two institutions in Germany which still retained some independence. The first was the Churches." (Bullock, 1991)

---

[74] Hence the murders of the likes of Pastor Paul Schneider, The Blessed Otto Neururer, Pastor Dietrich Bonhoeffer, Friar Maximilian Kolbe, Nun Edith Stein to name but a few who the Nazi Machine needed to exterminate due to their intolerable Christian and thus anti Nazi views, come to mind as tragic testimony to the anti theistic, atheist stance of the National Socialist German Workers Party: The Nazi Party, that atheist killing machine.

The other was the professional Army.

In addition, the flavor of the National Socialism of Hitler and his German National Socialist Workers' Party was his racial commitment to advancing what he deemed to be his race, over and above any other. This is a socialist, Darwinian war of all against all. For the record, I am in no way suggesting Darwin would have agreed with this, neither that any atheist would - just that this is what Hitler believed. A reading of "Mein Kampf" clearly demonstrates this (Hitler, 1925). He was devoid of any religious belief, and was a throrough, out and out, secular mass murderer.

Stalin

Likewise, Stalin was a great admirer of Darwin and his own form of social Darwinism was more at the class struggle end of the spectrum. He did not racially select; rather, he party politically selected and externimated anyone who did not agree, or demonstrated nonconformity. The historian Paul Johnson comments :

> "Stalin had Darwin's 'struggle' and 'survival of the fittest' in mind when dealing with the Kulaks and when relocating the minorities of Greater Russia: extermination of groups was a natural event if the party, redefined as the politically 'fit,' was to survive"
> (Johnson, 2012)

In his early life, Satlin had wanted to be a priest. However, one noted biographer of Stalin cites his reading of the Origin of Species, as his descent into a godless, atheistic world view took hold. This was obviously prior to initiating his regime of mass murder:

> "If he coveted a volume , he was happy to steal it from another schoolboy ....he paid a 5 kopeck subscription and borrowed a book that was probably Darwin's Origin of Species .

Stalin read it all night, forgetting to sleep, until Keke found him. 'Time to go to bed,' she said . 'Go to sleep-dawn is breaking.' 'I loved the book so much, Mummy, I couldn't stop reading ....' As his reading intensified , he piety wavered. One day Sos and some friends , including Grisha Glurjidze, lay on the grass in town talking about the injustice of there being rich and poor when he amazed all of them by suddenly saying: 'God's not unjust, he doesn't actually exist. We've been decieved. If God existed, he'd have made the world more just.'" (Sebag Montefiore, 2007)

By 1930, with the collectivisation of farms in progress at an accelerating pace, the quest to enlighten the backward peasantry on the modernity of socialism, the "fierce campaign against the Orthodox Church" had begun. The Orthodox Church was:

"the centre of traditional peasant culture , which was seen by the Stalisint leasdership as one of the main obstacles to collectivisation. In village after village , not only was the church closed, but the cross was knocked from the cupola, the bells removed and icons burned. Historic Russian churches were the object of destruction and many priests were arrested. The monasteries were closed ...., and thousands of monks and nuns were deported to Siberia. By the end of 1930, roughly 80 per cent of village churches are said to have been closed." (Bullock, 1991)

Like Hitler when he needeed all the support he could get during in his darkest hours, Stalin cynically created a reconcillaition with the Church in 1943 in order to motivate nationalism in what he termed "The Great Patriotic War" against Hitler:

"The invasion and the terrible causalties awakened a strong tide of religious feeling in the country and the Metropolitia Sergei issued an appeal to all beleivers, calling on them to defend the country. In September 1943-four months after he abolished the Communist International –Stalin received the three metropolitains and concluded what ammounted to a concordat with them, allowing them for the first time since the revolution to elect a Patriarch of Moscow and All Russia as well as a Holy Synod, and to open a theological institute." (Bullock, 1991)

Concernng the other mass murdering secular killers of the brutal 20th century -

Mao, and Pol Pot - I could not establish whether they were or were not influenced by Darwin. However, I am not aware of it being disputed that they were atheists. Godless types. A summary list of their blood letting will follow to illustrate my point. A must-read book which lists these secular killings was the French publishing sensation translated as "The Black Book of Communism" which tracks the murderous deeds of the socialist pioneers:

> *"The following rough approximation, based on unofficial estimates, gives some sense of the scale and gravity of these crimes:*
>
> *U.S.S.R.: 20 million deaths*
> *China: 65 million deaths*
> *Vietnam: 1 million deaths*
> *North Korea: 2 million deaths*
> *Cambodia: 1 million deaths*
> *Eastern Europe: 1 million deaths*
> *Latin America: 150,000 deaths*
> *Africa: 1.7 million deaths*
> *Afghanistan: 1.5 million deaths*
> *Communist movement and Communist parties not in power: about 10,000 deaths*
>
> *The Total approaches 100 million people killed."* (Courtois, 2000)

The authors of the above statistics don't equate - as I do - the socialism of the above with the socialism of Hitler. I don't make a distinction between the socialist, the national, or the international variety of motivation. The Nazis killed six million Jews, and approximately another 20 million were killed in World War II; Round it off at 125 million deaths, give or take a few million: such is the value of human life to war mongers. Give or take *a few million souls* here and there and you won't be far off anyway.

Is it correct to call these atheist-inspired or Darwin-inspired deaths? No, they are neither, just tragic, human blood-letting on political, cultural or ethnic grounds. I write this to goad my holier-than-thou humanist, rationalist, atheist friends who seem to think their world view produces harmony whereas religion does not. I also use it as a way to illustrate that the problem is not the ideas themselves, but people and their employment of them. Socialism - national or international, with its secular anchorage - was a bad idea from the outset.

Granted, the small unit of a family can be run on socialist lines with success. But what is for sure is that when you advance beyond that stage and start to apply such an ideology to large communities then the ability, say, to understand the price signals that tell an entrepreneur what to produce, when, in what combinations of factors of production, over what period of time with what combination of factors of production are decided by the central planners in the socialist system is lost. Let me expand upon this a little. The impossibility of calculating and replacing price signals was well documented by Mises in 1922 (Mises L. v., 1922) & (Mises L. v., Socialism , 1936) and during the 1920s was called 'The Socialist Calculation Debate'. Hayek's variation on this theme was in labeling this the 'knowledge problem' (Hayek F. , 1935) which arises by looking at any one planner's limitations to absorbing all the knowledge necessary to be able to instruct production of goods and services for whole nations. You cannot replicate the market with all its dispersed participants making their best rational decisions about what to produce, with what, and for what, prices etc and expect to get a better allocation of resources or a better wealth creation process than the market left to its own devices. Interestingly, Hayek's Nobel lecture on "The Pretense of Knowledge"[75] 40 odd years later was to be on this very subject.

It is not acceptable to say you are a Nazi today, as the racial element in the socialist program of Hitler is universally deemed odious. But it seems you can be accepted as a former supporter of these mass extermination communist regimes because they were after all trying to 'do it for the poor'. A noble cause, then, and we can politely gloss over the gulags, prison camps, dissident murder programs and the lot of it. It is peculiar that those 'religious' wars, the Crusades and the Inquisition, the wars of the Protestant Reformation and so on, attract

---

[75] http://www.nobelprize.org/nobel_prizes/economic-sciences/laureates/1974/hayek-lecture.html

opprobrium almost equal to the genocide caused by Hitler, despite being but a fraction in size and terror - while all is apparently forgiven as far as the atheistic, socialistic, intellectual apologists are concerned. These are double standards I truly detest. An enforced death, by whatever it is motivated - whether it be religious, political, ideological, fanatical - is to be condemned and resisted.

Let us now move on very briefly to another atheist monster.

Mao

"Today, two big mountains lie like a dead weight on the Chinese people. One is imperialism, the other is feudalism. The Chinese Communist Party has long made up its mind to dig them up. We must preserve and work unceasingly, and we, too, will touch God's heart. Our God is none other than the masses of the Chinese people. If they stand up and dig together with us, why can't these two mountains be cleared away." (Mao, 1945)

"Saying Good-bye to the God of Disease (1)
Mauve waters and green mountains are nothing
when the great ancient doctor Hua Tuo
could not defeat a tiny worm.
A thousand villages collapsed, were choked with weeds,
men were lost arrows.
Ghosts sang in the doorway of a few desolate houses.
Yet now in a day we leap around the earth
or explore a thousand Milky Ways.
And if the cowherd who lives on a star
asks about the god of plagues,
tell him, happy or sad, the god is gone,
washed away in the waters."

JULY 1, 1958[76] (Mao C. Z., 1972)

---

[76] MAO ZEDONG'S NOTE "After reading in the People's Daily of June 30, 1958, that in Yukiang county the parasitic leech the schistosome had been eliminated, my head was so filled with thoughts that I could not sleep. As a slight breeze came and blew in the dawn, and early morning sun came and knocked at the window, I looked at the distant southern skies and happily guided my pen into composing a poem." TITLE This poem and the one following are

Saying Good-bye to the God of Disease (2)

> "Thousands of willow branches in a spring wind.
> Six hundred million of China, land of the gods,
> and exemplary like the emperors Shun and Yao.
> A scarlet rain of peach blossoms turned into waves
> and emerald mountains into bridges.
> Summits touch the sky.
> We dig with silver shovels
> and iron arms shake the earth and the Three Rivers.
> God of plagues, where are you going?
> We burn paper boats and bright candles (Mao C. Z., 1972)
> to light his way to heaven."

JULY I, 1958

Ironically, since the demise of Mao China has experienced an explosion in the growth of Christianity, which was illegal until recently, and currently there is a minimum of 70 million practising members of churches in China. By 2030, following the current growth pattern, it will be the largest Christian country in the world.[77] This Christianty business just won't go away!

---

separate yet related poems, each on the subject of eliminating disease. Schistosomiasis, found also in Egypt and North Africa, had plagued many districts south of the Yangzi. A commission was set up in 1956 and in June 1958 it was reported that the parasites and the disease had been eradicated in Yujiang county in Jiangxi, as a result of filling in infected ponds, irrigation projects, and a new cure which shortened the disease's duration from months to a few days. The referenceto southern skies is to the areas most troubled by the disease. (Mao C. Z., 1972)

[77] http://www.telegraph.co.uk/news/worldnews/asia/china/10776023/China-on-course-to-become-worlds-most-Christian-nation-within-15-years.html I am grateful for Alan McCormick of The Legatum Foundation for pointing out this article .

Child Sacrifice and the Bible

It is interesting to note that the bible contains 58 verses condeming child sacrifice. [78] Regretably, in the most modern wars we are still scarificing our children on a large scale but we don't do this on the altar, like the Cannanites once did, we do it on the battlefield. One of the most striking Bible passages is in Genesis 22:1-19, the story of Abraham and the confirmation of his faith concerning the command to sacrifice Issac, his son, which is the most stark warning against child sacrifice ever made in the Bible. The story unfolds as God tells Abraham three times he must sacrifice his son (verses 2, 12 &16). However, he knows that as he leaves he will return with his son Issac (v5). in Herbews, 11:17-19, it is explained that he knew that either way he was coming back with the boy. This is because Abraham trusted in God, and thus a scapegoat is provided at the last minute showing that ultimately it is only God who who can sacrifice a son, and, when viewed in hindsight, this son of God is Jesus, in a one off sacrifice for all mankind. So we have one known, God-driven sacrifice of a son in the last 2000 years, yet there are countless unaccountable deaths of our our sons and daughters caused by the collateral damage of non-religious wars. The claim that religion is responsible for most wars is simply untenable, as discussed above. The fact that we still partake in child sacrifice during wars shows we have not learnt much in 4000 odd years since Abraham and Isaac.

---

[78] http://www.openbible.info/topics/child_sacrifice

Conclusion

Undoubtedly, I have to conclude that the secular juggernaut is in the ascendancy. The atheists lead the charge. They keep sowing the seeds of doubt wherever they can. In answer to this, I hope I have demonstrated that it is still rational to hold faith in the most perfect being: God. I hope also that I have shown that there is no real conflict between faith and science - indeed, both support each other. More to the point, I hope I have sown a few seeds to show that these leading high priests of what is actually a deeply religious belief system, that of atheism, hold their views on blind faith - and they don't even know it. They are sophisticated, patronising, and pretentious pagan mystics and should be recognised as such. People who acknowledge the Deity should have the complete confidence to cede no ground to them.

In Book Two of the Series, "Against Atheism: The Case for Christ", I will offer some of the empirical evidence in scripture that supports the Jewish and then the Christian view of God. Once again, this is for the rational believer. It is not a spiritual investigation into the Godhead. It might help people who, in the midst of this secular nothingness, where every value is as good as the next one, to acquire more secure footings - *reasonable* ones - for them to stand on as they embark upon their spiritual journey of becoming.

Toby Baxendale,
Hertfordshire UK, June 2015

Acknowledgments

To Dr Jane Taylor, who has read this work on many occasions and offered suggestions and some proof reading. To my wife, Catherine, for her support in this project. To my colleague at the Legatum Institute, the historian Hywel Williams, for his review and comments. And to Professor J Guido Huslmann and his fellow professors and PhD students at the University of Angers who kindly took part in a seminar on two of my chapters. Also, I would like to thank our local priest, the Rev Dr David Munchin, for his reading of parts of this book as well as Canon Rev Alistair MacDonald-Radcliff for his helpful criticism.

Appendix: The Body Count

"Crusades (1095-1291) **3,000,000**
Estimated totals:
Robertson, John M., *A Short History of Christianity* (1902) p.278: 9,000,000
Aletheia, *The Rationalist's Manual*: 5,000,000
Henry William Elson, *Modern Times and the Living Past*, (1921) p. 261: 5,000,000
Om Prakesh Jaggi, *Religion, Practice and Science of Non-violence*, (1974) p. 40:
"The crusades cost Europe five million young men"
Fielding Hudson Garrison, *Notes on the History of Military Medicine*, Association of Military Surgeons, (1922) p. 106: 3,000,000 total, incl. 2,000,000 Europeans
MEDIAN: 3 million
Philip Alexander Prince, *Parallel universal history, an outline of the history and biography of the world divided into ...* (1838) p.207: "Although two million souls perished in the Crusades..."
Charles Mackay, *Memoirs of Extraordinary Popular Delusions and the Madness of Crowds* (1841): 2,000,000 Europeans killed.
[http://www.bootlegbooks.com/NonFiction/Mackay/PopDelusions/chap09.html]
Wertham: 1,000,000
John Shertzer Hittell, *A Brief History of Culture* (1874) p.137: "In the two centuries of this warfare one million persons had been slain..."
NOTE: No scholar has ever published a death toll of less than one million or more than nine million, so the order of magnitude is generally accepted even if the precise number is unknown.
Individual Events:
Davies: Crusaders killed up to 8,000 Jews in Rhineland
Paul Johnson *A History of the Jews* (1987): 1,000 Jewish women in Rhineland comm. suicide to avoid the mob, 1096.
Gibbon, *Decline and Fall of the Roman Empire*, v.5, 6
1st Crusade: 300,000 Eur. k at Battle of Nice [Nicea].
Crusaders vs. Solimon of Roum: 4,000 Christians, 3,000 Moslems
1098, Fall of Antioch: 100,000 Moslems massacred.
50,000 Pilgrims died of disease.
1099, Fall of Jerusalem: 70,000 Moslems massacred.
Siege of Tiberias: 30,000 Christians k.
Siege of Tyre: 1,000 Turks
Richard the Lionhearted executes 3,000 Moslem POWs.
1291: 100,000 Christians k after fall of Acre.
Fall of Christian Antioch: 17,000 massacred.
[TOTAL: 677,000 listed in these episodes here.]
Catholic Encyclopedia (1910) [http://www.newadvent.org/cathen/]
Jaffa: 20,000 Christians massacred, 1197
Sorokin estimates that French, English & Imperial German Crusaders lost a total of 3,600 in battle.
1st C (1096-99): 400
2nd C (1147-49): 750
3rd C (1189-91): 930
4th C (1202-04): 120
5th C (1228-29): 600
7th C (1248-54): 700
James Trager, *The People's Chronology* (1992)
1099: Crusaders slaughter 40,000 inhabs of Jerusalem. Dis/starv reduced Crusaders from 300,000 to 60,000.
1147: 2nd Crusades begins with 500,000. "Most" lost to starv./disease/battle.
1190: 500 Jews massacred in York.

1192: 3rd Crusade reduced from 100,000 to 5,000 through famine, plagues and desertions in campaign vs Antioch.
1212: Children's Crusade loses some 50,000.
[TOTAL: Just in these incidents, it appears the Europeans lost around 650,000.]
Albigensian Crusade (1208-49) **1,000,000**
The traditional death toll given for the war against the Cathars is one million, which is repeated in these:
John M. Robertson, *A Short History of Christianity*, London: Watts, 1902, p.254 ("It has been reckoned that a million of all ages and both sexes were slain.")
Christopher Brookmyre, *Not the End of the World* (New York: Grove Press, 1998) p.39
Max Dimont, *Jews, God, and History*, (New York: Penguin, 1994) p.225: 1,000,000 Frenchmen suspected of being Albigensians slain
Dizerega Gus, *Pagans & Christians: The Personal Spiritual Experience* (St. Paul, MN: Llewellyn, 2001) p.195
Helen Ellerbe, *The Dark Side of Christian History* (Orlando, FL: Morningstar & Lark, 1995) p.74
Michael Newton, *Holy Homicide* (Port Townsend, WA: Loompanics Unlimited, 1998) p.117
Rummel: 200,000 democides
Individual incidents:
Flexner, *Pessimist's Guide to History*: 20,000 massacred in Beziers.
Ellerbe:
Beziers: 20-100,000
St. Nazair: 12,000
Tolouse: 10,000
Newton: 20-100,000 massacred in Beziers.
Sumption, *Albigensian Crusade* (1978): <5,000 k. by Inquisition [ca. 1229-1279]

Spanish Inquisition (1478-1834)
Cited in Will Durant, *The Reformation* (1957):
Juan Antonio Llorente, General Secretary of the Inquisition from 1789 to 1801, estimated that 31,912 were executed, 1480-1808.
In contrast to the high estimate cited above, Durant tosses his support to the following low estimates:
Hernando de Pagar, secretary to Queen Isabella, estimated 2,000 burned before 1490.
An unnamed "Catholic historian" estimated 2,000 burned, 1480-1504, and 2,000 burned, 1504-1758.
Flexner, *Pessimist's Guide to History*: 8,800 deaths by burning, 1478-1496
Philip Schaff, *History of the Christian Church* (1910): 8,800 burnt in 18 years of Torquemada. (acc2 Buckle and Friedländer)
4. Motley, *Rise of the Dutch Republic*: 10,220 burnt in 18 years of Torquemada
Britannica: 2,000
Aletheia, *The Rationalist's Manual*: 35,534 burned.
Fox's Book of Martyrs, Ch.IV: 32,000 burned
Paul Johnson *A History of the Jews* (1987): 32,000 k. by burning; 20,226 k. before 1540
Wertham: 250,000
Rummel: 350,000 deaths overall.
MEDIAN: 8,800 under Torq.; 32,000 all told.
Punished by all means, not death.
Fox: 309,000
P. Johnson: 341,000
Motley: 114,401

Bibliography

Alford, H. (1863). *The Greek Testament, With a Critically Revised Text* (5th Edition considerably Revised ed., Vol. 1). London, UK: Rivingtons.
Anselm, S. o. (2001). *Proslogion.* (T. Williams, Trans.) Hackett Publishing Compnay Inc Indianapolis.
Aristotle. (1995). *The Complete Works of Aristotle The Revised Oxford Translation* (6th Printing with corrections ed., Vol. Vol II). (J. Barnes, Ed.) Princeton: Princeton University Press.
Armstrong, K. (1994). *A History of God, The 4,000 Year Quest if Judaism, Christianity and Islam* (Peperback ed.). Ballantine Books New York.
Ayer, A. (1936). *Language, Truth and Logic* (First ed.). Victor Gollancz.
Ayer, A. (1977). *Part of My Life* (Vol. Vol I). London: Collins.
Ayer, A. (1982). *Philosophy in the Tewntieth Century* (First ed.). London, UK: Weidenfeld and Nicolson Ltd.
Ayer, A. (1971). *Russell and Moore: The Analytical Heritage* (First ed.). Cambridge, Massachusetts: Harvard University Press.
Barrow, J. T. (2009). *The Anthropic Cosmological Principle* (Reprint of 1986 Edition ed.). Oxford, UK: Oxford University Press.
Baxendale, T. (2015). Did Jesus in His Own Words Describe or Reveal His Divinity?
Blaiklock, E. (1951). *The Tyndale New Testament Lecture for 1951 The Christian in Pagan Society*. London, UK: The Tyndale Press.
Bradley, F. (1893). *Appearance and Reality A Metaphysical Essay* (First ed.). Swan Sonnenschein & Son.
Bruce, F. (1965). *Commentary on the Book of the Acts* (Special Edition published with W M Eerdmans Publishing Co ed.). London, UK: Marshall, Morgan & Scott.
Bullock, A. (1991). *Hitler and Stalin Parallel Lives* (First ed.). Harper Collins.
Collingwood, R. (1928). *Affirmation Series "Faith and Reason"* (1st ed.). UK: London Ernest Benn.
Collingwood, R. (1940). *Metaphysics* (First ed.). Oxford, The Clarendon Press 1940.
Collingwood, R. *Philosophical Method* (First ed.). Oxford, The Clarendon Press.
Collingwood, R. (1933). *Philosophical Method*. Oxford: Clarendon Press.
Collingwood, R. (1927). *Reason is Faith Cultivating Itself* (1st Edition ed., Vol. XXVI). Hibbert Journal.
Collingwood, R. (1916). *Religion and Philosophy.* MacMillan.
Collingwood, R. (1946). *The Idea of History* (First ed.). Oxford: Clarendon Press, Oxford University.
Collingwood, R. (1942). *The New Leviathan or Man, Society and Barbarism* (First ed.). Oxford, UK: Clarendon Press.
Collingwood, R. *The Principles of Art* (First ed.). Oxford, The Claren don Press.
Conway, D. *Philosophy and the Rediscovery of Wisdom, the Quest for Sophia.* MacMillan.

Corey, M. (2007). *The God Hypothesis Discovering Design in Our "Just Right" Goldilocks Universe* (First Paperback ed.). Plymouth, UK: Rowman & Littlefield Publishing Inc.
Courtois, W. P. (2000). *The Black Book of Communism* (First English Edition, Third Printing ed.). (M. Kramer, Ed., & J. K. Murphy, Trans.) Harvard.
Cusa, N. (2001). *Complete Philosophical and Theological Treatises of Nicholas Cusa* (First ed., Vol. Vol1). (J. Hopkins, Trans.) Minneapolis, Minnesota, USA: The Arthur J Banning Press.
Darwin, C. (1859). *On the Origin of Species or the Preservation of Favoured Races in the Struggle for Life* (First Edition ed.). London: John Murray.
Darwin, C. (1896). *The Descent of Man And Selection in Relation to Sex* (Second, Revised and Augmented Thirty-Third Thousand ed.). London, UK: John Murray.
David, D. A. (1928). *Affirmations, God in the Modern World* (1St ed.). Ernest Benn Ltd.
Davies, J. B. (2013). *God Versus Particle Physics A No-Score Draw.* Imprint Academic.
Davies, W. (1948). *Paul and Rabbinic Judaism Some Rabbinic Elements in Pauline Theology* (First ed.). London, UK: S.P.C.K.
Dawkins, R. (2013). *An Appetite for Wonder The Making of a Scientist A Memoir* (First ed., Vol. I). London, UK: Bantam Press.
Dawkins, R. (1981). In Defence of Selfish Genes. *Philosophy, Vol 56.*
Dawkins, R. (1986). *The Blind Watch Maker.* London, UK: Longmans.
Dawkins, R. (2006). *The God Delusion* (First ed.). Bantam Press.
Dawkins, R. (1976). *The Selfish Gene* (First ed.). Oxford University Press.
Dawkins, R. *The Selfish Gene 30th Anniversary Edition* (30th Anniversary Edition ed.). Oxford University Press.
de Botton, A. (2012). *Religion for Atheists* (First ed.). Hamish Hamilton.
Dennett, D. (1996). *Darwins' Dangerous Idea Rvolution and the Meaning of Life.* Penguin.
Denton, M. (1986). *Evolution: A Theory in Crisis New Developments in Scirnce are Challenging Orthodox Darwinism* (First USA Edition, Originally Published by Burnett Books UK 1985 ed.). Bethseda, Maryland, USA: Adler & Adler.
Dombrowski, D. (2006). *Rethinking the Ontological Argument, A Neoclassical Theistic Response.* CAmbridge University Press.
Dunn, J. D. (2003). *Eerdmans Commentary on the Bible* (First ed.). Grand Rapids, Michigan/Cambridge, UK: William B Eerdmans Publishing Company.
Flew, A. w. (2007). *There is a God How the World's Most Notorious Atheist Changed His Mind.* Harper One An Imprint of Harper Collins Publishers.
Freedman, D. (2000). *Eerdmans Dictionary of the Bible* (First ed.). Grand Rapids, Michigan, USA: W B Eerdmans Publishing Company.
Grayling, A. (2013). *The God Argument The Case Against Religion and for Humanism* (First ed.). New York: Bloomsbury.
Grayling, A. (2011). *The Good Book A Secular Bible* (First ed.). (A. Grayling, Ed., & A. Grayling, Trans.) London, UK: Bloomsbury.
Grayling, A. (2010). *Thinking of Answers* (First ed.). Bloomsbury.
Grayling, A. (2009). *To Set Prometheus Free.* Oberon Books.
Greene, B. (2005). *The Fabric of the Cosmos* (1st Paper Back UK ed.). Penguin Books.

Guthrie, D. (1970). *New Testament Intrioduction* (3rd (revised) in one Volume ed., Vol. 1). Illinois , USA: Inter-Varsity Press.
Hannam, J. (2010). *God's Philosophers* (1st Edition ed.). Icon Books.
Hare, R. M. (2004). *Essays on Religion and Education* (Reprinted 2004 ed.). Clarendon Press Oxford .
Harris, E. E. (1936). Mr Ryle: The Ontological Argument. (G. E. Moore, Ed.) *Mind: A Quaterly Review of Pscychology and Philosophy , XLV.*
Hayek, F. M. (1935). *Collectivist Economic Planning* (First ed.). London: Routledge & Sons.
Hayek, F. (1952). *The Sensory Order.* Chicago.
Hitler, A. (1925). *Mein Kampf: Eine Abrechnung.* Munchen: Franz Eher.
Hopkins, J. (2001). *Complete Philosophical and Theological Treatises of Nicholas of Cusa.* Minneapolis, USA: Banning.
Hume, D. (1779). *Dialogues Concerning Natural Religion.* UK.
Hume, D. (1978). *Treatise of Human Nature .* (L. A. Bigge, Ed.) UK: Oxford .
Johnson, P. (2012). *Darwin: A Portriat of a Genius .* Viking Penguin.
Josephus, F. *The Works of Flavius Josephus* (PDF ed.). (W. Whiston, Trans.)
Krauss, L. (2012). *Why There is Something Rather than Nothing With an Afterword by Richard Dawkins* (First ed.). UK: Simon & Schuster.
Long, R. T. (2006). Realism and Abstraction in Economics: Aristotle and Mises Versus Friedman. *Vol 9* (3).
MacArthur, J. (1997). *The Macarther Study Bibile* (New King James Version ed.). Thomas Nelson.
Mao, C. (1945). *Selected Works* (Vol. Vol III).
Mao, C. Z. (1972). *The Poems of Mao Zedong.* (W. Barnstone, Trans.) New York: Harper & Row.
McGrath, A. &. (2008). *Alistair McGrath & Daniel Dennett in Dialog.* (R. B. Stewart, Ed.) UK: Fortress Press.
McTaggart, J. E. (1908). The Unreality of Time. (P. G. Stout, Ed.) *Mind a Quaterly Review of Psychology and Philosophy , XVII* (68).
Midgley, M. (1979). Gene-Juggling. *Philosophy , 54* (210).
Midgley, M. (1983). Selfish Genes and Social Darwinism. *Philosophy , Vol 58* (225).
Mill, J. (1981). *Principles of Evidence and the Methods of Scientific Investigation* (Vols. Books I-II). (J. M. Robson, Ed.)
Mises, L. v. (1922). *Die Gemeinwirtfchaft Unterfuchungen uber den Sozialismus* (First ed.). Jena: Verlag von Guftav Fifcher .
Mises, L. V. (1949). *Human Action* (First ed.). Yale University Press.
Mises, L. v. (1936). *Socialism* (First English Language Edition ed.). (J. Kahane, Trans.) London: Jonathan Cape.
Moore, G. E. (1899). The Nature of Judgment. *Mind .*
Moore, G. (1939). *Proof of an External World* (1st Reading ed.). Aristotle Society.
Nagel, T. (2012). *Mind and Cosmos.* Oxford .
Oakeshott, M. (1993). *Religion, Politics and the Moral Life* (First ed.). (T. Fuller, Ed.) New Haven: Yale University Press.
Pelikan, J. *The Christian Tradition A History of the Development of Doctrine* (Vol. Vol 3).
Pelikan, J. *The Christian Tradition of the Development of Doctrine* (Vol. Vol 4).

Pelikan, J. *The Christian Tradition, A History of the Development of Doctrine* (Paper Back Edition ed., Vol. 2). University of Chicago Press.

Pelikan, J. *The Christian Tradition, A History of the Development of Doctrine* (Vol. 1).

Penrose, R. (1989). *The Emperor's New Mind Concerning Computers, Minds, and the Laws of Physics* (First Published 1989 Reprinted (with corrections) 1989 ed.). Oxford, UK: Oxford University Press.

Plantinga, A. (2011). *Where the Conflict Really Lies* (1st ed.). Oxford University Press.

Plato. (1997). *Plato Complete Works.* (J. M. Cooper, Ed.) Cambridge, Indianapolis: Hackett.

Plato. (1997). *Plato Complete Works.* (J. Cooper, Ed.) Cambridge , Indianapolis : Hackett.

Prayer, T. B. (1662). *The 325 AD Nicene Creed from the First Council of Nicaea , updated First Council of Constantinople 381 AD.*

Ramsay, W. (1898). *Was Christ Born in Bethlehem* (First ed.). Hodder and Stoughton.

Runciman, S. S. (1990). *A History of the Crusades Vol III The Kingdom of Acre and the Later Crusades* (Reprinted Penguin Books (of 1954 Cambridge University Press First Edition) ed., Vol. Vol III). Penguin Books.

Russell, B. (1903). *The Principles of Mathematics.* London: W W Norton.

Ryle, G. (1937). Back to the Ontological Argument . (G. E. Moore, Ed.) *Mind: A Quaterly Review of Psychology and Philosophy , XLIV.*

Ryle, G. (1935). Mr Collingwood and the Ontological Argument . (G. E. Moore, Ed.) *Mind : A Quarterley Review of Psychology and Philosophy , XLIV.*

Sebag Montefiore, S. (2007). *Young Stalin* (Vol. 1). London: Weidenfeld & Nicolson.

Sedley, D. (2007). *Creationism and its Critics in Antiquity* (First ed.). University of California Press.

Smolin, L. (2013). *Time Reborn From the Crisis in Physics to the Future of the Universe.* Allan Lane Imprint of Penguin Books .

Swinburne, R. (2005). *Faith and Reason* (Second Edition ed.). Oxford: Clarendon Press.

Swinburne, R. (1992). *Revelation From Metaphor to Analogy.* Clarendon Paperbacks .

Swinburne, R. (1977). *The Coherence of Theism* (First ed.). Oxford : Clarendon Library of Logic and Philosophy .

Swinburne, R. (2004). *The Existence of God* (Second Edition ed.). Oxford: Clarendon Press.

Young, E. J. (1992). *The Book of Isaiah Vol 1 Chapters 1-18* (1992 Reprint of 1965 First Edition ed., Vol. Vol I). Grand Rapids, Michigan: Eerdmans Printing Company .

Young, E. J. (1992). *The Book of Isaiah Vol II / Chaptwers 19-39* (Reprint of 1969 First ed., Vol. Vol II). Grand Rapids, Michigan : Eerdmans Publishing .

Young, E. J. (1992). *The Book of Isaiah Vol III / Chapters 40-66* (Reprint of 1972 First Edition ed., Vol. Vol III). Eerdmans Publishing.

Young, R. (1963). *Analytical Concordance To the Holy Bible* (Reprint of 8th Revised Edition ed.). London, UK: Lutterworth Press.

Index

1

1 Chronicles 29:14 · 165
1 Peter · 226
1 Timothy · 168

2

2 Maccabees 14:35 · 166

3

3 Maccabees 2:9 · 166

A

A Priori Judgments · 169
A Synthetic Judgment · 169
Abraham · 136, 212, 249
Abrahamic faiths · 134, 136
Absolute · 189, 190
absolute presuppositions · 37, 118, 121, 174, 185
Acts · 215
Adelard of Bath · 62
agape · 221, 224
Albans · 68
Alcuin · 58
altruism · 71, 72
Amos · 61
Anselm · 33, 144, 168, 170, 171, 172, 173, 174, 175, 176, 177, 178, 179, 185, 190, 196, 197
anthropic · 118, 119, 120
anthropic arguments · 118
anthropic principle · 118
Appearance and Reality · 90, 99
apriori · 80, 130, 141, 182
Aquinas · 60, 64, 66, 68, 196
Aratus · 166
Archbishop of Atheism · 210
Areopagus · 164
Aristarchus of Samos · 75
Aristotelian · 32
Aristotle · 30, 31, 32, 64, 65, 68, 71, 76, 82, 83, 84, 118, 153, 183, 211
Armenians · 234
Astrolabe · 59
astrology · 61, 89, 241
atheist · 8, 23, 47, 62, 68, 86, 123, 124, 139, 202, 218, 219, 227, 228, 230, 231, 239, 240, 245
Atran · 55, 76

Augustine · 76, 169
Averroes · 65
axiom · 37, 85, 109, 183, 184, 191
Ayer · 26, 28, 29

B

babbler · 164
Barmen Declaration · 242
Barrow and Tipler · 132
Barth · 242
Behold · 158
Being · 83, 103, 106, 107, 110, 131, 163, 169, 170, 179, 199
Bellarmine · 76
Benedetti · 76
Bible · 52, 60, 61, 69, 70, 73, 74, 76, 86, 158, 205, 213, 215, 229, 249
Big Bang · 88, 98, 99, 107, 112, 113, 114, 127, 133, 147, 217
Bishop of Paris · 65
black holes · 115, 117
Blackfriars · 60, 64
blasphemies · 214
Block Universe · 101
Boethius · 59
Bohr · 56, 103
Bonhoeffer · 242
Book of Job · 61, 69, 70, 110, 136
Bradley · 50, 90, 92, 93, 94, 99, 143
Bradwardine · 65, 76
Bright · 206, 207, 208
Bright Movement · 206
British Humanist Association · 231
Buchannan · 63
Bullock · 240, 241, 242, 244
Buridan · 65, 75
Byzantines · 58

C

Caldwell · 74
Caliphate · 235
Cannanites · 249
Carroll · 43, 44
Catholic Church · 56, 77
Catholicism · 230
causality · 34, 82, 84, 106, 120, 121, 126, 129
Charlemagne · 58
Chesterfield · 215
child sacrifice · 249
China · 63, 218, 245, 248
Christ · 41, 61, 112, 168, 221, 225, 226, 238

259

Christian · 31, 32, 38, 44, 45, 64, 85, 88, 146, 187, 202, 216, 219, 220, 221, 235, 236, 237, 238, 240, 241, 248, 252, 253
Christianity · 30, 31, 32, 35, 54, 65, 173, 209, 225, 230, 231, 236, 237, 241, 248, 252, 253
Christology · 225
Church · 26, 56, 62, 63, 64, 65, 67, 76, 78, 86, 170, 221, 226, 229, 230, 233, 237, 242, 244, 253
Cicero · 68
circular reasoning · 140
Clavius · 76
Cleanthes · 167
Cogito · 35, 36
coincidence of opposites · 105
Collingwood · 31, 32, 33, 35, 36, 37, 38, 39, 40, 43, 67, 152, 154, 155, 156, 162, 168, 171, 181, 182, 185, 186, 190
Congregation of the Index · 77
consciousness · 71, 72, 89, 140, 188
Constantinople · 55, 64, 235
constants · 47, 92, 119, 131, 132, 135, 140, 141, 144, 209
Controversies in Scripture · 41, 124, 194, 196
Conway · 124, 125, 130, 187
co-operation · 87, 146, 235
Copenhagen Interpretation · 103
Copernicus · 56, 66, 70, 75, 76, 77
Corinth · 222
corporation · 62, 147
cosmic constants · 118, 138
Cosmological Argument · 124, 125, 127, 128, 131, 190
Council of Laodicea · 221
Courtois · 240, 245
Cox · 150
creation · 32, 51, 53, 61, 70, 81, 82, 83, 85, 86, 87, 88, 107, 109, 112, 133, 138, 143, 180, 181, 201, 210, 246
creator · 73, 74, 86, 87, 98, 105, 106, 108, 109, 123, 124, 180, 202, 205
Critique of Pure Reason · 27, 128
Cromwell · 68
Crusades · 63, 233, 235, 236, 237, 246, 252
Cusa · 75, 105, 107, 211

D

Daniel · 79, 173, 203
Dark Ages · 53, 54
dark energy · 142, 143
dark matter · 142, 143
Darwin · 51, 52, 72, 79, 80, 81, 82, 85, 123, 138, 184, 195, 207, 208, 243, 244, 245
Darwinists · 72
David · 44, 82, 123, 124, 125, 172, 187
Davies · 43, 45, 46, 47, 252
Dawkins · 38, 48, 51, 52, 53, 67, 71, 72, 73, 74, 84, 123, 124, 141, 168, 170, 171, 179, 190, 201, 202, 203, 204, 220, 238
de Botton · 213, 218, 225, 226, 227, 228, 229, 231
De Sepulturis · 67
de Sousa · 203

Decalogue · 146, 215
De-coherence · 109
deductively · 25
Deep Thought · 73, 74
deity · 32, 85, 86, 126, 199
Dennett · 79, 80, 81, 82, 203, 204, 205, 206
Denton · 139
Descartes · 28, 35, 36, 37
Design Argument · 130, 131
Design arguments · 124, 187
deterministic · 56, 95, 106, 121
Dialogues · 124, 130, 174
Dialogues Concerning Natural Religion · 124, 174
Didache · 225
diplomatic bag of immunity · 28, 130, 140
division of labour · 147
Dombrowski · 173, 175
Domesday Book · 57
Dominicans · 65
Dragon in the Garage · 194

E

Ecclesiastes · 81
economics · 86, 182, 183, 184, 185, 186, 187, 191
Edge.org · 54
Einstein · 56, 90, 95, 96, 97, 99, 100, 101, 103, 106, 107, 122
Eleusinian Mysteries · 223
Emergent Universes · 88
Empirical Judgment · 169
Enlightenment · 53, 54, 56, 57, 61, 64, 65, 69, 70, 103
entrepreneurs · 38
Epicurean · 84
Epimenides · 166
Eucharist · 220, 221, 225, 238
Euclid's Elements · 62
Euclidian geometry · 119, 182, 184
eugenics · 207
Everett Many World Interpretation · 109
Everett Many Worlds Interpretation · 107
Evil · 151, 152, 157, 158, 214
evolution · 79, 84, 85, 86, 87, 88, 109, 115, 117, 120, 201, 210, 217
external relations · 92, 93
external world · 25, 26, 27, 28, 29, 30, 48

F

fairies · 10, 23, 24, 85
faith · 8, 10, 23, 24, 25, 26, 27, 28, 29, 30, 31, 32, 33, 34, 35, 36, 37, 38, 39, 40, 43, 44, 45, 46, 48, 51, 54, 55, 56, 64, 65, 68, 76, 112, 113, 114, 128, 140, 144, 168, 169, 185, 196, 201, 203, 205, 208, 209, 211, 216, 217, 218, 219, 229, 236, 238, 241, 249
fallacy of false disjunction · 155
Feynman · 104, 105
first cause · 34, 86, 123, 124, 128, 143
Flew · 124, 202

260

fool · 168, 172, 177, 179
force fields · 142, 151
Forshaw · 150
free will · 106, 121
fundamental ground for being · 32, 34, 145, 147

G

Galileo · 56, 57, 76, 77
Gasking · 180
Gaunilo · 16, 177, 178, 179, 180, 190
Genesis · 51, 52, 60, 74, 81, 134, 210, 249
Gentiles · 61, 221
Gerbert of Aurillac · 59
Ghirardi-Rimini-Weber Theory · 109
Gibbon · 55, 57, 252
God · 23, 26, 31, 32, 33, 34, 36, 39, 41, 48, 56, 59, 60, 61, 63, 64, 65, 66, 69, 74, 81, 82, 85, 86, 98, 103, 107, 121, 122, 123, 124, 125, 128, 129, 131, 134, 135, 136, 140, 143, 144, 145, 147, 158, 159, 162, 163, 168, 170, 171, 172, 173, 174, 175, 176, 177, 178, 179, 180, 181, 182, 186, 187, 189, 190, 192, 195, 196, 197, 198, 199, 201, 202, 203, 204, 209, 211, 212, 213, 214, 215, 217, 218, 219, 220, 221, 228, 231, 236, 237, 238, 243, 247, 248, 249, 253
God Delusion · 168
Golden Rule · 146
goodness · 26, 135, 156, 158, 159, 162, 163
Gospel · 88, 121, 147, 148, 211
grace · 26, 121, 168
Grayling · 23, 24, 30, 85, 142, 177, 192, 195, 197, 199, 208, 210, 212, 213, 214, 216, 220, 229
Greek · 30, 31, 32, 55, 58, 61, 62, 69, 86, 145, 215, 221
Greene · 89, 97, 98, 103, 104, 105, 110, 111, 113
Gutenberg · 68
Guzmen · 64

H

ham sandwich · 203
handmaiden of faith · 24
Hannam · 55, 56, 57, 59, 61, 75, 78
Hare · 38, 44, 45
harmony · 138, 245
Harris · 181, 186, 187, 188, 190, 191, 238, 239
Hayek · 74, 246
Hegel · 48, 179, 186, 187, 190
Heisenberg · 103
heliocentric · 69, 75, 76, 107
Herbews · 249
heresy · 62
Herodotus · 213
High Priests · 45, 54, 112, 140, 177, 203
Histories · 213, 215
Hitler · 239, 240, 241, 242, 244, 245, 246
Humanism · 218
Humanists · 54, 68
Hume · 123, 124, 125, 127, 128, 130, 131, 133, 134, 135, 136, 138, 141, 174, 175, 179, 182

hundred Taler · 190

I

idealism · 26, 48
identical coincidents · 152, 154
Ignatius · 225
immaterial first cause · 86, 126
induction · 25, 38, 47, 115, 120, 121, 183, 211
inductively · 25
infinite · 31, 32, 33, 34, 35, 37, 39, 52, 79, 84, 108, 112, 120, 123, 127, 161, 164, 217
infinity · 84, 85, 86, 108, 109, 120, 133, 217
Inflationary Cosmology · 113
Inn at the World End · 41
Inquisition · 56, 62, 76, 77, 233, 237, 246, 253
internal relations · 93
Isaiah · 69, 70, 134
Islamic State · 234
Islamists · 54, 58
Issac · 249

J

James · 55, 56, 63, 123, 252
Jeremiah · 61, 205
Jeremiah 10 · 61
Jesus · 64, 168, 221, 249
Jews · 203, 225, 237, 242, 245, 252, 253
Jihad · 234
Job · 69, 70, 136, 158
John · 76, 85, 216, 228, 252, 253
John of Damascus · 58
Johnson · 243, 252, 253
Justin Martyr · 223, 225
Justinian · 55

K

Kant · 27, 29, 36, 119, 124, 128, 129, 130, 131, 179, 182, 184, 186, 190
Kelper · 76
Killing Fields of Cambodia · 63
knowledge problem · 246
Krauss · 46, 123, 124, 126, 127, 129, 141, 143, 144, 145, 147

L

Lancet Flukes · 204
laws of motion · 89, 95, 105
Learned Ignorance · 105
Leibniz · 89, 90, 93, 114
logarithms · 65
Long · 39
Lucretius · 84, 85, 108
Luke · 8
Luther · 26

M

magic · 88, 212
Maier · 57
Mao · 63, 239, 244, 247, 248
Mappe Mundi · 59
Martyr · 225
Mary · 71
Mary Midgley · 71
mata law · 120
material · 34, 41, 83, 84, 86, 96, 104, 108, 110, 120, 126, 128, 143, 189, 218, 227
materialists · 92
maths · 54, 58, 93, 128, 151, 153, 154, 159, 163, 183, 184, 195, 217
Matthew · 219, 237
McTaggart · 99, 100, 101, 102
mechanistic · 95
Mengele · 208
Merton Calculators · 65
metaphysics · 36, 49, 51, 52, 53, 88, 121, 170, 181, 201, 204
Middle Ages · 32, 33, 53, 54, 56, 57
Mill · 57
Mind · 100, 168, 181, 190, 196
Mises · 44, 183, 246
Moore · 26, 27, 28, 29, 30, 93
Moses · 70, 215
multiverse · 88
mumbo jumbo · 40
Muslim · 58, 237

N

Nagel · 5, 20, 47, 48
National Socialist · 63, 240, 241, 243
Natural Selection · 80
naturalistic world-view · 208
New Testament · 212
Newton · 56, 65, 89, 95, 97, 105, 142, 210, 253
Newtonian · 65, 90, 104, 105, 106, 131, 132
Nicomachean Ethics · 82, 153
nisus · 71
Noah · 134
Nobel · 74, 246
Nominalist · 66
Norman's · 57
Northern Hemisphere · 69
nothingness · 113, 143, 147
nows · 97, 98, 102, 122
Nuremberg Trial · 240

O

Ockham · 66, 68, 86, 199, 218
Ockham's Razor · 66
Old Testament · 69, 70, 134
omnipotence · 198
omnipotent · 174, 197, 198
omniscient · 98
Oneness · 105, 107, 150
oneness of reality · 104, 151, 176, 178, 186

Ontological Argument · 127, 162, 168, 170, 173, 174, 175, 181, 185, 186, 189, 190, 191, 196, 197, 199
Ontological Deduction · 19, 182
ontological proof · 33
Ontology · 169
Origin of Species · 243
Orseme · 76
overlapping classes · 154
Oxford · 62, 65, 181, 202

P

pagan school in Athens · 55
Papal Bull · 67
parables · 229
parallax · 75
Parmanides · 161
Passover · 225
Patrizi · 76
Paul · 25, 43, 45, 47, 56, 168, 216, 221, 226, 227, 228, 243, 252, 253
Pelikan · 26, 55
Penrose · 133
perfect island · 161
performative contradiction · 35, 196
Peter · 141, 216, 226
phenotypic · 51
Philoponus · 76
philosophy · 23, 26, 27, 31, 32, 55, 58, 61, 64, 65, 119, 125, 145, 151, 154, 155, 160, 162, 171, 181, 182, 186, 195, 215, 216, 227
Plank time · 112
Plantinga · 88
Plato · 25, 48, 68, 82, 151, 160, 171, 182
plough · 57
Pol Pot · 244
Polylogism · 46
Polynaturalism · 46
Pope Urban VIII · 77
Popper · 195
precarious margins · 154, 155
Primordial Soup · 88
Process Theology · 16
prophet · 70
Proslogion · 168, 171
prosperity · 150, 152, 154, 155, 156, 157, 159, 160, 162
Protestant Reformation · 62, 77, 246
Proverbs · 214, 215
Psalm · 59, 60, 61, 172
Psalm 50:9-12 · 165
Psalm 96 · 60
pseudo metaphysics · 12, 88, 170
pure being · 151, 162, 163, 164, 170, 174, 178, 182
Pythagoras · 83, 110, 111, 184
Pythagoreans · 110

Q

quantum mechanics · 88, 103, 104, 106
Qur'an · 234

262

R

rationality · 9, 23, 38, 39, 43, 47, 58, 64, 87, 191, 202, 205, 209, 217
reason · 10, 23, 24, 25, 26, 28, 29, 30, 31, 32, 33, 34, 35, 36, 37, 38, 39, 40, 43, 46, 48, 51, 55, 62, 64, 66, 73, 82, 87, 100, 116, 122, 125, 152, 168, 171, 183, 185, 186, 191, 195, 196, 203, 205, 208, 212, 217, 218, 232
Relativity · 66
religious · 23, 24, 29, 34, 38, 41, 43, 44, 45, 46, 56, 58, 59, 68, 89, 92, 103, 107, 123, 128, 134, 146, 195, 202, 209, 210, 212, 214, 216, 218, 219, 220, 227, 231, 233, 235, 237, 238, 240, 241, 243, 244, 246, 249
Renaissance · 56, 58
Revelation · 59, 60, 88, 187, 239
Richard of Wallingford · 68
righteous · 136
Roman Empire · 56, 236, 252
Romans · 226
Runciman · 233, 235, 236
Russell · 26, 93, 123
Russia · 63, 243, 244
Ryle · 26, 80, 181, 182, 185, 186, 187, 188, 189, 190, 191, 203

S

Sagan · 193, 194
Satan · 157, 158
Saul · 168
Scale of Forms · 152, 156
science · 10, 32, 36, 39, 40, 43, 44, 45, 46, 48, 51, 53, 54, 56, 57, 60, 61, 66, 69, 75, 78, 81, 88, 90, 92, 104, 106, 114, 118, 120, 121, 140, 144, 145, 148, 151, 152, 153, 154, 159, 160, 162, 163, 174, 178, 182, 192, 195, 208, 210, 217
scientist · 37, 38, 39, 40, 41, 44, 48, 51, 55, 71, 89, 99, 107, 112, 115, 118, 123, 139, 144, 151, 164, 202
Scotus · 66, 68
scripture · 41, 124, 187
Sebag Montefiore · 244
Sedley · 83
self interested genes · 67
selfish gene · 72
selfish genes · 67, 72
Sidereal Messenger · 76
Simplicio · 77
Smolin · 46, 47, 90, 106, 114, 116, 117, 118, 119, 120, 121, 122
Socialism · 241, 242, 245
Socialist · 63, 246
Socialists · 63
Socrates · 25, 30, 151, 161, 211
Solomon · 81, 138, 172
something from something · 143
source · 214, 215
Southern Hemisphere · 69
Soviet Union · 63
spacetime · 95, 97, 98, 142

Special Relativity · 96
Spectacles · 68
St Augustine · 60
Stalin · 239, 240, 243, 244
Stephen · 141
stirrup · 57
String Theory · 110, 111
Sum Over Histories · 104
super · 131, 207
superstition · 32, 39, 54, 170, 229
superstring theory · 111
Surah · 234
Swinburne · 41, 59, 60, 125, 187, 198
syllogism · 30, 31, 118, 120, 192
syllogistic proofs · 30
Synthetic A Priori Judgement · 169

T

Talmud · 70
tautological · 184
teleological · 72, 82
teleology · 72
The Black Book of Communism · 245
The Good · 151, 214
The Great Patriotic War · 244
the law of demand · 184
The Law School of Bologa · 62
The Mathematical Pope · 59
The Philosophers' Mail · 231
The School of Life · 230
The Simple Believer · 44
The Socialist Calculation Debate · 246
The Sunday Assembly · 231
The Unreality of Time · 99
Theologians · 39
theoria · 145
Thorndike · 57
Time Reborn · 114
timeless · 98
Trebuchet · 63
Trial · 77
Tuberculosis · 67

U

unicorn · 194, 195
uniformity of nature · 38, 47
uniformity of the laws of nature · 10
uniformity of the laws of the universe · 10
universal · 35, 36, 37, 40, 67, 71, 104, 152, 155, 252
universal laws · 40
Universalist · 66
universals · 66, 67, 152, 153
Universe from Nothing · 88, 123, 141
University of Padua · 62
unmoved first mover · 72

263

V

vacuum · 65, 76, 126, 132
Virgin Birth · 112

W

Wallingford's clock · 68
War and Peace · 98
Waugh · 230
Wisdom · 124, 125, 177, 211, 214
witch doctor · 40, 44, 144

witness testimony · 196

Z

Zeh · 109
Zephaniah · 61

Σ

σπερμολόγος · 164

Poorly researched → relying on popular presentations of Scientific + theological thought +, occasionally, Wikipedia!

Tendency to serious oversimplification of serious complexity.
→ Admits at times, that he is forming opinions based on one book (p. 18)

Very poor writing style — often v. hard to follow
Book jumps around, no logical structure
— no references
— Strange Style

All the passion of an armchair theologian...
Claiming Scripture is not interested in science and then proceeding to show that Job believed in a round earth + Solomon understood evolution.

→ Talks a lot about "logical" and "rational" and yet his arguments are not logical or rational
e.g.
→ P.89 — The fruit of his inquisitive mind.
→ Rude towards his opponents (p 188)
  ↳ Accuses Dawkins of setting up straw men... But..

Printed in Great Britain by Amazon